THE PITTSBURGH THEOLOGICAL
MONOGRAPH SERIES

Dikran Y. Hadidian
General Editor

28

THE REFORMED ROOTS OF THE
ENGLISH NEW TESTAMENT

The Influence of Theodore Beza
on the English New Testament

THE REFORMED ROOTS OF THE ENGLISH NEW TESTAMENT

The Influence of Theodore Beza on the English New Testament

by
Irena Dorota Backus

Preface by
BASIL HALL

PICKWICK PUBLICATIONS
An imprint of *Wipf and Stock Publishers*
199 West 8th Avenue • Eugene OR 97401

Pickwick Publications
An imprint of Wipf and Stock Publishers
199 W 8th Ave, Suite 3
Eugene, OR 97401

The Reformed Roots of the English New Testament
The Influence of Theodore Beza on the English New Testament
By Backus, Irena Doruta
Copyright©1980 Pickwick
ISBN 13: 978-0-915138-36-6
ISBN 10: 0-915138-36-0
Publication date 1/1/1980

To my husband

CONTENTS

PREFACE ix

INTRODUCTION. xvii

ACKNOWLEDGEMENTS. xxi

LIST OF ABBREVIATIONS xxii

I. GENERAL SURVEY OF MATERIAL.   1

    Beza's Manuscript Sources   1
    Beza's Use of the Church Fathers.   8
    Beza's Influence on the English Geneva Bible. . . 13
    *Laurence Tomson's Translation of Beza's
        Latin New Testament*. 18
    *Use of Beza's New Testament by the
        Authorized Translators* 28
    *The Bodleian Copy of the Bishops' Bible 1602
        Printed by Robert Barker* 28

II. INFLUENCE OF BEZA ON THE ENGLISH
        SYNOPTIC GOSPELS 43

    St. Matthew 44
    St. Mark. 65
    St. Luke. 76
    *Relationship Between Bodleian Bishops'
        and the Theology of Two Members
        of the Oxford Company*. 93

III. INFLUENCE OF BEZA ON THE PAULINE EPISTLES
        AND HEBREWS 109

    Romans. 113
    1 Corinthians 123
    Galatians 132
    Hebrews 139

GENERAL CONCLUSIONS 169
APPENDIX: *Laurence Tomson 1539-1608*. 173
BIBLIOGRAPHY. 203
INDEX 211

PREFACE

Dr. Irena Backus has produced a thorough and significant contribution in a field of increasing interest among scholars, that of the historical study of the development in the quest for a better biblical text in the original languages, and of the impact of this improved learning on vernacular translations. *The Cambridge History of the Bible* published over several years in three volumes is one major indication of this interest. One aspect of these studies has been the investigation of the making of the English versions of the Bible, a history which has covered nearly two hundred years from Herbert Marsh to recent investigators like C. C. Butterworth, Bruce Metzger, F. F. Bruce and A. C. Partridge. Few of these attained the concisely expressed but remarkable learning of B. F. Westcott (especially in the edition revised by W. A. Wright in 1905), and few of the authors concerned over that period gave a thorough investigation of the use made of particular editions of the original Hebrew or Greek texts upon particular English versions. Too often an author reproduced the views of previous investigators including their errors and remained content with occasional soundings, and because they were frequently scholars of repute, some sound judgments. Writing as one who has endeavoured to make some small contribution to these studies I have been sometimes uneasy about the lack of thoroughness in many of these investigations which are too frequently directed to a popular readership. What Dr. Backus has done is to provide, in work of scholarly weight covering a large area of the New Testament following a precise method, a careful study in depth establishing the nature and extent of the influence of Théodore de Bèze (Beza) on the Genevan Version of the New Testament, and then after casting some new light on the revisers' use of the Bishops' Bible, giving full treatment to his influence on the making of the Authorized [or King James'] Version of the New Testament. What elsewhere has been referred to in three or four pages, rather than thoroughly discussed, has now been provided at book length. This method of study is peculiarly difficult because of the degree of painstaking care in sifting the material, in deciding whether a particular example is directly based on Beza, and if so in what edition of his work, and in what way that example was used. This task is formidable and requires not only ability in linguistic and exegetical skills but also scholarly insight in the shifting variations of the materials studied.

    That the English-speaking world of literary and historical as well as biblical scholars rightly shows an interest in the Authorized [or King James'] Version and the influence on it of its predecessors, is admirable, but it still needs to have available more thorough studies of the influence of the extraordinary increase in and achievements of biblical linguistic scholarship in the sixteenth century especially those made by European scholars other than English. Why, nevertheless, select Beza from these others who include for the New Testament Erasmus; the editors of the Greek text of the Complutensian Polyglot Bible; Robert and Henri Estienne; Arias Montano, the chief editor of the Royal or Polyglot Bible of Antwerp? Whether Beza was abler than the Spanish scholars may be arguable but it is beyond dispute that for the Protestant world to which the English translators belonged from the Geneva editors who succeeded the Tyndale-Coverdale Bible to the makers of the Authorized Version it was Beza who became the major figure, from the appearance of his Latin version, based on his revision of the Greek text (though this was not extensive), through to the final edition of the Greek text with his Latin version and his extensive annotations in which variant readings of the Greek manuscripts were discussed.

In the *Registre de la Compagnie des Pasteurs de Genève*, in course of publication the name Théodore de Bèze in the index to volumes IV and V is followed by the word *passim* which makes him unique among all the other names mentioned. This may stand as a sufficient symbol of his pervasive if not dominating influence not only at Geneva but in the Reformed Churches in the Europe of his time. His influence was felt everywhere among these Churches in organizing what were to become the distinctive forms and spirit of Presbyterianism which owed much of its success to its theologically and politically aggressive defense against the extension of Tridentine Catholicism. It speaks much for the respect in which Beza was held in the Church of England, which had to struggle against presbyterianizing attacks, that in spite of his positive commitment to Presbyterianism (though it was guardedly expressed in writing to Englishmen) that his fame as a theologican and biblical scholar was hardly impaired. Whether the makers of the English ·Genevan version and the revision of its New Testament, almost entirely approved of Beza's ecclesiological and political views, which for the English government represented a dangerous challenge to the Elizabethan Settlement of Religion, or whether, on the other hand, the makers of the Authorized Version mostly Bishops or vigorous anti-Puritans like John Bois disapproved of those views of Beza, made apparently little difference to the high regard which scholarly Englishmen gave to Beza's theological learning (which even the Bishops adopted) and his New Testament biblical scholarship. Beza, of course, had not only great natural ability, but he was given a solid foundation upon which to build in theology by the work of Calvin, and in New Testament studies by the work of his predecessors especially the revision of the Greek New Testament text of Erasmus by the Estiennes. That he was no great innovator who followed with courage and insight the possibilities for the text raised by the manuscripts he had acquired, as well as the collations made from manuscripts by Henri Estienne, has been shown more than once. Dr. Backus gives the most recent account of this caution, or perhaps, inadequacy in Beza, while at the same time drawing attention to the considerable discussion by Beza of the manuscripts as well as citations of the New Testament in the Church Fathers in his annotations, and does so succinctly and from personal investigation. If Beza's caution could be defended it would require pointing to the fact that a major Catholic attack on Protestantism lay in asserting that Protestants varied in their views and were constantly changing their versions of the biblical texts: Beza in helping to establish what became the *Textus Receptus* was seeking to avoid what were at the time potentially challengeable proposals on readings which we now know he could have made.

Dr. Backus moves from describing Beza's work to its influence on the English versions giving useful though not extensive space to the Genevan version of the New Testament of 1560, and to the revision of this by Laurence Tomson in 1576. The Genevan version ran eventually into close to one hundred and fifty editions, and it was for almost a century the most popular Bible version in English, and through its prefaces to the biblical Books and its marginal annotations it was to bring the Genevan version of the Reformed faith into great prominence in the lives of not only clergy but laity, for this Bible either complete, or as a New Testament only, was frequently available in small sized editions easily handled,

and often printed in the easily legible Roman type (as against
the traditional Black Letter). Dr. Backus shows us more
thoroughly (what Westcott had first demonstrated) the nature
of the contribution of Beza's Latin version, Greek text, and
discussions in his annotations particularly on doctrinal
points, to this popular and influential version which the
Bishops' Bible was unable to challenge in readership, and
which it took the Authorized Version, and some degree of suppression, years to overcome. Beza addressed the English speaking world in a particular tone and with specific theological
themes for much of his life-time and even after his death
through this version. It is a strange gap in the history of
the Genevan English version (and there are many accounts of
it though all brief) that Laurence Tomson whose version of the
New Testament of 1576 continued to be printed for years to
come, separately and in the complete Bibles, with its additions of positively protestant notes ('...very partiall, un-
true, seditious, and savouring too much of daungerous and
trayterous conceites' as King James is reported to have said
in 1604, probably referring particularly to the addition of
the French scholar Junius' notes to *Revelation*) has very
little space given to him by scholars. We are indebted to
Dr. Backus for the extended--because thorough--account of him
in the appendix to her book. In providing this she has given
adequate space to showing what hitherto has not been fully demonstrated: what Tomson took from Beza and also what he gave,
in the event not much, to the makers of the Authorized Version; and more than this she has added a chapter to the history of Elizabethan Puritanism which has not hitherto been
written. Patrick Collinson's book *The Elizabethan Puritan
Movement* gave little reference to Tomson, perhaps in view of
his thesis that the presbyterian party has been over-rated by

scholars in discussing Puritanism. Dr. Backus not only fills in this gap in our knowledge, but also she does something to redress the undue tilting of the balance which Collinson made against overstressing the presbyterianizing group. For a linguistic scholar, who is not primarily a historian, this appendix shows indeed professional skill in a field where many ploughs have furrowed not always with such fruitful results.

Apart from Westcott's useful study the only analytical account of the influence of editions of the Greek text, including that of Beza, on the making of the Authorized Version of the New Testament is that of F. H. A. Scrivener as long ago as 1884, and that was contained in a few pages of an Appendix. The major part of Dr. Backus' book now provides (what Scrivener merely indicated so briefly) a full account of Beza's influence in the readings adopted by the revisers who produced the version of 1611; and this has been done not merely by citing phrases as did Scrivener but by a fully-rounded description of the background to the arguments presumably made, and the balancing of possibilities between readings before the revisers made their final decisions. It is necessary to repeat how impressive is the achievement of Dr. Backus when every paragraph she has written in this closely argued study has involved long examination of editions, annotations, the Latin version and citations of variant readings, accompanied by the comparison of these with the evidence from the surviving manuscripts and marginalia of the revisers and the ultimate product in the text of the first and second issues of the edition of 1611. Work of this nature is not only testing because of the need for constant re-checking to see that the material is correctly and lucidly presented but also because it requires a degree of theological and historical competence in interpreting the evidence. Some incautious generalizations that have appeared in writings on the making of the English version of 1611 will now have to disappear.

Dr. Backus has also investigated two manuscript sources which represent stages in the making of the final version. In so doing she has established that the manuscript annotations in the Bishops' Bible of 1602 (the edition used as the basis by the 1611 revisers for their work) in the Bodleian Library give evidence of how certain revisers were working and that these annotations precede in time the stage of revision shown by Bois' annotations in the Fulman Manuscript edited by Ward Allen. She has used the Bodleian Bible's annotations, and other evidence, in helping to establish the influence of Beza among revisers for the Synoptic Gospels; and then for the Pauline Epistles and Hebrews she has used the annotations of Bois, with other materials, to show that influence once again. From such comparatively minor points as the significance of the words printed in Roman type, and the suggestions made by the Bodleian annotations, as indicators, she builds up evidence concerning the stage of advance those annotations represent; and equally she shows from pointers in the Bois annotations concerning choices of readings and versions of these readings how these represent an earlier stage towards 1611.

One of the most interesting results of her work is her demonstration of the strong theological influence (though on some important issues he was set aside), which controlled the ultimate choice of readings, which Beza had on the Authorized Version. Scrivener had suggested this: Dr. Backus fully demonstrates it and shows the influence to be concerned with meaning and therefore theological. She adds, though inevitably more speculatively, evidence from two books by Oxford revisers which also show the magnetic attraction of Beza's views. This study undermines thereby a common assumption about the clear differentiation of the Church of England from Lutheran and Reformed churches by showing how the makers of so fundamental a basis for Anglican theology as the Bible text leaned positively towards the Genevan orthodoxy of the Reformed churches. When Beza received a very flattering letter of thanks from the University of Cambridge for his gift of the Codex Bezae in 1581 it was a sign of what his influence was to become, for in that letter he and Calvin were described as the most memorable of all writers for their knowledge of Scripture to be preferred before all others.

All who wish to investigate the quality of Beza as an editor and annotator on the Greek text of the New Testament will find a great deal of material in this book to help them on their way. All who wish to know how the Authorized Version came to be made will find here a study worthy to stand beside the best of other investigators in this field. All who have worked on this subject will know how much worthwhile effort has gone into the making of this book.

Basil Hall
St. John's College
Cambridge, England

INTRODUCTION

Our aim, in this work, is to establish the influence of Theodore Beza on the English New Testament, particularly the Authorized Version of 1611. However, as the reader can see, reference is made throughout to other English versions both earlier and (occasionally) later. Reference is made also to New Testament scholars contemporary with Beza who appear to have had some influence on the English versions.

In the first chapter the following material is discussed: manuscript variants used by Beza, the availability of Patristic material in the late sixteenth century, and Beza's attitude to the theology and text of the Fathers. We then briefly examine the type of influence Beza had on the English Geneva Bible of 1560, and give an account of L'Oiseleur's 1574 edition of Beza's Latin New Testament and of Tomson's 1576 English translation of it. We conclude that both Geneva 1560 and Tomson's 1576 N.T. were influenced by Beza primarily in their doctrine. Finally, in the first chapter we describe the Bodleian copy of the 1602 Bishops' Bible, examining in some detail what appear to be typographical annotations in the volume. We suggest that there is a close link between Bodleian Bishops' and the AV since the typographical annotations correspond to the AV's use of italics.

In the second chapter we are concerned with the influence of Beza on the English Synoptic Gospels. We examine the annotations on the text of Matthew, Mark and Luke in the Bodleian Bishops', we relate those to the corresponding readings in the AV and we examine the influence of Beza on the two sets of readings, referring throughout to other English versions. We conclude that the influence of Beza on the AV Synoptic Gospels is considerable especially in matters of text and style, and although there is a slight difference between the Bodleian Annotator's and the AV's use of Beza this difference points to two different stages in the process of Revision. This slight difference in the use of Beza and the actual differences in readings in the two versions mean that the Bodleian Bishops' cannot be a later collation of the Bishops' and Royal text, especially as some of the readings in the Bodleian Bishops' are not supported by any other English version. A short section is appended giving an account of theological views of two members of the Oxford Company of translators and comparing their theology with that of Bodleian Bishops' and the AV. This short enquiry shows there is good reason to suppose that a member of the Oxford Company owned the Bodleian Bishops'.

In the third chapter we deal with the influence of Beza on Paul's epistles to the Romans, (I) Corinthians and Galatians and on the epistle to the Hebrews. As well as examining selected readings from the AV 1611 from the point of view of Beza's influence, we also relate those to the remarks made by the Revisers in the Fulman manuscript. The Fulman MS (Professor Ward Allen's edition) contains translation notes made by the Final Revision Committee and is supposed to represent the very last stage in the making of the AV. We discover that Beza has a crucial influence on the AV epistles so far as text and style is concerned. In matters of doctrine the Revisers tend to moderate Beza's more extreme pronouncements. The same applies to style and to text in places where Beza's version is idiosyncratic or inadequately supported. We also notice that there is a difference between the Final Committee's and the Revisers' attitude to Beza, the latter showing a more marked preference for Bezan readings.

We finally conclude that the difference between the Fulman MS and AV 1611 is greater (so far as Bezan readings are

concerned) than the difference between the Bodleian Bishops'
and AV 1611. We therefore suggest, taking into account the
additional evidence of the typographical annotations in Bodleian Bishops' and the theology of the Oxford Company, that
it represents a later stage in the making of the AV than the
Fulman MS. We also conclude that, in spite of the Revisers
tendency to 'moderate' Beza's doctrine and some of his un-
supported textual and stylistic pronouncements, Beza's 1598
N.T. had a crucial influence on AV 1611 and that his influence
seemed to increase as Revision progressed.

We add an appendix which contains a short biography of
Laurence Tomson, together with an account of his works and a
summary of the relationship between his New Testament and the
AV. This is intended as an example of the English Puritans'
attitude to Beza during the late sixteenth century.

ACKNOWLEDGEMENTS

I should like to express my gratitude to the late Reverend Dr. S. L. Greenslade from whose supervision, throughout the course of this work, I have benefited more than I can say. My thanks also go to the Principal and the Governing Body of Somerville College who financed my graduate studies, and to the Leverhulme Trust Fund which made it possible for me to visit Geneva and work on Beza and sixteenth-century English New Testament exegesis during the year 1974/75. Further, I would like to thank Dr. Pierre Fraenkel and Jean-Blaise Fellay of the Institut d'histoire de la Réformation for their advice on the Patristic material in this thesis. Finally, I extend my thanks to Father Peter Levi S.J. of Campion Hall who first brought the Bodleian copy of the Bishops' Bible to my attention.

Geneva,
December, 1974   I.D.B.

ABBREVIATIONS

AV: Authorized Version of the Bible, 1611.

D.N.B.:   *Dictionary of National Biography*

Gregory: C. R. Gregory, ed., *Prolegomena*, (Leipzig, 1894). Vol. III of Tischendorf's *Novum Testamentum Graece*.

Legg: S. C. E. Legg, ed., *Novum Testamentum Graece; Evangelium Secundum Matthaeum*, (1940); *Evangelium Secundum Marcum*, (1935).

Liddell &   *A Greek-English Lexicon*, compiled by H. G.
Scott: Liddell and R. Scott, revised by Sir Henry Stuart Jones, (9th edition, 1940 with Supplement, 1968)

Nestle &   E. Nestle & K. Aland, ed., *Novum Testamentum*
Aland: *Graece*, (25th edition. United Bible Societies, London, 1971).

S.O.E.D.:   *Shorter Oxford English Dictionary*.

Souter: A. Souter, ed., *Novum Testamentum Graece*, (2nd edition, 1947).

TR: *Textus Receptus*.

Tischendorf: C. Tischendorf, ed., *Novum Testamentum Graece*, 2 vols., (Leipzig, 1869).

CHAPTER I

General Survey of Material

Our purpose in this chapter is, firstly, by discussing the manuscript material at Beza's disposal and assessing his attitude to the Church Fathers, to obtain some idea of the nature and scope of his New Testament Scholarship. Secondly, we shall delineate his influence on the English Geneva Bible of 1560 and on Laurence Tomson's New Testament of 1576. Thirdly, we shall describe the material which will be our main concern in the subsequent chapters of this work. This material will consist of (a) the Bodleian copy of the Robert Barker 1602 edition of the Bishops' Bible,[1] with the marginal annotations which are considered to represent a stage in the making of the AV and (b) the notes made by John Bois as member of the Final Revision Committee; the notes now known as the Fulman Manuscript.

In subsequent chapters we shall examine Beza's influence on the Bodleian Bishops' and the Fulman MS and relate it to his influence on the final version of the AV.[2]

Beza's Manuscript Sources

In his lifetime, Theodore Beza produced one Latin and four Greek-Latin editions of the New Testament.[3] Robert Stephanus (Estienne) printed the Latin edition in Geneva in 1557 as the third volume of his *Biblia utriusque Testamenti*. This volume contained the Vulgate as well as Theodore Beza's Latin New Testament with his marginal annotations. It was also Robert Stephanus who, in 1565, printed the first edition of Beza's Greek-Latin New Testament. The Greek text of this edition was based on the text of Stephanus' 1550 New Testament,[4] even though Beza differed from Stephanus in about twenty-five places. Beza's second edition of the Greek-Latin New Testament came out in Geneva in 1582. For this, he used Tremellius' Latin version of the Syriac New Testament,[5] Junius' edition of the Arabic version of Acts and 1 & 2 Corinthians,[6] Codex Bezae (D) and the Codex Claromontanus (D*) as well as the material which he had incorporated into his previous editions of the New Testament.

Beza's 1582 version differed from Stephanus in about 40 places. The third and fourth editions of Beza's Greek-Latin New Testament came out in 1589 and 1598. Those differed little from the third edition.[7]

Unfortunately it is not possible, at least within the scope of this work, to identify all the individual MSS which Beza referred to for his editions of the New Testament. We can, however, give the reader an idea of some of the variants at Beza's disposal and of his attitude to Greek MS sources generally. In this discussion (and in the subsequent chapters) our principal concern will be his edition of 1598.

This 1598 edition printed in Geneva by Eustathius Vignon, contains both Beza's dedicatory epistle to Queen Elizabeth I and also a preface addressed to the Christian reader. In both these preambles Beza makes a statement concerning the Greek MSS and his use of them. We find that the information he gives in the dedicatory epistle is supplemented by the information contained in the preface. Thus, in the epistle Beza says that, as well as referring to the works of his contemporaries and Greek and Latin fathers (all of which he diligently collated), he also had access to an 'exemplar'[8] from the library of Robert Stephanus. This 'exemplar' had been collated by Henri Stephanus (Robert's son) with 'more or less' twenty-five[9] Greek MSS and nearly all the printed versions. Beza says that this 'exemplar' provided the sole source for his minuscule MS variants.

In the preface, Beza is more specific stating that he referred to nineteen ancient MSS.[10] Although he does not further identify them in the preface, he does enumerate a few in the body of the annotations. He singles out D (which he calls 'meus vetustissimus exemplar'), D* and the 'versio Arabica'.[11] We know that he had all three at his disposal, as opposed to merely having knowledge of their variant readings.[12]

This accounts for either two or three of the ancient MSS but the identity of the other sixteen MSS remains undisclosed. Once we remember, however, that Robert Stephanus[13] also used Henri's collations as the sole source of Greek variants for his 1550 edition of the New Testament, some of the sixteen MSS can be identified. Unlike Beza, Robert Stephanus numbered the MS variants at his disposal with Greek symbols from α' to ις'. These have been identified by Gregory in the following way: α' = the Complutensian Polyglot, β' = D, γ' = Evv4, δ' = Evv5, ε' = Evv6, ς' = Evv7, ζ' = Evv8, η' = Levv, θ' = Evv38, ι' = Act 7, ια' = Act 8, ιβ' = Evv9, ιγ' = Act 9, ιδ' = Evv120, ιε' = Act 10, ις' = Apoc 3, making a total of sixteen sources. Bearing in mind that the Complutensian Polyglot is a printed source we can see that Robert Stephanus used fifteen sources from Henri's collations as against Beza's nineteen. We shall not attempt here to isolate the MSS which were used by Beza and not Stephanus. We can, however, determine which of the variants collated by Henri were used by both Robert Stephanus and Beza. To do this we have compared variants cited by the elder Stephanus with variants cited by Beza[14] in the first ten chapters of the book of Matthew. We then tabulated the instances where the two scholars agree, in the following way.

	T. Beza	R. Stephanus
II.11	In omnibus vetustis codicibus εἰδον	εἰδον ἐν πασι
III.11	Vetustum quoddam exemplar (habet) ἐγω μεν οὐν βαπτιζω	ἐγυ μεν οὐν βαπτιζω ιδ'
IV.10	Octo vetusti codices habet ὀπισω μου	ὀπισω μου β' δ' ς' ζ' η' θ' ιβ' ιδ'
V.18	Quintum exemplar bis habet ἀμην	ἀμην ἀμην ε'
V.33	In uno exemplari πλην i.e. caeterea vel praeterea	πλην ιβ'
V.36	Octavum exemplar tollit particulum ἡ	-ἡ η'
V.44	τοις μισουσιν ut in vetustis exemplaribus omnibus	τοις μισουσιν ἐν πασι
V.47	τους φιλους in omnibus vetustis exemplaribus	τους φιλους ἐν πασι
VII.1	In uno exemplari Graeco legimus μη καταδικαζετε και οὐ μη καταδικασθηται	μη καταδικαζετε και οὐ μη καταδικασθηται η'
VII.6	In duobus vetustis codicibus legimus τα ἁγια	τα ἁγια δ' θ'
VII.13	Vetusta exemplaria tria habent ἐρχομενοι	ἐρχομενοι δ' η' ιβ'
VII.14	Siquidem in vetustis codicibus legimus τι στενη	τι στενη ἐν πασι
VII.19	Unum vetus exemplar habet οὐν	οὐν ς'
VIII.8	In quibusdam codicibus εἰπε λογῳ	εἰπε λογῳ α' γ' ε' ς' ζ' η' θ' ιβ'
IX.11	Vetus quoddam exemplar habet και πινει	και πινει ιδ'

The agreement of Beza with Stephanus at Matthew II.11, V.44, V.47, VII.14[15] does not, by itself, indicate that Beza, in fact, referred to the same fourteen Greek variants as Stephanus. But the belief that they did use the same variants receives some confirmation from instances of more precise agreement between the two scholars. Thus at IV.10 where Beza points out that ὀπισω μου now occurs in eight old codices, Stephanus enumerates β' δ' ς' ζ' η' θ' ιβ' ιδ' as containing that same variant. The same measure of agreement between Stephanus and Beza occurs at III.11, IV.10, V.33, VII.1, VII.6, VII.13, VII.19, and IX.11.[16] Although only the first chapters of Matthew have been considered, nonetheless the accord between Stephanus and Beza in those chapters appears too great to be accounted for by mere coincidence. Crucial evidence here is provided by V.18 and V.36. Commenting on these verses Beza points out respectively "Quintum exemplar ἀμην bis habet" and "Octavum exemplar tollit particulum ἡ". Stephanus makes the same points; variant ε' (5) is quoted as repeating ἀμην and variant η' (8) as leaving out ἡ.[17]

In the light of this evidence it is reasonable to conclude that Beza definitely overlapped with Stephanus in using Greek MSS Evv6 and Levv. Moreover, the cases of numerical agreement between the two scholars seem too many to be dismissed by the assumption of coincidence. We can thus say that Beza almost certainly overlapped with Stephanus in using δ' ς' ζ' θ' ιβ' ιδ' (i.e. Evv5, Evv7, Evv8, Evv38, Evv9, Evv120) as well as Evv6 and Levv. The two cases where Beza and Stephanus agree in identifying a particular MS and the six cases where they agree in quoting the same number of MS variants give us a good reason to believe that their agreement at Matth. II.11, V.44, V.47, VII.14 is a real one (i.e. Beza also overlapped with Stephanus in using γ' ι' ια' ιε' and ις' (Evv4, Act 7, Act 8, Act 9, Act 10 and Apoc 3). Thus we can say that, in the book of Matthew at least, Beza used thirteen miniscules, L and D, in other words the same variants as Stephanus.

We can thus conclude that Beza used D^*, D, L and Evv6 as four of his nineteen variants, and we have good evidence to believe that he used Evv4, Evv5, Evv7, Evv8, Evv38, Evv9, Evv120, Act 7, Act 8, Act 9, Act 10 and Apoc 3 as another twelve variants.

This suggests that Beza was very largely dependent on the collations of the two Stephani for his MS variants. As has already been pointed out[18] the variants used by the two Stephani were very largely taken from miniscule MSS the earliest of which (Act 10) dated from the tenth century.[19] The text of L reckoned by Gregory to be "optimae notae" was treated by Stephanus in the same way as that of any other variant. Although Stephanus' addition of the apparatus criticus to the text was an improvement upon Erasmus' editions of the N.T., the changes in the actual text were small. The text with its preponderance of late and "Byzantine" readings was finally affirmed as authoritative in 1633 by the Elzevir brothers and became known as the Textus Receptus.[20]

Beza, as we shall see, followed this text but his attitude to his MS sources as expressed in his notes is somewhat ambiguous. In the dedicatory epistle of his 1598 edition he points out that, while using Henri Stephanus' collations, he noticed on occasions "quae alioqui sola interpretum coniectura nitebantur alicuius codicis autoritate ad cognoscendam veritatem nobis patefieret; in quo tamen hunc modum tenuimus ut admonitione contenti ex ingenio aut simplici coniectura ne apicem quidem mutaremus". This suggests that Beza had some appreciation of manuscripts as witnesses to the text. On the other hand, he had no method of evaluating his witnesses and it is interesting to note that, although he mentions 'veritas' he makes no reference to any criteria for it. Moreover, he states openly that he was very unwilling to amend the basic text[21] and was interested largely in readings which confirm it. This statement reflects Beza's practice in referring to his Greek MS sources. He does not weigh up the manuscripts in terms of right and wrong readings. On the other hand we cannot say with full justice that he merely lists his variants without assessing them in any way.[22] Here we shall briefly examine Beza's attitude to 3 of the MS sources which he quoted explicitly; D and the Syriac and Arabic versions.

When referring to D readings in the annotations, Beza frequently approves them as being clearer in the context than the corresponding TR readings (Mk. V.23, Mk. IX.16, Acts, II.46, XIV.17, XV.20). He does so, however, with the support of other witnesses, usually Syriac and Vetus. On occasions a D reading seems to influence either his Latin (Mk. IX.16, Acts II.46) or his Greek text (Mk. VIII.24, Acts XIV.17). On other occasions he expressly dismisses a D reading as either inapposite in the context (Mk. VIII.26) or theologically unacceptable (Luke VI.4-6). At other times Beza makes no reference at all to a D reading (Luke VII.36, Acts XIII.23, Matth. II.16).[23]

Similarly he often quotes the Syriac and Arabic N.T. as supporting his own interpretation of a particular passage (Mark VII.3, Luke I.38, Rom. I.20) but sometimes turns down the Syriac/Arabic readings as giving an inaccurate interpretation of the Greek (Acts I.3, VII.20, XVII.31, Heb. VII.19, XII.23).[24]

Throughout Beza is more concerned with accurate interpretation of particular passages than with establishing a correct reading and thus shows considerable unwillingness to tamper with the Greek text of Robert Stephanus.

Beza's Use of the Church Fathers

As well as having access to several new MSS sources, Beza also had at his disposal editions of Church Fathers which had come out in the latter half of the sixteenth century.

Although Beza refers to the fathers not as copiously as Erasmus he nonetheless mentions them a lot more frequently than Calvin. We may point out here that Beza's annotations are set out on the Erasmian model. In other words they are *notes* (as opposed to any kind of continuous commentary) which sometimes explain only minute philological points.

However, whereas Erasmus was in general concerned with simply citing patristic evidence as much for the clues it gave to the Greek text as for its theology, Beza was much more critical in his attitude to the Fathers' theology, while showing considerable respect for their textual evidence. Erasmus himself had edited several patristic works,[25] most of which were re-edited or re-printed by Beza's time. The 1570 Catalogue of Calvin's Academy[26] shows that the following main patristic works were at least available to Beza having been purchased during Calvin's time. Of the Latin editions the following were at his disposal; there was the 1555 version of the complete works of Ambrose corrected by Gelenius after Erasmus;[27] also a Latin edition of Cyprian's works printed by Hervagius in Basle in 1540. Moreover there were editions of Hilary of Poitiers (*Lucubrationes quotquot extant* printed by Froben in 1550), Jerome (Froben, 1553), Chrysostom (*Opera Omnia*, Chevallon, Paris, 1536), Origen (Froben, 1545), Augustine (Froben, 1543), Theophylactus (*In Quattuor Evangelia Erarrationes*, Hervagius, Basle, 1554), Tertullian (Froben, 1550) and Basil (Froben, 1552). Most of these were Erasmian editions, or based on his.

In addition, the library of Calvin's Academy contained the following Greek editions of the Fathers; an edition of

Chrysostom (*In Omnes Pauli Apostoli epistolas*, Verona, 1529), in three volumes, the *Liturgiae* of Chrysostom and Basil (*una cum canonibus Apostolorum*)[28] *Catalogus* of Basil's Greek works with a preface by Erasmus (Froben, 1532), an edition of the works of Gregory of Nazianzus in Greek and Latin (Hervagius, 1550), the Greek dialogues of Theodoret (Rome, 1547), a copy of *Oecumenii opera* (Basle, 1553), a Greek edition of Damascenus' *Orthodoxae fidei accurata explicatio* containing a parallel Latin translation by Lefèvre d'Etaples (Basle, 1548) and a copy of Eusebius' work in two volumes (R. Estienne, Paris, 1544-1545).

Even though these editions were available to him, it is not necessarily the case that Beza would have used them all, and, as most of them were purchased during the time of Calvin, they can only give us an indication of the attitude to the Fathers prevalent in Geneva. They do not give us any clue as to Beza's personal outlook. However the 1605 Catalogue of Calvin's Academy[29] is more helpful here since it contains, among other titles, a list of patristic works which would have been purchased during Beza's rectorship. The most striking additions are a Greek edition of Theophylactus,[30] a copy of Chrysostom's homilies in Greek and Latin as well as a separate Greek-Latin copy of his *De Sacerdotio* and *Homiliae contra Judaeos*, a six-volume edition of the complete works of Augustine (Printed in Paris) in addition to the ten-volume version already in the library, and a separate copy of Augustine's *De Civitate Dei*. Other accessions number the Greek-Latin works of Clement of Alexandria, and the Latin version of Theophylactus' commentaries on St. Paul's epistles.

From this we may assume that Beza approved of Theophylactus' collations and Chrysostom's works and that he was in theological outlook an Augustinian. We may further say (on the combined evidence of the two catalogues) that Beza had a large corpus of Patristic evidence to draw upon, but the small number of accessions made during his own time suggests that he was not altogether in favour of the Fathers.

This assumption is borne out by an examination[31] of Beza's exegetical notes in his editions of the New Testament, where although showing a wide knowledge of Patristic writings, he is usually critical of the Fathers' viewpoint. Thus, one striking feature of Beza's annotations on the Romans is his attack on Origen. His particular objections to Origen are to do with the Law, its definition and its relation to Christ, and with the question of free will.[32] Thus at Romans II.27 Beza objects to Origen's differentiation between πραττειν, φυλαττειν and τελειν. Origen associates the first two verbs with an observation of an external cult, while applying τελειν to the perfect keeping of the Law. Beza replies that there is only one Law which demonstrates the δικαιοκρισια of God and that all the three verbs apply to the keeping of that law.

At Romans IV.2 Origen claims that Abraham was justified by faith and thus he had "gloriam apud Deum". Beza objects to this saying that men, although justified freely, have nothing of their own in which they might glory. Hence, Abraham's faith could not account for his glory since Faith itself is a free gift of God.

Jerome, the exegete, as opposed to Jerome, the translator is also frequently criticized. Thus at 1 Cor. VII.1 Beza condemns Jerome for interpreting καλον in such a way that he relegates marriage "a Spiritu Sancto toties comprobatum" to the realm of things evil. As against that, Beza approves the interpretation of Clement, Epiphanius and Augustine, all of whom suggest that chastity has a place within marriage.[33]

Ambrose is treated rather less severely even though Beza criticizes him for thinking that Zacharias was a Pontifex maximus (Luke I.5) and for assuming that, when Paul was writing,

"Romanos...nondum fidem Christi recte tenuisse" (Rom. I.12). However it is more important to see that Beza uses Ambrose and Tertullian to support the homoousian notion of the divinity of Christ (Rom. I.4). Similarly, it is Ambrose whom Beza quotes in support of his doctrine of the Eucharist.[34]

There can be little doubt that Beza's theology was, on the whole, Augustinian and that, from among the Fathers, it is Augustine who is accorded the greatest measure of respect in Beza's quotations. This does not mean to say that the Bishop of Hippo[35] escapes censure altogether. For instance at Rom. V.14 Beza suggests that Augustine is right in saying that newly born children are mortal because of the original sin. However, he considers Augustine's interpretation too harsh because he underestimates the connection between Baptism and salvation. Moreover, at Rom. VI.12 he suggests that Augustine's definition of sin should not be wholly accepted, as Augustine does not call "illa vitiositas 'peccatum' nisi quum Spiritum re ipsa in aliquo motu superat". Beza, on the contrary, suggests that sin remains an evil independently of its interaction with men. On the other hand, Augustine's views on predestination and "permissio mali" are quoted at length by Beza in support of his own. Origen's views, particularly on 'permissio mali' are found to be "most impure".[36]

As we have seen from the instances quoted above, Beza's attitude to the Fathers is critical and not even Augustine escapes this. This, however, does not seem to have any bearing on Beza's serious consideration of the Fathers as witnesses to the Greek text. A few instances of this will be examined here.

At Matthew I.11 Beza explains that he has changed Stephanus' text for two reasons. Firstly, it appears from the writings of Epiphanius, Chrysostom, Jerome, Augustine "et aliis probatissimis patribus" that Stephanus' reading was not the oldest 'recepta lectio'. Secondly the "sacrae historiae" do not refer to Jechonias as having any brothers. As the final authority for this latter statement he quotes Jerome's account[37] with which, he says, he agrees totally.

At Matthew X.1 Beza inserts κατα before πνευματων on the authority of two Greek MSS and Theophylactus' commentaries on the Gospels.

At John XII.32 Beza accepts the reading παντας (Vulgate, παντα) on the authority of Chrysostom and Theophylactus. He also refers to Cyril's exploitation of παντα (lib. in Joan 8 vers. 17) as indicating "all kinds of men".

At Rom. IV.9 Beza supplies the verb "cadit" on the authority of Theophylactus,[38] and the word μονον on the authority of Jerome (Vulgate). However he occasionally also criticizes the Patristic readings.

At Rom. IV.17 he points out that Ambrose reads "credidisti" not "credidit" (ἐπιστευσε). This, Beza says, is wrong since it does not appear in any manuscripts or in the Vulgate. At Luke XVIII.7 he objects to Chrysostom's reading και μακροθυμει ἐπ' αὐτοις ("et iram cohibebit super ipsis") which also occurs in D, Vetus versions and the Vulgate,[39] for doctrinal reasons; the Scripture itself and innumerable histories of the Saints show that the Lord will defer his anger against the Church's enemies, *not* that he will restrain it altogether. As against Chrysostom,[40] Beza quotes Theophylactus' suggestion that και ahould be taken in the sense of καν before μακροθυμων which supports his own interpretation.[41]

From this brief survey of Beza's attitude to the Fathers we can draw the following conclusions. Beza undoubtedly had a wide and thorough knowledge of Patristic writings. However, he made few accessions to the Library, and his attitude to the Fathers' theology was much more critical than that of Erasmus.

In spite of that, however, he values the Fathers as guides to the Greek text.

Naturally, in modern terms Beza appears somewhat conservative as a textual critic. He was reluctant to amend radically and the Greek text he presents, in spite of the new MSS and the Patristic evidence available to him is the Textus Receptus with a few revisions. On the other hand, we must remember that a surprising amount of the new material which Beza had at his disposal was incorporated into his exegetical notes[42] and that these notes as well as Beza's Greek text and his translation of it had a powerful influence on the English New Testament from the 1560 Genevan to the Authorized version.[43] In the chapters to follow, we shall be considering the exact nature of this influence, but firstly, we shall take a brief look at the versions themselves.

Beza's Influence on the English Geneva Bible

The English version of the Geneva Bible, probably the work of Gilby, Whittingham and Sampson[44] was printed in Geneva by Roland Hall in 1560, in quarto. The translators were Marian exiles in a Calvinist environment.

Their work was considerably influenced by the French Geneva Bible which was revised by Calvin in 1558 and their main Greek text for the New Testament translation was the 1550 text of Stephanus. Although the translators had access to Beza's 1557 Latin New Testament to which the annotationes majores were appended, no edition of Beza's Greek New Testament had as yet appeared.

There is no doubt about the strong influence which the French Geneva Bible had on the text of English Geneva. This has already been adequately shown by Westcott[45] and can hardly be disputed. However, it seems that so far as the marginal notes in the English Geneva Bible are concerned, the influence of Beza was more significant than it might at first appear.

Professor Metzger in an article in *New Testament Studies*[46] (vol. 8, pp. 72-77) discusses the relationship between the 1560 English Geneva Bible and Codex Bezae. Twenty variant Western readings appear in the margins of the English Bible, and *four* of these (John VIII.5, Acts XIV.8, Acts XIV.9, 1 Cor. XV.55) did not appear in Stephanus' edition of 1550. Professor Metzger concludes from this that, before 1562, when the Codices finally came into his possession, Beza must have had access to a larger body of MS evidence than that contained in the printed form of Stephanus' text, and this he made available to the English translators.

If this conclusion is right,[47] this would suggest strong connections between Beza and the translators of the English Geneva Bible.

Here we propose to give a brief survey of the marginal notes in the 1560 Geneva Bible, then compare them with notes on the same passages in the French Bible and in Beza's 1557 New Testament. The English marginal notes are of two types; those marked with " denote a textual variant and those marked with // denote a comment on a difficult place. It is the latter type that we shall be principally concerned with here having selected some notes on the principle of (a) their theology and (b) their style.

At Matth. VI.7 the Geneva translators stress that "superfluous repetes" as opposed to mere "repetes" are being condemned. Beza also specifically condemns unnecessary repetitions in his annotationes majores making the point that "longae preces non damnant sed vanae inanes et superstisiosae". The French Geneva version has no marginal note here but translates the Greek as "N̕ usez de vaines redites" thus making the same point as Beza in his annotation and the English Geneva in both its text and its note.[48]

At Rom. I.9 the English translators gloss "in my spirit" as "earnestly and from the heart". The other possible interpretation would have been "in spirit" as opposed to "ceremonies". Beza also did not think that Paul meant the latter and he himself glosses the phrase as "plane volens et ex animo illi addictus". The French version has no note here and its text reads simply "en mon esprit".

At Rom. I.28 the Geneva version explains "reprobat mind" as "such one as was destitute of all judgement". Beza has here "mentem omnis iudicii expertem" in his text as translation of ἀδόκιμον νουν. The French Geneva also reads "un esprit despourveu de tout jugement" which is glossed "reprouvé" in the margin.

At 1 Cor. X.17 the Geneva translators offer the following marginal explanation. "If we that are many in number are but one bodie in effect, joyned with our head Christ, as many corners make but one loaf, let us renounce idolatrie which doeth separate our unitie." The loaf metaphor originated with Ambrose and was also used by Beza in his annotation on 1 Cor. X.17[49] to emphasize that our union with Christ is corporeal[50] not spiritual. The French Geneva version has no note here and translates the Greek "Car nous qui sommes plusieurs, sommes un pain et un corps d'autant que nous sommes tous participans d'un mesme pain",[51] thus leaving open the question of corporeal union with Christ.

At Heb. III.1 the English translators gloss their text "our profession" with "that doctrine which we believe and ought to confesse". Beza's text reads here "professionis" and his marginal note "eius doctrinae quam profitemur". There is no annotation in the French Geneva Bible here and their text reads "de nostre confession".

At Heb. XII.13 the English translators elucidate "lest

that which is halting" as "partly declaring their sloeness and partely their inconstancie in doctrine". This seems to be a paraphrase of Beza's note who points out that the lame are not only those who are slow and negligent about doing their duty but also those who waver between the Old Covenant and the New. The French version has no annotation here, reading "afin que ce qui cloche" in the text.

At Heb. X.26 the Geneva Bible explains "if we sinne willingly" to mean "that is forsake Jesus Christ, as Judas, Saul, Arius, Julian the apostat did". Beza in his exposition on this passage draws a distinction between those who sin and those who delight in forsaking Jesus Christ and the truth. Among the latter he specifically mentions "Saul, Julianus Apostata, Arius". It seems from this as if the Geneva annotation was a simplified version of Beza's note with the name of Judas added. The French version has no annotation here translating the Greek as "car si nous pechons volontairement".

At Acts II.46 the reading "from house to house" is suggested as marginal alternative by the translators. They read "at home" in the text. The version "from house to house" was adopted by Beza but not until 1589. The French Geneva Bible however, has "de maison en maison" in its 1558 text.

At Acts XVII.11 the translators explain that "more noble" does not mean "more excellent of birth but more prompt and couragious in receiving the word of God; for he compareth them of Berea with them of Thessalonica who persecuted the Apostles in Berea". Both Beza and the French Geneva take εὐγενεστεροι in this sense. The French version has the marginal explanation "Et ceulx ci furent plus courageux que ceulx de Thessalonique."

At Acts XX.7 the English version reads "the first day of the weeke" agreeing with both Beza and the French Geneva ("le premier jour de la septmaine"). The French Geneva adds no marginal annotation but the English translators comment "Of this place and also of 1 Cor. XVI.2 we gather that the Christians used to have their solemn assemblies this day laying aside the ceremonie of the Jewish Sabbath." This, in fact, is an exact translation of Beza's note.[52]

At Acts XXII.14 the English translators comment that "this may be referred to the eternal counsel of God, or els to the execution and declaration of the same which semeth here to be more proper". This again is an exact translation of Beza's comment on the same passage, "Potest autem hoc vel ad aeternum Dei consilium, vel ad eius exequutionem ac deliberationem referri; quod posterius malo." The French Geneva version has no annotation here.

The selection of notes discussed above is by no means exhaustive. However, the following observations may be made on the basis of it. Of the eleven marginal annotations in the English Geneva Bible which we have examined here, four (Matth. VI.7, Rom. I.28, Heb. III.1, Acts XVII.11) agree with Beza's annotations but could equally well be based on the French Geneva version or, at least, have its additional support. Six (Rom. I.9, 1 Cor. X.17, Heb. XII.13, X.26; Acts XX.7, XXII.14) appear to be based on Beza's annotations but, it must be pointed out that none of them (with the possible exception of 1 Cor. X.17) goes against the French text. In one case (Acts II.46) the English translators' marginal note is based directly on the French text.

To conclude, we may say that the English Geneva translators tended to use Bezan annotations simply for purposes of elucidation rather than to contravene the French text. Indeed, they show an opposition to the French Bible only in the case of the doctrine of the Eucharist. However, it can be seen from the instances adduced above that the English translators took from Beza a larger proportion of their marginal annotations than might be expected in view of their general reliance on the French version.

Laurence Tomson's Translation of Beza's Latin New Testament (1576)

In 1574 Pierre L'Oiseleur de Villers, a Huguenot refugee in London, produced an edition of Beza's Latin New Testament. L'Oiseleur originally came from Paris but was forced to move from there on account of persecutions against those who professed the Reformed faith.[53] He stayed in Geneva during the late 1550's and 60's. Sometime during that period Beza asked him to translate his "rubric annotations" into French.[54] L'Oiseleur then took up a ministry at Rouen, in which he continued until the Massacre of St. Bartholomew forced him to seek refuge in England. It was not until after his arrival in England that he embarked on the task entrusted to him by Beza.

In his dedicatory epistle to the 1574[55] edition L'Oiseleur makes no mention of altering Beza's Latin text. He does, however, explain that sometime ago Beza had left him the task of changing his *shorter* (breviores) annotations into French and of explaining the more difficult and less common phrases with brief notes. L'Oiseleur, however, felt that to take such liberty would be something of an insult to Beza, so he published the shorter annotations as they stood in Latin, and added the explanations of the harder passages (printed in italics in Vautrollier's publication) from Beza's own "majores annotationes". He claims that he followed his own judgement on very few occasions indeed merely adding some notes from Camerarius in Gospels and Acts where Beza's annotations were not very full. Altogether, his principal concern, he says, was to produce a work which could pass for Beza's own.

It is difficult to ascertain exactly what sources L'Oiseleur used, but we can have a good idea of the sources which were available to him. By the 1570's Beza had produced two sets of New Testament annotations both of which were to undergo several editions and reprints. The 'Majores Annotationes' were first published separately in folio by Robert Stephanus in 1557. The 'Minores Annotationes', summaries of points of doctrine inserted in the N.T. margin were printed for the first time in 1565 in octavo. Beza's *Latin* New Testament, originally published in 1557 had its second printing in 1565 and L'Oiseleur includes Beza's prefatory epistle to the 1565 version in his 1574 edition. It is placed there so that it follows L'Oiseleur's dedication. On the strength of this we may assume that L'Oiseleur based his edition on Beza's 1565 Latin version. And a closer examination shows *no* difference between the two Latin texts. Johannes Camerarius, a German humanist and classical scholar produced two works of New Testament Annotations, *Commentarius in Novum Foedus* published in 1570 and *Notatio Figurarum Sermonis* published in 1572.

The two quite often have an identical or similar annotation on a particular passage and L'Oiseleur appears to have referred to both. It is much more difficult to see which of Beza's annotations L'Oiseleur referred to. He appears to have straightforwardly reprinted the 'Minores Annotationes' since they do not differ in any way from those published in 1565. In Vautrollier's publication they are printed in lower case.

In Gospels and Acts L'Oiseleur sometimes glosses difficult points of text and style with an extract from an "Annotatio Major". On other occasions he supplies a note from Camerarius even though a Bezan annotation was available.

When L'Oiseleur supplies a note out of the 'Annotationes Majores' he either paraphrases Beza's note in order to make it more concise, or extracts the crucial phrase from an "annotatio". Thus in Matthew VI.2 Beza has "quod vocabulum theologi retinuerunt. Dicitur autem proprie de Histrionibus personam aliquam sustinentibus in fabula." Which L'Oiseleur abbreviates to "hypocritae enim erant histriones qui personam aliquam in fabula sustinerent". He extracts the main part of the annotation, omitting the peripheral idea that the word "histrio" was adopted into theological vocabulary. At Matthew VI.6 Beza has "significat locum secretiorem in quo recondimus aliquid" which is shortened by L'Oiseleur to "in locum interiorem et conditum". At Matthew VI.16 Beza has "ipsa vultus externa specie cui isti quoque hypocritae comptum et munditiem omnem subtrahebant illuvie et squalore foedi prodeuntes quasi nativum vultum e medio tollerent". L'Oiseleur paraphrases this to read "Non sinunt conspici faciem priorem i.e. colorem faciei nativum vitiant ut appareant macra et pallida facie." These examples illustrate a practice which L'Oiseleur adopts consistently in dealing with the 'Annotationes Majores'.

There are occasions, however, in Gospels and Acts when he prefers Camerarius to Beza. His reason for doing this is sometimes of a doctrinal nature as in John VII.16 where Beza's annotation reads "mihi non est quaesita et ex doctorum disciplina sed data divinitus a Patre" thus emphasizing that Jesus drew his teaching from the Father as opposed to the Rabbis. Camerarius (*Notatio Figurarum*) has here "quasi dicat Mea doctrina non est mea, id est eius, quem vos hominem unum ex multis putatis esse, atqua adeo contemnitis, sed eius a quo missus sum", laying stress on the fact that Jesus was not a self-taught upstart. The antithesis between the Rabbinic learning and the New Learning is omitted. L'Oiseleur presumably preferred Camerarius' emphasis here.

In other instances, however, L'Oiseleur chooses Camerarius where there is no doctrinal difference between his note and

Beza's. To give just one example of this at Mark XVI.15 Beza annotates "Hinc vero pro humano omni genere accipitur sive pro omnibus gentibus" whereas Camerarius has "Non Judaeo nec in Judaea tantum sed omnibus hominibus." L'Oiseleur preferred Camerarius. There is a remarkable similarity between the notes of Camerarius and Beza in several other instances. In fact some of Beza's notes are so similar to Camerarius' that it seems extremely unlikely that they could have been produced independently.

Moreover, L'Oiseleur justifies his using of Camerarius by saying that he was "vir (Bezae) amantissimus". Those facts in conjunction with the already established similarity of the two scholars' notes in Gospels and Acts would lead us to believe that Beza himself had referred to Camerarius for his 'Annotationes Majores'. This, however, does not explain why L'Oiseleur should have used Camerarius' notes in preference to Beza's especially after having claimed to use Camerarius only where there are *no* annotations in Beza.

The internal evidence here would suggest style as a possible solution to this problem. Camerarius' notes both in the *Commentarius* and in the *Notatio* are considerably shorter than Beza's notes, having been designed for a relatively small work. Their style is therefore correspondingly more concise although, in some cases, very similar to Beza's.

Thus at Matthew IX.38 Beza's full annotation reads, "Ad verb. eiiciat quam vocis huius prophetam si sequi voluimus, intelligemus operarios vel celeriter mittendos in opus Dei, vel etiam invitos et cunctantes extrudendos, sumus enim omnes in istis praesertim rebus tardissimi", whereas the full note in Camerarius adopted by L'Oiseleur is "Ad verb. eiiciat nam in tam sancto opere homines sunt tardissimi." While he was working on the annotations L'Oiseleur probably had copies of both Camerarius and Beza before him. On seeing that Beza's content was sometimes expressed much more concisely in Camerarius, he would quite likely copy the latter, thereby saving himself the labour of cutting Beza's lengthy notes and at the same time remaining faithful to his aim of producing a work as close as possible to Beza's own. Camerarius had done no expository work on the Epistles, and there L'Oiseleur confined himself almost entirely to summarizing Beza's 'Annotationes Majores'.

Occasions in Gospels and Epistles where L'Oiseleur used his own judgement are very few. Thus for instance at Rom. VII.7 he explains that "desire here does not signify desires guilty because of their object 'sed fontem earum', i.e. a desire which is guilty in itself".

L'Oiseleur's edition of Beza's New Testament was translated into English by Laurence Tomson (then secretary to Walsingham[56]) in 1576 and was printed in London by Christopher Barker in octavo-size. It received several reprints and by 1586 it had replaced the 1560 New Testament in the English Geneva Bible (with notes). Tomson based his work very largely on L'Oiseleur's referring also to the 1565 edition of Beza's *Greek* N.T. In some instances he preferred to follow the 1560 Geneva readings as against Beza. In matters of text he seems to have used his own judgement very rarely. So far as the marginal notes were concerned, he retained those of L'Oiseleur's annotations which he considered the most important. For instance in Matthew VI Tomson has 11 annotations where L'Oiseleur has 27. In Matthew IX he has seven annotations to L'Oiseleur's 16. In Matthew XIII he only retains one annotation out of L'Oiseleur's 24. In Mark XV Tomson has 6 annotations to L'Oiseleur's 8; in John III Tomson keeps all the notes with the exception of one. In Acts II Tomson has 25 annotations to L'Oiseleur's 31. At Romans V and VII Tomson keeps all the annotations of his original. Since Tomson's practice is consistent it is possible to obtain some idea of the principles which guided him in selecting annotations. In Matthew VI Tomson keeps the note "Long praiers are not condemned but vaine, needlesse, and superstitious". This annotation is (a) of doctrinal significance because of its anti-Catholic tone, and (b) has the backing of the 1560 Geneva version. Tomson, in the same chapter discards note at v. 7 which paraphrases "loquacitate" as "verbositate". He himself translates "loquacitate" as "babbling" so there is no need for an explanatory note. In note on v. 14 L'Oiseleur gives "aequalibus vestris" as synonym for "hominibus". Tomson translates simply "men" discarding the annotation as superfluous. In Luke I Tomson keeps the more important notes such as the historical elucidations at v. 36, "Though Elizabeth were of the tribe of Levi..." and v. 39, "that is to say, Hebron: which was in times past called Cariantharbe...". He also retains the doctrinal notes such as the one at v. 50 which explains the text "them that feare him" as "them that live godly and religiously". In Romans VII where all the annotations are of a doctrinal nature, Tomson is seen to retain them all. The rubric notes explaining sections of chapters are also preserved by him in their entirety. We can thus say that Tomson keeps L'Oiseleur's doctrinal and historical annotations whilst dispensing with the inessential linguistic points.

So far as Tomson's text and his interpretation is concerned he agrees with Beza as against the 1560 Geneva version in the following cases. At John XIV.1 Tyndale, Whittingham and 1560 Geneva all read "And he sayde unto his disciples". This reading is confirmed by D and Erasmus.[57] Beza, however, followed Stephanus here omitting καὶ εἶπεν τοις μαθηταις αὐτου and starting the verse with "Μη ταρασσεσθω ὑμων ἡ καρδια--ne turbetur cor vestrum." Tomson followed Beza here translating "Let not your heart be troubled" as the first sentence of the verse.

At Romans VII.6 Tyndale has "dead from that whereunto we were in bondage", Whittingham and Geneva 1560 read "being dead until it wherein we were holden". Beza's 2nd Latin edition has "mortuo eo in quo detinebamur" and this is followed by Tomson who translates "he being dead in whom we were holden". The Greek variants here are as follows: Codex Bezae and some Vetus MSS read του θανατου for αποθανοντες.[58] αποθανοντες is the reading adopted by the majority of Greek MSS and followed by both Stephanus and Erasmus. Chrysostom, however, reads αποθανοντος. This is the reading Beza follows in his *Latin* version on the grounds that Paul never speaks about death in the Law without mentioning sin. Of the English versions, Whittingham, Tyndale and Geneva follow the αποθανοντες reading. Tomson, however, follows Beza in translating αποθανοντος i.e. "sin being dead we are free from the Law". This suggests that both Beza and Tomson were associating Paul's concept of the Law with his concept of Sin. Before the coming of Christ we served God by observance of the written Law. Sin was consequent upon the Law and thus we were bound to it (married). But now through Christ's death we are freed from Sin, and thus freed from the Law. According to Beza and Tomson it is Sin not the Law which is the dead husband in v. 2.

At Romans V.12 και ουτως εις παντας ανθρωπους ο θανατος διηλθεν εφ' ᾧ παντες ημαρτον is rendered by Beza as "et ita in omnes homines mors transiit in quo omnes peccarunt". Erasmus has here "in quo" in the sense of "quatenus". Tyndale, Whittingham and Geneva all agree with Erasmus and translate "insomuch that all men have sinned". Tomson, however, agrees with Beza and reads "in whom all men have sinned". Beza had read εφ' ᾧ as εν' ᾧ[59] thereby following the teaching of Ambrose and Augustine on the original sin. St. Ambrose taught the solidarity of the whole human race with Adam not only in the consequences of his sin but also in the sin itself which is trans-

mitted through natural generation. Augustine agreed with this
claiming that Adam's guilt is transmitted to his descendents
by concupiscence. Man is therefore not free; he necessarily
follows the attractions of either concupiscence or grace.
Beza rejected out of hand Origen's view that only the un-
righteous shared in the consequences of Adam's act. The other
versions translating ἐφ' ᾧ as "insomuch that" would seem to
incline to the Thomist view that the Original Sin is transmitted not as the permanent fault of Adam but as state of
human nature. It still constitutes a fault since all men are
regarded as members of one great organism of which Adam was
the first mover. In his 1565 Greek-Latin edition Beza has a
short note by this verse. "Ab Adamo in quo omnes peccarunt
reatus et mors (quae est reorum poena) in omnes pervasit" and
the same annotation appears in L'Oiseleur's Latin edition.
Although Tomson follows Beza's *reading* he edits the marginal
note to make it *less explicit* and says simply "(in whom) that
is, in Adam".

At 1 Peter III.18 Beza translates ζωοποιηθεὶς δε τῳ πνευματι as "vivificatus autem Spiritu". Of the English versions
Tyndale, Whittingham and 1560 Geneva agree with Erasmus and
translate "was quickened in the Spirit". Tomson agrees with
Beza and has "was quickened by the Spirit". Beza in his 1565
edition raises the doctrinal point that "Spiritus" here indicates the power or Divine nature joined onto the human frame
when it is opposed by the weaker, the fleshly nature. Therefore, Beza says, the passage interpreted correctly means
"Crucifixus est ex infirmitate sed vivit ex Dei potentia".
To support this he quotes Paul at Rom. I.3 and at 2 Cor. IV
and XIII. The interpretation that Christ was killed in the
flesh but his soul was restored to life is regarded by Beza
as "foul corruption". He subscribes to the view that regards
Christ's new spiritual activity as beginning immediately after

death and even before the Resurrection. Tomson evidently supported this view and so did Whittingham, who translating "in the spirit" added a marginal note to specify "the power of God".

On the following occasions Tomson seems to use his own judgement as against both Beza and Geneva 1560. At John I.15 Beza reads "is qui pone me venit ante me fuit quia prior me erat". Tyndale has "he that cometh after me is proferred before me, for he was more excellent than I". The Geneva version reads "He that cometh after me is proferred before me for he was before me". Tomson has "He that cometh after me was before me, for he was better than I". Tomson evidently chose this particular reading to emphasize the doctrinal point. If πρωτος is translated as "better", the emphasis is placed on Jesus' supremacy over John by reason of his status; if it is translated as "first" the emphasis is placed on Jesus' pre-existence. On consulting L'Oiseleur's edition of Beza we find that the marginal annotation here states "Ad verbum Prior, illud autem non ad tempus sed ad dignitatem refertur". Tomson has inserted his *own* annotation here saying "This sentence hath in it a turning of the reason as we call it, as who would say a setting of that first which should be last and that last which should be first; for in plain speech this is it 'He that commeth after me is better than I am, for he was before me' (cf. Luke VII.47)." We can see from this that whereas Beza preferred to keep the literal Greek meaning in the text and explain its doctrinal meaning in the margin, Tomson preferred to bring out the doctrinal significance of the text and give the literal rendition in the margin. At Philippians I.10 εις το δοκιμαζειν υμας τα διαφεροντα is translated by Beza as "ut dignoscatis quae discrepant". This translation seems to be followed by Whittingham and Geneva 1560 both reading "that ye may discerne things that differ one from another". Tyndale ("that ye might accept things most excellent") and Tomson ("that ye may alowe those things which are best") agree with Erasmus' rendering "ut probetis quae sunt praestantia". Beza had commented here that good judgement is that whereby we can not only recognize what is pleasing but also distinguish right from wrong. Hence his own translation suggests that judgement consists in accepting those things which are objectively acknowledged to be excellent.

From this we can see that Tomson's New Testament was more influenced by Beza than the 1560 Geneva version. Most of Tomson's marginal notes, especially in the Epistles come from Beza via L'Oiseleur. His text showed a closer agreement with Beza's Latin than had the 1560 version. But it must be remembered that although Tomson used his *own* judgement rarely, he did, however, on occasions refer to the English Geneva version and adopted *its* reading as against Beza. This will be seen in later chapters.

So far in this chapter the following ground has been covered. We have discussed the material Beza himself used for his editions of the Greek-Latin New Testament. We have outlined the influence of Beza's 1557 Latin edition with Annotations on the 1560 Geneva Bible. We then discussed L'Oiseleur's edition of Beza's Latin New Testament, establishing that L'Oiseleur used the text of 1565 edition of Beza's Greek-Latin New Testament (printed by Robert Stephanus) and a mixture of notes from Camerarius and Beza himself. Laurence Tomson translated L'Oiseleur's work in 1576 thus producing a New Testament dependent almost entirely upon Beza's version, although, as has been mentioned he did refer to other sources. From this we can see that Beza's influence on the English Geneva and Laurence Tomson's version was largely that of his *Latin* versions. Although Tomson certainly would have consulted Beza's Greek he does not refer to it explicitly. In conclusion it was Beza's doctrinal notes and his Latin wording which were of principal interest to the Geneva translators, and even more so to Tomson.

Use of Beza's New Testament by the Authorized Translators

The influence of Beza on the Authorized Version was of a different type.[60] Scrivener has pointed out that "On certain occasions, it may be the Translators yielded too much to Beza's somewhat arbitrary decisions; but they lived at a time when his name was the very highest among Reformed theologians, when means for arriving at an independent judgement were few and scattered, and when the first principles of textual criticism had yet to be gathered from a long process of painful induction." Recently some new material has come to light which may help us to define more closely the exact nature of Beza's influence on the AV.

We know from their preface to the first edition that the translators (47 or 54) were divided into 6 companies. Two of those were to work at Westminster, two in Cambridge and two in Oxford.[61] The translators were issued with forty-two copies of the Bishops' Bible, printed in folio by Robert Barker in 1602. The completed work was then handed over to the Final Revision Committee, which included John Bois and Andrew Downs working in the Stationers' Hall from 1610-1611.[62] The finishing touches to the work were apparently put by Bishop Bilson and Dr. Smith.

The Bodleian Copy of the Bishops' Bible 1602 printed by Robert Barker

A copy of the 1602 issue of the Bishops' Bible is found in the Bodleian. The volume is remarkable for its MS annotations which occur in the Old Testament,[63] in books (1) from Genesis to the Song of Solomon, (2) the twelve Minor Prophets. In the New Testament, which concerns us here, the Synoptic Gospels are annotated fully throughout. St. John's Gospel has annotations in chapters 17-21, and isolated notes occur at Ephesians IV.8, II Thessalonians II.15, 1 Cor. IX.5, Gal. III.15, II Peter I.10. Some passages of the unannotated text are marked with / evidently to denote a place where a note could be inserted.

The handwriting of the notes does not provide any clues as to the identity of their executor. Although the Old Testament hand is different and probably earlier than that in the New Testament, in both parts the notes are in the Elizabethan Secretary hand, such as would be used by an amanuensis. Leaving aside the nature of the O.T. annotations, since they do not concern us here, let us consider the nature of the N.T. ones. Those are of two main types; first, notes in the Elizabethan secretary hand denote changes in the text. In each case the relevant portion of the printed text is either underlined or crossed out and the 'new reading' is inserted either in the margin or, in some cases, between the lines of the printed text, above the section which has been crossed out. All the 'new readings' are marked with letters of the Greek alphabet from α to ω, α beginning the first annotation of each book. Secondly, there are the annotations 'Ang' and 'Rom' executed in the italic hand; these suggest typographical instructions, and here we shall consider in detail their appearance in the Synoptic Gospels. We shall endeavour to establish a principle governing the insertion of those notes and examine whether they relate in any way to the text of the second issue of AV 1611.[64]

In Matthew there are 16 'Ang' annotations (X.2, XV.33, XVI.8, XVIII.8 (2), XIX.23.26, XXI.39.41, XXII.35.42, XXIII.27,

XXIV.41, XXV.40, XXVI.17.71). All of those are done in the same way; the relevant words in the text *printed in italics* in every case are underlined 'Ang' is written above the word in the text and then again in the margin. In three cases the word in the text is underlined and 'Ang' occurs above it only and not in the margin (XIII.41, XVIII.9, XXVIII.6). There are also two cases where the word is underlined, and 'Ang' is inserted in the margin only. This would suggest either simple forgetfulness on the part of the writer or an omission made in *copying*. There are three cases of 'Rom' appearing in text and margin. In each case the words underlined are printed in ordinary letters. There is one instance of 'Rom' appearing *above* the underlined word and not in the margin (X.9).

In all cases the italic words marked by 'Ang' in Bodleian Bishops' are printed in ordinary letters in the second issue of the AV. At XXVI.71 the Bishops' text has 'wench' in italics with an 'Ang' annotation. The AV has substituted 'maiden' for 'wench', and printed it in ordinary letters. All the words in Matthew marked with 'Rom' are printed in italics in AV.

There are 13 'Ang' annotations in Mark (III.8, IV.35, V.1, V.21, V.24, VI.5.40, IX.18, X.19.33, XIII.29, XIV.54) and the technique adopted here is slightly different from that in Matthew. Instead of inserting 'Ang' in both text and margin, the annotator marked the relevant italicized words in the text with a Greek symbol as well as underlining them. The same Greek symbol is then inserted in the margin beside 'Ang'. The only exception to that seems to be X.19 where 'no' in the text is underlined and crossed out and 'not' is inserted in the margin with 'Angl' after it in brackets. The 'Rom' annotations occur 4 times in Mark (VI.16, VI.26, XII.1, XV.45). All the words marked with 'Ang' in the Bishops' text are printed in ordinary type in the AV. All the words marked with 'Rom' the AV prints in italics.

In Luke there are 12 'Ang' annotations; in each case the relevant italicized word is marked with a Greek symbol, underlined and written again in the margin with the Greek symbol and the annotation 'Ang' (III.23, VI.15, VII.15, VIII.13, XII.47.48, XV.12, XV.23, XV.28, XVII.14.24.35). There are 4 'Rom' annotations (II.37.38, VI.16.22). In each case the relevant word is crossed out and underlined in the text, and marked with a Greek symbol. It is then rewritten in the margin in imitation italic print with 'Rom' following. The words marked with 'Ang' are printed in ordinary letters by the AV in all cases except one. At Luke III.23 AV prints 'the sonne' (of Heli) in italics. All the words marked with 'Rom' are printed in italics by the AV.

A study of the Greek text may reveal the principle behind the 'Ang' and 'Rom' annotations in the Bodleian copy of the Bishops' Bible. It may be useful to remember here that the principle behind italics in the Bishops' Bible was the same as in 1560 Geneva Bible, i.e. the italics were to be "put to that word which lacking made the sentence obscure, but...(so that) it may easily be discerned from the common text".[65] The Bishops' Bible applied this principle very freely to the extent that most words *not contained* in a particular Greek sentence were italicized even though they might be essential to the English construction. Conversely, words not appearing in the Greek and *not* essential to the English construction were sometimes put in, wrongly, in ordinary print.

It seems that the 'Ang' and 'Rom' annotations in Bodleian Bishops' represent an attempt made by the AV translators to establish more rigorous principles for italicizing words. This can be seen from the following table. Parentheses are used to indicate context.

1. *'Ang' Annotations in Matthew*

WORDS MARKED WITH 'ANG'		CORRESPONDING WORDS PRINTED IN ORDINARY PRINT BY AV	GREEK TEXT
X.2	sonne of	✓	ὁ τοῦ Ζεβεδαίου
XV.33	should we get	should we have	ποθεν ἡμιν... ἀρτοι τοσουτοι
XVI.8	which	✓	γνους δε ὁ 'Ιησους
XVIII.8	(cast) them (from)	✓	βαλε ἀπο σου
XVIII.8	rather (than thou having)	✓	ἠ
XIX.23	man	✓	πλουσιος
26	(beheld) them	✓	ἐμβλεψας
XXI.39	(slue) him	✓	ἀπεκταιναν
XXI.41	(wicked) men	✓	κακους
XXII.35	one (of them)	✓	ἐξ αὐτων
XXII.42	the sonne (of David)	✓	του Δαυιδ
XXIII.27	(dead) mens' (bones)	✓	νεκρων
XXIV.41	women	✓	δυο
XXV.40	(done) it (unto me)	✓	ἐποιησατε
XXVI.17	(the first) day	✓	πρωτῃ
XXVI.71	(another) wench	maide	ἀλλη

2. *'Rom' Annotations in Matthew*

WORDS MARKED WITH 'ROM'		CORRESPONDING WORDS PRINTED IN ITALICS BY AV	GREEK TEXT
XVI.14	that thou art (already printed in italics)	say that thou art	οἱ μεν 'Ιωαννην
XXIV.33	even (at the dores)	✓	ἐπι θυραις
XXVI.25	be (on us)	✓	ἐφ' ἡμας

Since the same rule applies throughout the Synoptic Gospels we shall refer to the Matthew table as illustrative of the *typographical* principles in Bodleian Bishops'.

The 'Ang' annotations in Matthew seem to, on the whole, concern words which provide a noun or pronoun essential to the English construction. For instance at XVI.8 it could not be said in English 'but Jesus knowing' without some reference to the object of his knowledge. The Greek, however, is quite explicit as it stands, 'it' or 'which' being understood in the participle γνους. At XIX.26 and XXI.39 the same applies. It is not necessary to state the pronominal object to make the sentence clear in Greek but in English (beheld) 'them' and (slue) 'him' has to be added for complete clarity. At XIX.23 and XX.41 the Greek endings make it plain that πλουσιος and κακους mean 'rich man' and 'wicked men' respectively. In English, however, the noun had to be supplied. This leads us to believe that the corrector of the Bodleian Bishops' text was removing italics where the 'extra word' was (a) implicit in the Greek, (b) essential to the English syntax.

The insertion of italics on the other hand, seemed to follow the converse of this principle. At XVI.14 the Greek text οἱ μεν 'Ιωαννην (some indeed John the Baptist) is incomprehensible if translated literally into English. The English translators therefore had to supply an ellipsis some *say that thou art* John the Baptist. This ellipsis is not implicit in the Greek and its purpose is to do with meaning rather than syntax. The same applies at XXIV.33 where the English text adds *even* (at the dores) for ἐπι θυραις and at XXVII.25 *be* (on us) for ἐφ' ἡμας.

This principle for the insertion of italics and black letter print would agree with Bp. Turton's, Westcott's and Scrivener's[66] view of principles for italics adopted by the AV. The three scholars all agreed that the AV on the whole[67] was much more careful than its predecessors (particularly Bishops') in inserting italics, especially in distinguishing between a rendering and an ellipsis.

This would seem to point to *Bodleian Bishops'* as representing a stage in the making of the AV. Admittedly not enough evidence has been adduced here to make this a *proof*. On the other hand it is most unlikely that a scholar making a collation of AV and Bishops' text would put in typographical instructions in different hand, especially, as in Luke III.23, AV did not follow the 'Ang' instructions and retained the Bishops' italics. For the moment we assume that Bodleian Bishops' represents a stage in Revision, at some time before the work of the Final Revision Committee.

In the following chapter we shall compare readings from Beza's 1598 N.T. (the one most frequently consulted by AV translators) with readings from Geneva 1560, Tomson 1576, *Bodleian Bishops' 1602*, and AV 1611 (second issue, printed by Robert Barker). The chapter will be concerned with the Synoptic Gospels and its object will be to assess Beza's influence on the various versions of the English Synoptic Gospels, including the stage of AV revision represented by the Bodleian Bishops'.

In later chapters we shall consider Beza's influence on the English versions of Acts, Pauline Epistles and Hebrews. For Pauline Epistles and Hebrews close reference shall be made to Ward-Allen's edition of the 'Fulman MS',[68] which, as Ward-Allen has proved, represents an eighteenth century copy of the notes made by John Bois on the work of the Final Revision Committee.

Altogether we shall hope to establish not only the influence of Beza on the several final versions of the English N.T. but also his influence on AV translators at various stages of their Revision.

NOTES

1. Henceforth referred to as the Bodleian Bishops'.

2. Moreover, an examination of the influence of Beza on the works of two members of the Oxford Company will be used to assess the likelihood of a member of that Company owning the Bodleian Bishops'.

3. See Gregory, *Prolegomena*, (Leipzig, 1894), pp. 214-215 and F. Gardy, ed., *Bibliographie des oeuvres de Théodore de Bèze*, (Geneva, 1960).

4. της καινης διαθηκης ἀπαντα *Novum Jesu Christi... Testamentum*, (R. Stephanus, Lutetia, 1550).

5. See bibliography.

6. Junius' *Apostolorum Acta ex Arabica translatione Latine reddita cum notis* and *Pauli apostoli ad Corinthios apistulae duae ex Arabica translatione Latinae factae cum notis* were printed at Leyden in 1578. A complete Arabic N.T. came out in 1616 (*Novum Testamentum Arab. bibliotheca Leidensi*, edente Thos. Erpensis, Leidae).

7. Gregory, *Prolegomena*, p. 215, claims on the evidence of Reuss (*Bibliotheca Novi Testamenti Graeci*, Brunswick, 1872) that Beza's 1582 edition differed from Stephanus in c. 40 places. Scrivener, however, maintains that Beza's 1589 N.T. differs from Stephanus in c. 80 places [*The Authorized Version of the Bible*, (1884)]. I have not attempted to reconcile these two statements, as this would mean touching on material lying outside the scope and purpose of this work.

8. It is difficult to see whether Beza means a MS or a printed book. He uses the word 'codex' to mean both. Thus 'Theophylacti codex Romae impressus' (Matth. X.1) and 'manuscripti codices' (Mk. IV.40). He tends to use 'exemplar' in the sense of 'manuscript' (meus vetustissimus exemplar [sic]) but the full sentence in the epistle is '...exemplar ex Stephani nostri bibliotheca cum vigintiquinque plus minus manuscriptis codicibus et omnibus paene impressis...collatum'. This suggests either a printed book containing MS collations or simply, a single copy either MS or printed. Dr. Greenslade informs me that Erasmus is equally ambiguous as regards the use of the word *codex*.

9. As the table, p. 4, demonstrates, Beza is usually accurate in both counting and numbering the MSS. Thus 'more

or less twenty-five' would denote here no more than a slight uncertainty about the number of MSS collated by Henri Stephanus.

10. He mentions the printed version of Tremellius' Syriac N.T. separately. He also refers to the Complutensian Polyglot by name in the annotations although he does not change Stephanus's system of numbering the MSS (see p. 4ff.).

11. Junius' version is treated by Beza as a witness to the Greek text, but it is difficult to see whether he includes it among the nineteen manuscripts.

12. See Gregory, *Prolegomena*, pp. 410, 419.

13. Gregory, p. 213, but see also E. Armstrong, *Robert Estienne Royal Printer*, (Cambridge, 1954), p. 137, for MSS which R. Stephanus actually consulted.

14. References to D have been omitted since it is established that Beza used it.

15. Legg quotes the following variants here:

Matth. II.11   ειδον Uncs omn. fam^1. 22. 1582. 346. 543. 28. 33. 157. 349. 565. 700. 1278. al. *a d f k* (viderent sic*) q Sy omn Cop$^{sa. bo.}$ Aeth Arm. : ευρον 474. 892 al.plu *b.c. ff' g'* aur vg Aug. ^{cons} Sed.

Matth. V.44   ευλογειτε τους καταρωμενους υμας καλως ποιειτε τοις μισουσιν υμας (τους μισουντας υμας 472. 474 al pauc) D L W Δ Θ Π Σ ϕ fam^{13} 543. 28. 33. 157. 565. 700. 892. al pler. *t f h m vg.* Sy. $^{pesh hl}$ (etc.)

Matth. V.47   τους φιλους L W Δ Θ Π Σ ϕ 346. 28. 33. 157. 243. 349. 485. 517. 565. 692. 700. al plur.

Matth. VII.14   τι ℵ^b etc B** Uncs rell. 1* 1582. 22. fam^{13}. 543. 71. 349. 517. 565. 700*. 892 al pler. cf. quam it. (pler) vg. (pler).

16. Legg quotes the following variants:

Matth. III.11   εγω μεν ουν 13. 543. 999. 1093. 1588.

IV.10 + οπισω μου C^2 D E L M U Z Γ Ω *l* 1355. 209. 346. 5432. 28. 33. 71. 157. 248. 349. 482. 517. 692. 892^2. al pler.

V.33   −

VII.1 + μη καταδικαζετε και ου μη καταδικασθηται
L item vg. (edd. aliqui).

VII.6   τα αγια   118. 209. 157. 243. 245. 1689.
Eph.73.

VII.13 ερχομενοι   L. 13. 124. 543. 238. 482. 544.
1093. 1375. *l* 47. *l* 183.

VII.19+ ουν   C** L Z Φ 13. 543. 33. 66. 157. 230.
241. 479. 566. 1555. al mu. item *b c g*^{1} *h vg*
(1MS) Sy.^{c} Cop. $^{sa.\ bo.}$

IX.11 + και πινει (πινη 346) M(346). 248. 273. 482.
489. 544. 565. 660. 1555. 1689. al pauc. g^2
vg.

17. Legg quotes the following variants:

V. 18   amen amen Sy. hier *semel*

V. 36   λευκην ποιησαι η   (om. L)

This agreement suggests that Beza's numbering system was identical with Stephanus' (cf. Matth. IX.26: Beza refers to the second exemplar as adding αὐτου--a variant which in fact occurs in Stephanus' β', (D)).

18. Armstrong, p. 137.

19. For full identification see Gregory, pp. 345-686.

20. From a phrase in the preface to the 1633 Elzevir edition, "Textum ergo habes nunc ab omnibus receptum."

21. This confirms the view held by all modern scholars that Beza was unwilling to tamper with the TR and that he affirmed it in his few editions of the Greek-Latin N.T. (see Gregory, p. 218; Bruce Metzger, *The Text of the New Testament*, (New York: Oxford University Press, 1968), pp. 105-6.

22. This was claimed by S. Berger, *La Bible au seizième siècle*, (Paris, Berger-Levrault, 1879), p. 134.

23. See Chapter II for full discussion of the following, Mk. V.23, IX.16, VIII.24, Matth. II.

24. See Chapter II for full discussion, Mark VII.3 and Chapter III for Rom. I.20, Heb. VII.19 and their bearing on the English versions.

25. For full list see Allen, XII, Index II.B.

26. A. Ganoczy, *La Bibliothèque de l'Académie de Calvin*, (Geneva, Droz, 1969).

27. Erasmus suspected the style of Ambrose's commentaries on the Pauline Epistles and attributed them to another author (nowadays called Ambrosiaster). Beza, however, shows no knowledge of this distinction (cf. note on Romans IV.17, Ch. III), and so refers to both Ambrose and Ambrosiaster as 'Ambrose'.

28. Lost from the library at Geneva, see Ganoczy, *Bibliothèque*, p. 170.

29. Unpublished. Bound together with the 1570 catalogue in a MS folio volume. Unfortunately entries only contain authors' names and titles. Places and dates of publication are hardly ever mentioned. Both the 1570 and the 1605 Catalogue (as well as the 1620 MS Catalogue bound separately) are found in Geneva, Bibliothèque publique et universitaire (Archives, BPUI; Archives, BPU3).

30. Beza in his 1598 version frequently refers to the "*Theophylacti* codex Romae impressus". This refers to *two* works of Theophylactus; firstly there were Theophylacti *Enarrationes in Quatuor Evangelia*, first published in Rome in 1542. But the Bulgarian Bishop's commentaries on the Pauline Epistles were first translated into Latin by Christophorus Porsena (Persona) who attributed them to Athanasius. They were published in Rome in 1477. The error was noticed by Erasmus who, in the preface to the *Lucubrationes* of Chrysostom and Athanasius rejects the Athanasian authorship of *Enarrationes* (cf. Allen, VI. no. 1790, p. 467).

31. A table of Beza's references to the Fathers in the Romans (1557 N.T.) looks as follows:

Fathers Referred To		*Favourably*	*Unfavourably*	*Discussed*
Origen	80	1	75	4
Ambrose	37	5	20	12
Chrysostom	31	5	20	6
Augustine	31	19	7	5
Theophylactus	14	8	6	–
Jerome	7	1	6	–
Tertullian	5	5	–	–

(I owe this information to J. B. Fellay of the Institut d'histoire de la Réformation.)

32. Beza often refers to Erasmus being "too much under the influence of Origen" (1598). Erasmus in fact had a lot of admiration for Origen as exegete and he admits this openly in a letter to John Eck written from Basle in 1518; "plus me docet Christianae doctrinae unica Origenis pagina quam decem Augustini..." (Allen, III, 337). This, however, did not stop Erasmus from thinking Origen heretical on some doctrines. Thus in Erasmus' 1536 edition, *De Principiis* has many "caveats" in the margin concerning Origen's theology.

33. Erasmus here prefers Jerome's interpretation considering it to be closer to the Greek text (N.T. 1535). For bearing on English versions cf. comments on 1 Cor. VII.35, IX.5 in Ch. III.

34. Cf. comment on 1 Cor. X.17, Ch. III, for bearing of this on English versions.

35. Sometimes his criticisms of Augustine are anonymous viz. criticism of the translation "a lege evacuati sumus" at Rom. VII.6 (1598).

36. Origen says here (Rom. IX.18) that God deliberately hardens some people because of their lack of merit.

37. "Sciamus...Jechoniam priorem ipsum esse quem et Joakim; secundum autem filium non patrem; quorum prior per K + M, sequens per CH + N scribitur; Quod scriptorum vitio et longitudine temporum apud Graecos Latinosque confusum est" (1598), cf. comment on Matthew I.11, Ch. II.

38. Cf. Rom. IV.9 in AV 1611.

39. According to Nestle & Aland, μακροθυμων, the reading which Beza follows after the TR occurs only in $\aleph$ pm (cf. comment on Luke XVIII.7, Ch. II). Tischendorf, II specifies ΓΔΛR unc^8 al pler syr^{sch} with the same reading.

40. Beza knew that Theophylactus was a compiler and that a large number of his citations came from Chrysostom, since elsewhere in his N.T. he refers to 'Theophylactus ex Chrysostomo'. Here there was evidently a difference between Theophylactus' and Chrysostom's readings.

41. All the English versions from Tyndale to AV agree with the Beza/Theophylactus reading.

42. It is interesting to mention, in this context, Beza's note at Acts XVIII.27 where he cites the full D reading even

though he does not consider it to be appropriate.

43. As Westcott pointed out, Beza also influenced William Whittingham's N.T. of 1557. Only occasional references to it will be made here. See B. F. Westcott, *A General View of the History of the English Bible*, (3rd ed. rev. by W. A. Wright, New York, Macmillan, 1905), pp. 274ff.

44. This is uncertain, see: S. L. Greenslade, ed., *Cambridge History of the Bible* (Cambridge, University Press, 1963), p. 157. The article includes a detailed description of the Geneva Bible.

45. Westcott, pp. 222-27.

46. B. M. Metzger, 'The Influence of Codex Bezae on the Geneva Version of the English Bible', now published in *Historical and Literary Studies; Pagan, Jewish, and Christian*, (Grand Rapids, Eerdman, 1968).

47. Our investigation above shows that Beza made little use of his new MS evidence in his own text.

48. English Geneva text "Use not vaine repetitions" is obviously a translation of the French Geneva.

49. The metaphor was also known to Calvin via Luther. See F. Wendel, *Calvin; the Origins and Development of His Religious Thought*, (New York, Harper & Row, 1963), p. 331.

50. This is possibly an instance of Beza's Aristotelianism. Calvin in his 1559 edition of the *Institutio* (IV.17, II) said that the spiritual truth of the Eucharist is not only symbolized by the signs but is also presented to the communicant. Beza put this more strongly saying that Christ offers himself *substantially* in the supper via the Holy Spirit since the benefits of Christ cannot be separated from Christ himself. [See Jill Raitt, *The Eucharistic Theology of Theodore Beza*, (Chambersburg, Pa., American Academy of Religion, 1972).]

51. Beza translates the Greek "Quoniam unus est panis unum corpus nos illi multi summus".

52. "...et ex hoc loco tum etiam ex eo quod scribitur. 1 Corinth. XVI.2 colligitur iam tum convenisse Christianos hoc die solennes conventus agere, paulatim evanescente Judaici Sabbati ceremonia."

53. Brief sketch of L'Oiseleur's life is given in: D. Gerdesius, *Miscellanea Groningana* (1736-45), IV, pp. 391-5. J. Ab Utrecht Dresselhuis, 'Pieter Lozeleur des Prinzen Raad en Hofprediker', *De Gids*, II (1846), 79-127 deals with L'Oiseleur largely in his capacity as adviser to William of Orange.

54. L'Oiseleur's preface to his edition of Beza's Latin New Testament published in London by Thomas Vautrollier (1574).

55. The edition was dedicated to the Earl of Huntingdon.

56. For Life and Theology of Laurence Tomson see appendix.

57. Nestle & Aland quote following support for και ειπεν τοις μαθηταις αυτου D a c (sy^5).

58. Nestle & Aland: του θανατου DG it vg^{cl}. Souter: του θανατου DG, Orig.lat, Ambst. Aug. Cf. Tischendorf, II, p. 395n. "αποθανοντος ex errore ut vdtr. Bezae Erasmum secuti male interpretatum verba Chrysostomi".

59. He does not alter the *Greek text* here (N.T. 1565).

60. The best account of the AV from this standpoint is found in F. Scrivener, *The Authorized Version of the Bible (1611)*, (Cambridge, University Press, 1884). It also contains references to Beza's influence on the AV and an appendix of passages where the text of the AV agrees with Beza as against Stephanus.

61. For full account of the external history of the AV see B. F. Westcott, *op. cit.*, pp. 145ff. A recent study of this appears in Ward Allen, ed., *Translating for King James*, (Nashville, Vanderbilt University Press, 1969), pp. 3ff. See also A. W. Pollard, *Records of the English Bible*, (New York, H. Froude, 1911), pp. 37-65, 336-379; Anderson, *Annals of the English Bible*, 2 vols., (London, William Pickering, 1845).

62. Ward Allen, pp. 6-7.

63. Mr. E. C. Jacobs of Louisiana Technical University has done work on the annotations in the Old Testament intending to prove that they represent a stage in the AV revision. His work is about to be published. The volume in question was known to Westcott who thought the annotations a *later* collation of the King James and Bishops' texts done by a scholar. It was also known to E. E. Willoughby who suggested

that the annotations might be an intermediate stage in the making of the AV. [*The Making of the King James Bible*, (Los Angeles, Printed for Dansoris Book Shop at the Plantin Press, 1956).]

64. For identification and description of the first and second issue of AV see Scrivener, pp. 3ff.

65. See Scrivener, pp. 61ff.

66. Thomas Turton, *The Text of the English Bible*, (Cambridge, 1833), B. F. Westcott, p. 363 n. Scrivener, pp. 61ff.

67. The 1611 editions of the AV were hastily printed so that several *inconsistencies* occur in their use of italics, see Scrivener, pp. 61ff.

68. Ward Allen, *op. cit.*

CHAPTER II

The Influence of Beza
on the English Synoptic Gospels

So far we have established the materials which Beza used for his 1589 and 1598 editions of the Greek-Latin N.T. We have also given a brief outline of the influence of Beza's 1565 Greek N.T. and his 1557 Latin N.T. on the English Geneva Bible and Tomson's New Testament. In this chapter we are primarily concerned with the influence of Beza's 1589 and 1598 editions on the Authorized version.[1] Important additional evidence here is provided by the manuscript annotations in the Bodleian copy of the Bishops' Bible printed by Robert Barker in 1602. As has already been pointed out, those annotations are of two types, typographical instructions, and emendations on the Bishops' text. The nature of the typographical instructions suggests that there is very good reason to think that the Bodleian Bishops' represents a late stage in the making of the AV. Here we shall examine the Secretary hand and italic annotations in the Synoptic Gospels with a twofold purpose. Firstly, we shall compare the annotations with the final readings of the second issue of the AV printed in 1611.[2] Reference will be made throughout to earlier English versions used by the Revisers. In this way we hope to select (1) Bodleian Bishops' readings which correspond exactly to those of the AV, (2) those readings in Bodleian Bishops' which are supported by some earlier English version, (3) the Bodleian Bishops' readings which do not appear to have the support of either the AV or of any other English version. The existence of such readings suggests that the annotations in the Bodleian Bishops' cannot represent a *later* collation of

King James and Bishops' text. Moreover if we find that these readings agree with *some principle* of revision adopted by AV translators, we shall have a clear indication that Bodleian Bishops' represents a stage in the making of the AV.

Secondly we shall attempt to trace the influence of Beza on Bodleian Bishops' and the AV, again with reference to earlier English versions. In this way we shall hope to establish (1) how Beza was used in the various versions of the English N.T., (2) how he was used by the AV Revisers, (3) how and whether the Bezan material in Bodleian Bishops' corresponds to the Bezan material in the AV.

Finally, a short section will be appended reviewing such theological works of members of the Oxford Company as proved to be still extant. This will be an attempt to see whether the theological outlook of the Bodleian Bishops' matches the theology of individual Oxford Company members. In this way we shall establish the likelihood of a Reviser owning the Bodleian Bishops'.

St. Matthew

I.11. Beza's 1598 N.T. reads 'Ιωσειας δε ἐγεννησεν τον 'Ιεχονιαν και τους ἀδελφους αὐτου which he translates "Josias autem genuit Jechoniam et fratres eius". He adds a note that "Itaque Robertus Stephanus ex vetustis codicibus excudit (quorum etiam fidem faciunt Stapulensis et Martinus Bucerus) 'Josias autem genuit Jakim. Jakim autem genuit Jechoniam' quam etiam lectionem in prioribus editionibus sum amplexus." The reading τον 'Ιωακιμ. 'Ιωακιμ δε ἐγεννησεν occurs in MΘλ33pmlr^{lat}Epiph.^{3} In his 1598 edition Beza then rejects this reading as a misconception quoting Augustine and Jerome in support (vid. supra). The "Iakim" reading did appear in Beza's 1574 N.T. and was translated by Tomson in 1576. "And

Josias begate Iakim. And Jakim begate Jechonias." Geneva 1560 also inserts 'Jakim' on the authority of Beza's early versions, since both Tyndale and Great had read "Josias begate Jechonias and his brethren". This was also the reading adopted by Bishops'. The only emendation made in the Bodleian Bishops' is the insertion of "And" before "Josias". This reading with the correction, is adopted by the AV. But the translators do suggest in the margin, "Some read, Josias begate Jakim and Jakim begate Jechonias." If the Bodleian Bishops' is taken as a stage in the making of the AV, we can assume that the marginal suggestion would have been inserted after the Bodleian Bishops' stage. This would make it the work of the very final revision committee.

At Matthew II.6 Beza's 1598 N.T. has "Ex te enim exibit dux qui pascet populum illum...." He translates ποιμανει as "pascet" rejecting the Vulgate reading "reget" which, he says, corresponds to εὐθυνειν (chastise, correct) and Erasmus' reading 'gubernaturus' from κυβερναν (to steer, to act as pilot, hence: to guide). English versions from Tyndale to Bishops' have "governe".[4] In the Bodleian Bishops' this becomes "rule" and this is the reading which appears in AV 1611 with "feede" inserted as marginal alternative. This insertion must have been made at a later stage than the Bodleian Bishops' emendations.

At Matthew II.11 Beza's 1598 N.T. has "Invenerunt puerulum", i.e. εὑρον το παιδιον. He explains that "In omnibus vetustis exemplaribus scriptum legimus ειδον--viderunt."[5] Of the English versions Tyndale reads "found" and so do Geneva and Tomson on the authority of Stephanus, Beza and Tyndale. The Great Bible also reads "found" but Bishops' has "sawe". In the Bodleian copy this is crossed out and "found" is written in above. "Or, sawe" is then inserted in the margin in italics. The AV, however, reads "saw" with no marginal

suggestions. The Revisers' decision here is not altogether
surprising as there was more support for εἶδον than for εὗρον
in variants which were available to them.

At Matthew II.16 Beza has "a bimulis et infra" (ἀπο διετους και κατωτερω). In the 1598 edition he points out that
some Greek MSS read κατω and that Vetus interpres appears to
have read ἀπο διετειας which he translated "a bimatu et infra". Beza prefers the reading ἀπο διετους since it has the
support of all the Greek MSS, and also of the Hebrew idiom.
The Hebrew, he suggests, would read here "a filio duorum an-
norum et infra". It is interesting to see that although Beza
refers to some MSS that read κατω and to the ἀπο διετειας
reading in Vetus, he makes no mention of the D reading ἀπο
διετειας και κατω. When we consider, however, that Beza
tended to refer to D for reasons of doctrine rather than just
text, the omission here is not altogether surprising. Erasmus' Latin text has "Quotquot essent bimuli et minores" which,
Beza thinks, "longius recedit a Graecis". Tyndale has "as
many as were two yere olde and under". This reading is also
adopted by the Great Bible and preserved by Bishops'. In the
Bodleian copy it is corrected to "from two years old and
under". This is the Bezan reading which also appears in
Geneva 1560 and Tomson, and is finally adopted by AV 1611.

At Matthew III.8 Beza's 1589 and 1598 N.T. read "Ferte
igitur fructus convenientes resipiscentiae" for ποιησατε οὖν
καρπον ἀξιον της[6] μετανοιας. In his earlier versions, however, Beza had read "Ferte igitur fructum dignum iis qui
resipuerint" (fruit worthy of those who have repented).
This reading was followed by Geneva 1560 and Tomson who render it "fruite worthie amendment of life", that is, such good
works as show that you have repented. The Vulgate reading is
neutral here and open to any interpretation as is the Greek--
"fructum dignum poenitentiae". Tyndale has "frutes belongynge

to repentaunce". Bishops' Bible has "fruits meete for repentance". In the Bodleian Bishops' this is corrected to "fruits worthy for repentance", i.e. good works consisting in repentance. The alternative reading "or, answerable to the amendment of life" is put in, in italics. The AV 1611 restores the more neutral rendition "fruits meete for repentance" but keeps the marginal alternative as in Bodleian Bishops'. The AV margin thus comes down almost on the early Beza/Geneva side, even though its actual text agrees with Bishops'/late Beza.

At Matthew III.9 Beza 1589 and 1598 has "Et ne putate vobis dicendum apud vosipsos" for καὶ μὴ δόξητε λέγειν. The Vulgate here reads "Et ne velitis dicere" and Erasmus "Ne hac mente sitis ut dicatis". Beza disagrees with both the translations on the grounds that "...το δοκειν neque hinc simpliciter significat videri quod vulgo dicimus *sembler* neque putare aut *Existimare* sicut Luc XII.40 item XIII.2 sed aliquid sibi per arrogantiam et animi elationem persuadere vel sibi de aliquo placere, sicut etiam accipitur Philip III.4 et Marc X.42. Itaque addidi pronomen *vobis* et λέγειν converti dicendum paulo liberius quam soleam, ut aliquo modo hoc dicendi genus saltem adumbrarem...."

We see here full agreement firstly between early and late Beza and secondly between Geneva 1560 and AV 1611. Tyndale had "And se that ye ons thynke not to saye in your selves" thus confirming Beza's authority so far as the Geneva translators were concerned. Tomson's translation "and presume not to say with yourselves" would seem to be based on Beza's explanation "aliquid sibi per arrogantiam et animi elationem persuadere" in the 1557 edition of his Latin N.T. Geneva 1560, however, has "And think not to say within yourselves". The Bishops' Bible agrees with Erasmus and has "And be not of such mind that...". In the Bodleian copy this is crossed out and "seem not to" inserted above. The AV, however, comes down

on the side of Tyndale/Beza/Geneva here. This is the stronger
translation; "Seeme not to say..." suggests merely a possibility of Pharisees and Sadducees relying on their descent from
Abraham, "think not to say within yourselves" emphasizes the
inadvisability of their doing so.

At Matthew IV.10 Beza has, in all his versions "Abi Satana" for ὑπαγε. He points out that "octo vetusti codices
habent ὀπισω μου quod videtur ex aliis locis additum". ὀπισω
μου did occur in some of the Koine MSS available to Beza.[7]
It also occurs in D which Beza does not mention here. The
Vulgate reads "Vade Satana". Tyndale, Great, Geneva, and
Tomson all read "Avoyde Satan". The Bishops' Bible has "Get
thee hence behind me" which is corrected in the Bodleian copy
to "Get thee hence",[8] the reading finally adopted by the AV.
As well as having the authority of Beza for the omission of
ὀπισω μου, the Revisers also had the backing of Origen, Jerome
and most earlier English versions.

At Matthew IV.12 Beza reads throughout "Quum audisset autem Jesus Joannem traditum esse *in custodiam*" for Ἀκουσας δε
ὁτι Ἰωαννης παρεδοθη. He comments that παρεδοθη implies "*in
carcerem*" which he actually inserts for the sake of clarity.
The Vulgate has no italics here and translates simply "quod
Joannes traditus esset". Geneva 1560 agrees with Vulgate here
reading "John was delivered up", in preference to Tyndale's
"that John was taken". Tomson follows Beza and has "John was
committed to prison".[9] Bishops' reads "John was delivered up"
and the marginal suggestion "that is, cast into prison" is inserted in italics in the Bodleian copy. AV reverses the order
of preference and has the Bezan reading "was cast into prison"
in the text and the Vulgate reading "delivered up" in the margin. Accordingly at Mark I.14 the AV has "put into prison"
for παραδοθηναι where the Bodleian annotator corrects "delivered into prison" to "delivered up", harmonizing this ren-

dering with that at Matthew IV.12. Evidently Beza's argument of clarity carried more weight with the Revisers than the more literal Vulgate translation.

At Matthew V.18[10] Beza has throughout "...iωta unum aut unus apex nequaquam praeterierit ex Lege, usquedum omnia facta fuerint". He justifies his rendering of οὐ μη by "nequaquam" saying that the double negative in Greek is stronger than the "negatio simplex". "Nos vero ita vertimus ut a simplici negatione distingueremus." This reading is not followed by either Geneva 1560 or Tomson both of whom have "one jote or one title of the Law shall not scape" (agreeing with Tyndale). Bishops' also reads "one jote or one title of the Law shall not scape" which is corrected in the Bodleian copy to "one jote or one title shall in no wise pass from the Law". This is the reading adopted by the AV. There is no doubt here that Beza's translation had a direct influence on both the Bodleian Bishops' annotator and on the AV. It is more difficult to decide, however, whether this was for a stylistic or for a doctrinal reason. At Matthew XXIV.34, Mark XII.30 and Luke XII.32 neither Beza nor AV translate οὐ μη by the strong negative where it appears in the context of "this generation shall not pass". This would suggest that the reason for literally translating οὐ μη at Matthew V.18 is not purely stylistic. It is useful to remember here Beza's attitude to the Law as outlined in the *Confessio*.[11] He regards Law and the Gospel as having the same efficient cause, i.e. God. They differ, however, in their effects, attributes and function. The Law teaches good works but does not give men strength to perform them. This, however, is given by the Gospel which teaches Faith. Law points out and condemns evil and reveals sin, which the Gospel removes. Thus, according to Beza, Law, although vastly inadequate on its own, does nonetheless play a part in the Christian faith when taken in conjunction with the Gospel. We may therefore conclude that in emphasizing the strong negative at v. 18 Beza wants to stress the permenent standing of the Jewish Law and the AV agrees with this.

This is confirmed by Matthew V.21. Beza's 1598 N.T. reads here "Audistis dictum fuisse a veteribus, Non occides; quisquis autem occiderit damnas erit iudicii." He does not explain why he changed his translation from that of his earlier versions. "Audistis dictum fuisse antiquis...quisquam autem occiderit, tenebitur iudicio." This earlier rendering was followed by Tomson and the Geneva version, "Ye have heard that it was said unto them...culpable of judgement." Tyndale had read "...unto them...danger of judgement", and the Bishops' Bible agreed with this, substituting "to them" for "unto them". In the Bodleian copy the reading "or, by them" is inserted in italics, and "in danger of" is emended to "liable to". The AV, however, restores Beza's 1598 reading here ("...by them...in danger of"); "to them" is suggested as marginal alternative. Beza explains his rendition of τοις ἀρχαιοις as ἀπο ἀρχαιων by suggesting that Jesus is referring not so much to the Law itself but to Jewish *corruptions* of it. An instance of such a corruption, he says, is the addition of the words ὁς δ'ἀν φονευσῃ, ἐνοχος ἐσται τῃ κρισει onto the sixth commandment. οἱ ἀρχαιοι, therefore, according to Beza, are not the people who heard the Law, which would warrant the rendition "to them of old", but the people who spoke in synagogues corrupting the Law. Christ is denouncing not the Law itself which still has a function to fulfill, but false interpretations of it.

Beza's interpretation, although in keeping with his general attitude to the Law, is nonetheless rather idiosyncratic here. Christ could equally well be merely pointing out the inadequacy of the Law. It is difficult to see whether the AV

in accepting Beza's phrasing, also accepts his exposition of
this passage.

At Matthew V.29 Beza throughout, has "Quod si oculus tuus
dexter facit ut tu offendas". Geneva and Tomson follow his
reading and translate "If thy right eye cause thee to offend".
The Vulgate has "scandalizat te", Tyndale, Bishops' and AV
seem to agree with this, in reading "If thy right eye offend
thee". The Bodleian Bishops' annotator inserts the Beza/
Geneva reading as marginal alternative and the AV appears to
follow this. Beza justifies his reading by saying that "...
ea faciunt ut offendamus quae impediunt quominus inoffenso
cursu pergamus in lege Domini. Peccata enim sunt veluti saxa
ad quae impingimus vel etiam corruimus...." He thus emphasizes the separation between us and the member which has
caused us to sin. The point is not simply one of style.
Beza seems to be implying that we are prone to sin even once
we have faith. Therefore faith needs to be constantly sustained.

At Matthew V.47 there are several problems. Beza and all
the English versions keep to the textual reading τους ἀδελφους.
Nonetheless, Beza points out "In omnibus vetustis codicibus
legimus τους φιλους amicos".[12] No mention of τους φιλους is
made in any English version except the Bodleian Bishops' where
"or friends" is inserted in the margin in italics. This suggestion was turned down by the AV. The Revisers probably did
not see any of the "vetusti codices" with φιλους and found
Beza's authority insufficient, especially as all the earlier
English versions have 'brothers'.

ἀσπασησθε is translated as "complexi fueritis" by Beza
in all his versions. Geneva 1560 appears to agree with Tyndale in reading "be friendlie". It is difficult to see why
Tomson should have followed Geneva here in preference to Beza,

since their translation, although expressing the emotion attached to ἀσπασηθε is nonetheless quite far removed from the Greek. The Vulgate has the more literal "salutaveritis". Beza objects to this on the grounds that ἀσπαζομαι "*salutare* quidem significat sed osculo et complexu; qui mos istarum gentium erat". In this context he thinks it essential to bring out the more emotional connotations of the Greek "alioqui contenti fuissemus vulgata versione quam frequenter in Epistolis Pauli sequuti sumus". His comment and translation evidently influenced the Bodleian Bishops' annotator who inserted "or greete with embracing" in the margin, in italics. This was crossed out, and the AV retained the Vulgate "salute", evidently for the sake of consistency.

For περισσον Beza has "amplius" in his early and late editions. In the 1598 N.T. he explains that "Idem hinc valet περισσον quod πλειον et subauditur 'quam alii'. Sic etiam infra XXVII.23." None of the earlier English versions follows Beza here. Geneva, Tomson and Bishops' all agree with Tyndale's "what singular thing do ye?" taking περισσος in the sense of "out of the common, extraordinary, strange". No correction of this reading appears in the Bodleian copy, but the AV adopts Beza's reading in full, translating "what do you more than others?"[13] At Matthew XXVII.23 the same construction occurs in οἱ δε περισσως ἐκραζον. Beza translates it as "eo amplius", and all the English versions with the exception of Bishops' ("exceedingly") have "all the more". This suggests a consistency in AV's translation of περισσον which does not occur in earlier English versions.

At Matthew VI.2 Beza has throughout "ne curato buccina cani coram te". Geneva and Tomson have here "thou shalt not make a trumpet to be blowen before thee" agreeing with Tyndale's reading. Beza insists that μη σαλπισῃς should be taken in the Hebrew Hiphil conjugation, even though the infinitive means no more than the Latin "buccinare". The Bodleian Bishops' annotator does not take up Beza's suggestion, merely correcting "do not blow" to "...sound".[14] This occurs in AV 1611 but Beza's phrase "cause not a trumpet to be sounded" is inserted in the margin. For ὁπως δοξασθωσιν Beza has "ut gloriam consequantur" throughout, but does not object to the Vulgate rendering "ut honorificentur", saying that as it's a question of earthly glory, δοξαζεσθαι is here equivalent in meaning to τιμασθαι.[15] Tomson and Geneva agree with Tyndale here and read "to be praysed of men". Bishops' has "that they might be esteemed of men" agreeing with the Vulgate in omitting any connotations of glory. The Bodleian annotator corrects the Bishops' text to "that they may have glory of men" and this Bezan reading is adopted by AV. By using the word "glory" in a secular context both Beza and AV emphasize that the δοξα received from men is full quittance of reward due to them; they will have no δοξα from God.

At Matthew VI.7 the 1560 Geneva version adopted the translation "use no vaine repetitions" for μη βατταλογησητε under the influence of Beza's 1557 comment on this verse; "Longae preces non damnantur sed vanae inanes et superstisiosae". This reading also followed by Tomson was inserted into the margin of Bodleian Bishops' to replace "bable not much",[16] and was adopted by the AV. In his 1598 edition where he translates μη βατταλογησητε as "ne blaterate" Beza condemns Roman Catholic prayers even more explicitly.[17] The AV here, coming down on the early Beza/Geneva side, also voices a condemnation of unnecessarily long Catholic prayers, as against the more neutral rendering of Bishops'.

At Matthew VI.34 Beza throughout takes his Greek reading from the Syriac versions; μεριμνησει τα ἑαυτης in preference to μεριμνησει ἑαυτης which appears in the majority of MSS. The latter struck all contemporary N.T. scholars as incorrect

since μεριμναν does not take a genitive anywhere else. The
Vulgate emended to the Latin "sollicitus erit sibi ipse", and
Erasmus translated μεριμνησει as though the Greek read φροντι-
σει in his Latin version since φρονιζω does take the genitive.[18]

Geneva 1560 agrees with the Tyndale 1535/Vulgate reading
and translates "for the morowe shall care for itself". Tomson follows this in preference to Beza. The Bishops' Bible
also adopts this reading but the Bodleian annotator corrects
this to "for the morowe shall take thought for the things of
itself". This exact translation of Beza's reading ("Nam
crastinus dies sollicitus erit de *rebus suis*") is adopted by
AV.

At Matthew VII.3 Beza has in the 1598 N.T.[19] "Quid autem
aspicis festucam...trabem vero...non animadvertis", giving
"aspicis" for βλεπεις as opposed to *"vides"* of Erasmus and
the Vulgate. He points out that βλεπειν means "to look at
with a purpose in mind" as opposed to ὁραν which means "to
see" generally. It is difficult to find illustrations for
Beza's pedantic distinction except for Matthew V.28 where
βλεπειν appears in the context "whosoever looketh on a woman
to lust after her". βλεπειν here obviously refers to a deliberate action of *looking* rather than the natural power of
seeing, but otherwise the two words appear to have been interchangeable.[20] Beza further supports his translation saying
that "Nec enim damnatur qui vel fratris vel suos errores vidit
et intelligit, sed qui in alienos intuetur studio reprehendendi, suos autem dissimulat...". All the English versions from
Tyndale to Bishops' 1602 go against Beza here and read "seest".
Correction of "seest" to "beholdest" occurs in Bodleian Bishops' and the AV also reads "beholdest". The Revisers were obviously convinced by Beza's somewhat arbitrary distinction.

At Matthew VII.14 Beza reads ὁτι στενη[21] throughout and
translates "Quia angusta est porta", "est" being understood

in the construction. Vetus interpres has "Quam angusta" which
led Erasmus to assume that he had read the Greek as ὡς στενη.
Beza disagrees with Erasmus thinking that it is far more likely to have been τι στενη as in Theophylactus and Syriac text.
Some Latin codices read "quoniam" for "quam" but Beza claims
"Ego receptam lectionem sum sequutus quam etiam sinceriorem
esse accipio". Unfortunately he does not say on what grounds
he finds the TR reading "sinceriorem". Presumably he considers that the τι versions structure a contrast between πυλη
and ὁδος of vv. 13 and 14, which is artificial and unnecessary.
He preferred to read the passage more simply; (v. 13) εἰσελ-
θατε is the basic injunction, (v. 13b) ὁτι πλατεια ἡ πυλη
constitutes one reason for the basic injunction, (v. 14) ὁτι
στενη ἡ πυλη constitutes the second reason for the basic injunction parallel to the first.

All the English versions follow Beza and TR here translating "because". There is no correction in Bodleian Bishops'
but AV 1611 inserts "or, how" in the margin.[22]

At Matthew VII.23 Beza translates ὁμολογησω here as
"profitebor" in all his versions, even though the more accurate meaning of ὁμολογειν is "confiteri". But, says Beza,
"hoc loco amplius aliquid declarat". Elsewhere in the N.T.,
for instance at Matthew X.32, Beza retains the translation
"confiteri" for ὁμολογειν. Tyndale here has "will acknowledge".[23] Geneva and Tomson agree with Beza and translate
"professe". The Bishops' Bible agrees with Erasmus and the
Vulgate ("will I confesse"). This, however, is corrected to
"will I professe" in the Bodleian Bishops', reading adopted
by the AV. It is clear why this was preferred by Geneva/Beza/
AV; although there are several references in the Synoptic Gospels to the last judgement and to judgement by the Son of Man,
only at this point in Matthew does Jesus openly claim that he
himself is the *judge*. Similar idea of voicing rather than ad-

mitting is expressed by the Tyndale/Great "will knowledge".[24]

At Matthew VIII.18 Beza in his N.T. versions until 1589 has "iussit *suos discipulos* abire in ulteriorem *ripam*" for ἐκελευσεν ἀπελθειν. In the 1589/98 editions he has "iussit ut abiretur in ulteriorem ripam" without referring to his earlier translation but condemning the Vulgate version for inserting *discipulos* and for translating εἰς το περαν as "trans fretum". This, Beza claims, would warrant the Greek reading περαν της θαλασσης.

Tyndale in 1534 had already had the translation "he commanded to go over the water". Geneva 1560 and Tomson agreed with this but supplied "them". Bishops' shows partial agreement with the Great Bible here reading "he commanded them to depart unto the other side".[25] The AV probably kept the Bishops' "unto the other side" but it is possible that their construction "he gave commandment to depart" was partly based on Beza's "iussit ut abiretur".

At Matthew VIII.32 Beza, in all his versions, has "ruit e praecipitio" for ὡρμησεν...κατα του κρημνου. He claims that the Vulgate/Erasmus "per praeceps" is "nec...quidem Latine, nec satis apposite" since κατα here is used in the sense of ἀπο as in Homer's *Odyssey* (14.399); κατα πετρης βαλεειν. Beza is right here as κατα + Genitive does usually denote motion from above as opposed to κατα + Accusative denoting downward motion, e.g. κατα ῥοον (*Od.* 14.254, *Il.* 12.33).[26]

Tyndale has "was caryed with violence hedlonge in to the see".[27] Geneva has "was caryed with violence from a steepe down place" accepting Beza's "e praecipitio". Tomson agrees with Bishops' reading "rushed headlong". In the Bodleian Bishops' this is corrected to "rushed violently from a steep place" and the AV has "ranne...down a steep place". In both cases Beza's reading is followed.

At Matthew IX.16 Beza translates αἰρει γαρ το πληρωμα

αὐτου (ἀπο του ἱματιου) as "illud enim ipsius supplementum". He identifies πληρωμα with ἐπιβλημα in 16a so that πληρωμα refers explicitly to the new patch. He also translates αὐτου as "his" not as "of it" on the grounds that ἱματιου is repeated soon afterwards. He rejects the Vulgate "Tollit enim plenitudinem eius a vestimento" and Erasmus' "Aufert enim supplementum illius a vestimento" as both take πληρωμα to be in the accusative agreeing with αἱρει, instead of in the nominative.

Tyndale has "For then taketh he awaye the pece agayne from the garment". Geneva and Tomson agree with Beza and read "for that that should fill it up (i.e. πληρωμα) takes away from the garment". Bishops' has "for then the piece... garment" but this is corrected in the Bodleian copy to "that which should fill it up". The AV makes it even more explicit that it follows Beza here and puts πληρωμα into the nominative by translating "that which is *put in* to fill it up". This was probably for partly theological reasons. In his annotation to this verse (1598) Beza draws a comparison between the new patch destroying the old material in this parable and the new wine destroying old bottles in the next parable. Both parables convey that the new teaching cannot be contained within the framework of the Law. In view of this it is better to translate the "new patch takes away from the garment" thus maintaining a direct parallel between the function of the new patch and of the new wine.

At Matthew X.9 Beza has "ne comparate" for μη κτησησθε in all his editions. The Vulgate has "noli possidere" which he considers wrong, as the Lord is not forbidding the possession of money (i.e. the disciples can accept anything that is given to them on the way) but the provision of it. The Apostles must have complete trust in the divine call. Beza disregards that the Vulgate could mean here "possidere" in the sense of "obtain possession of" which would not be notably different from his own reading.[28] All English versions from Tyndale to Bishops' read "possess". This is corrected in Bodleian Bishops' to "provide", the reading adopted by AV after Beza. AV 1611 supplies also the marginal alternative "get". This would suggest that they regarded the Vulgate "possidere" to mean "obtain possession", but "get" could be merely an alternative way of translating "comparate".

At Matthew X.18 Beza in all his versions reads "*ut hoc sit* eis et Gentibus testimonium" for εἰς μαρτυριον αὐτοις και τοις ἐθνεσιν. None of the English versions however, adopts his italics, all (including Bishops') reading "in witness to them". In the Bodleian Bishops' however, "in witness to them" is corrected to "that this may be a witness to them". This *correction* is then crossed out and "for a testimonie against them" is substituted, reading adopted by the AV. This suggests that whoever was correcting the Bodleian copy first of all adopted Beza's reading. At a later stage, however, the Revisers preferred to insert their own translation. The dative αὐτοις here was read as the dative of disadvantage --a testimony to their cost. In this way the Revisers emphasize that the "new" i.e. the teaching of Jesus will be detrimental to the old order, not only so far as the Jews are concerned but also further afield.

At Matthew XI.28 Beza has "et ego faciam ut requiescatis" in all versions. English translations from Tyndale to Bishops' 1602 agree with the Vulgate and translate "I will ease you". This is corrected in the Bodleian copy to "I will give you rest" reading adopted by the AV. Obviously the Revisers agreed with Beza in taking ἀναπαυσω to be the equivalent of the Hebrew conjugation Hiphil (nuah - to make to rest).

At Matthew XII.18 Beza has "servus" for ὁ παις as opposed to the Vulgate/Erasmus "puer". "Puer" is ambiguous in

Latin and can mean both 'son', 'child' and 'servant' so it is
difficult to see which sense was intended by the Vulgate.
Erasmus, however, makes it quite plain that he means 'son'
since the word 'son' is more apposite to Christ especially
as Chrysostom, among other Greek Fathers, "servi vocabulum
vereretur tribuere filio Dei".[29] Beza thinks such reluctance
unnecessary as Paul himself says at Philip. II.7 ἐν ὁμοιωματι
ἀνθρωπων γενομενος[30] and that παις in relation to Christ
"videtur ad immensam ipsius bonitatem magnopere pertinere".
Of the English versions Tyndale (34) has 'chylde',[31] Geneva
and Tomson have 'servant' after Beza. Bishops' reads 'child'
which is corrected in the Bodleian copy to 'servant' and the
AV reads 'servant' agreeing with Beza/Geneva exegesis.

At Matthew XIII.11 Beza translates μυστηρια as "mysteria"
in all versions, agreeing with the Vulgate. Tyndale, Geneva,
Tomson and Bishops' read 'secrets' and this remains uncorrected in the Bodleian copy. The AV, however, reads 'mysteries'. Some light on this can be thrown by considering
Beza's 1598 explanation of μυστηρια. He points out that
'mysteries' are revealed by Jesus only to his Church, whereas 'secrets' have a secular connotation and can be revealed to
anybody. Beza's interpretation here isn't very far removed
from that of some modern scholars who construe μυστηρια in the
sense of 'secrets *revealed* to the initiate'. It is difficult
to say here whether the AV adopted 'mysteries' under the influence of Beza or of the Vulgate or both.

At Matthew XIV.2 Beza has 'virtutes agunt in eo' for
ἐνεργουσιν. Vulgate and Vetus read 'virtutes operantur in eo'.
Beza (agreeing with Erasmus) prefers to use 'ago' on the
grounds that a parallel passage in Mark VI.14 refers not to
the miracles done by Christ but to his *power* to perform them
(i.e. powers which operate to produce miracles--so most modern
theologians). However, he does admit that δυναμεις here could

be taken to mean "great deeds", in which case ἐνεργουσιν can be read in the passive thus producing the translation "Efficiuntur istae virtutes ab eo".

It is interesting to observe here that Tyndale had the translation "...hys power ys so greate" as early as 1525, thus agreeing with Beza. Tyndale's 1534 version has the other possibility "Therefore are soche myracles wrought by him". Geneva and Tomson both read "great works are wrought by him". The Bishops' Bible has its own reading "great works do show forth themselves in him" which might have been adopted under Beza's influence. This reading is followed by the AV[32] with the Geneva version inserted as marginal alternative.

At Matthew XV.5/6 Beza in his versions up to 1589 has "Donum quodcunque a me erit tibi prodierit etiamsi nequaquam honoraverit patrem suum et matrem suam, *insons erit*". The Vulgate has "Munus quodcunque est ex me tibi prodiderit, et non honorificabit patrem suum aut matrem suam" thus treating the passage as an answer to a question rather than a vow. Erasmus reads "Quicquid doni a me [profecturum erat] id in tuum vertitur commodum".

In his 1598 version Beza translates δωρον ὁ ἐαν ἐξ ἐμου ὠφεληθης as "Donum est quocunque a me iuvari posses, *insons erit*..." thus interpreting, "I have consecrated to God the offering (since all vows are due to him and he has all the rights) which you could have otherwise taken from me in your need." He claims that ὁ ἐαν is more often used to mean "quodcunque" than the simple relative "quod", and goes on to say that the ellipsis in his literal translation, although difficult is nonetheless sensible. There is no doubt that Christ is talking about the sanction which the Scribes gave to the act, while knowing the wicked consequences of it. Beza supplies the word ἀναιτιος (*insons erit*) from Matthew XII.5 thus implying collusion between the Scribes and the Temple priests.

It could be argued³³ that this is not altogether correct; the δωρον was not really offered, it was *vowed*. The Temple priests therefore derived no advantage from it.

Tyndale has "that which thou desyrest of me to help the with: is given God; and so³⁴...mother" which can be interpreted in the same way as Beza 1598. Geneva and Tomson read "By the gift that is offered by me thou mayest have profite (b) though he honour not...*shall be fre*." Both seem to treat δωρον as preceding a vow of refusal to help one's parents, i.e. "On account of the offerings I made to God you will not profit." The Bishops' Bible has "By the gift that is offered of me thou shalt be helped" based on Erasmus' version. This is corrected in Bodleian Bishops' to "...thou mayst be benefited". The AV, however, adopts Beza's 1598 rendition, "It is a gift by whatsoever thou mightest bee profited by mee...." The AV follows early Beza/Geneva in inserting ἀναιτιος ("he shal be fre") after 'mother' not after "profited by mee". This is probably the simplest and clearest translation of the Greek. Mistake made by both Beza and AV is the allusion (albeit indirect) to collusion between Scribes and High Priests. If the δωρον is not really offered, the second half of the passage is not consistent with the first. (Cf. Mark VII.11 where δωρον is used to gloss the Hebrew κορβαν.)³⁵

At Matthew XVIII.19 Beza claims in his 1589 edition that "in antiquis omnibus codicibus additur ἀμην" (presumably from v. 18).³⁶ He does not add it himself. Tyndale does not insert ἀμην at v. 19, but possibly under the influence of Beza's note, both Geneva and Tomson read "Again *verely* I say unto you".³⁷ The Bishops' Bible reads "Again *truely*" which is corrected in Bodleian Bishops' to the Geneva reading "Again verily". The AV 1611, however, omits ἀμην probably under TR influence.

At Matthew XVIII.26 Beza has "adorabat" for the imperfect

προσεκυνει in all his versions. The Vulgate has "orabat". In the 1598 N.T. Beza comments that Erasmus had found MSS reading παρεκαλει here,[38] and that those were the source of the Vulgate/Vetus 'orabat'. Beza suspects that the παρεκαλει manuscripts were corrupted "a quopiam qui civilem adorationem in Oriente passim usurpatam non potuit a Dei cultu distinguere". It is equally likely, however, that the reading παρεκαλει arose as a result of confusion with v. 29. Moreover Beza is not necessarily right in attributing the Vulgate 'orabat' to παρεκαλει. It is possible that the Vulgate here distinguished between the imperfect "besought" and the aorist "did obeisance". If that was the case the Vulgate translation here is more adequate than Beza's. In connection with this it is interesting to see that Tyndale and Geneva both read "besought". Tomson preferred to follow Beza reading "worshipped". Bishops' reads "besought" which is corrected in Bodleian copy to "worshipped" under Beza's influence. The AV adopts the Bezan reading giving "besought" as marginal alternative.

At Matthew XIX.28 Beza, throughout his versions, associates "regenerate" with the time *after* the day of judgement saying, "Haec (verba) ita distincta sunt in 5 veteribus codicibus ut ad sententiam sequentem pertineant...id quod magis amplector." When sin has ceased "judgement will be the government of the ideal Israel" (cf. Ps. XVII.26). The AV follows the Beza/Vulgate rendition but none of the earlier versions do. Tyndale, Tomson, Geneva and Bishops all read "ye that have followed me in the regeneration" but this is corrected in the Bodleian copy to produce the AV reading "in the regeneration when the Son of Man".[39] In the 1598 version Beza points out that both readings are acceptable theologically, the Geneva/Erasmus reading signifying "Evangelii praedicationem quod ipse Christus in terras attulit quia tum veluti de integro conditus est mundus".

At Matthew XX.23 Beza supplies δοθησεται from the preceding δουναι in all his versions, thus reading "*dabitur* quibus paratum est a Patre meo". The Vulgate has "quibus paratum est a Patre meo" translating the ellipsis verbatim. Erasmus has "his continget quibus...". Tyndale has "but to them for when it is prepared". Geneva and Tomson follow Beza translating "it shall be given". The Bishops' Bible translates the Vulgate ellipsis. This is not corrected in Bodleian Bishops' but the AV follows the Beza/Geneva reading "it shall be given". As Beza makes no theological comment here the point is probably a purely stylistic one.

At Matthew XXI.37 Beza has "reverebuntur" for εντραπησονται in all his versions, which is followed by Geneva, Tomson and AV reading "reverence". The Bishops' Bible has "stand in awe of",[40] but this is corrected in the Bodleian copy to the eventual AV reading. Beza (1598) says that the addition of ισως is unnecessary here as he had not seen it in any Greek MSS.[41] He also mentions that this passage gave rise to the comment that "videtur Deus ignorare quid sit futurum, quum Iudaei Filium ipsius non sint reveriti. Unde postea curiosae quaestiones ortae sunt de providentia, de quibus multa Erasmus[42] hoc loco." Beza, however, considers these questions to be no more than "inanes...argutias. Loquitur enim hinc Deus in persona patris familias...affirmans quod est verisimile futurum. Sicut poenitere quoque Deum dicimus quum tamen consilium non mutet." He is making the sensible point that God foreordains even things that appear to denigrate his Name, i.e. the Fall or the Crucifixion.

At Matthew XXIII.2 Beza throughout interprets εκαθισαν (*aorist*) as having a present force like the Semitic perfect,[43] quoting Matthew III.17 as another instance of this. He says that the use of the present here suggests that the order of

Scribes as successors of Moses was divinely pre-ordained and therefore had to be taken as the source of truth "etiam ex ore mercenariorum et hypocritarum doctorum; sicut etiam nostra memoria in Papatu Deus conservavit verbum suum et Baptismum". However, now that the new way has become accessible with the coming of Christ, it is no longer necessary to adhere to the old truths in the same way. Beza then takes this opportunity to expand on the corruptions of the Roman Catholic Church, and on the right of magistrates to subdue all heretics and corrupt preachers.[44] Tyndale, Geneva and Tomson agree with Beza in reading the aorist as the present "sit". The Bishops' Bible agrees with the Vulgate and has "sate". In the Bodleian copy, however, "sate" is crossed out and there is a marginal note inserted, "Beza readeth 'sit'". "Sit" is also the reading adopted by the AV. The annotation in Bodleian Bishops' here, gives an explicit indication that Beza was being consulted.

At Matthew XXIV.31 Beza reads "Cum tubae voce magna" in all his versions, and all the English translations agree with this reading "with the great sound of a trumpet".[45] Beza (1598) points out that "in quatuor codicibus vetustis scribitur μετα σαλπιγγος και φωνης πολλης quomodo convertit Vetus interpres".[46] The Vulgate indeed has "cum tuba et voce magna" so it is difficult to say whether it was the Vulgate or Beza's annotation which caused the Revisers to adopt it as a marginal alternative.

At Matthew XXVI.26 Beza has "benedixisset" throughout and the Vulgate has "benedixit" for εὐλογησας. Beza points out in the 1598 N.T. that seven old codices[47] read εὐχαριστησας "gratiis actis, eodem sensu; et Marc VIII.6 et 7 haec duo εὐχαριστειν και εὐλογειν pro eodem usurpantur sicut hoc loco accipere necesse est; nisi velimus non poculum sed panem dumtaxat fuisse consecratum". In other words, Beza stresses that Jesus gave thanks to God for *both* the bread and the wine. If we are

to accept communion in both kinds, the action of blessing
(εὐλογειν) cannot be more important than the action of
giving thanks (εὐχαριστειν). Jesus did not bless the bread or the
wine but gave thanks to God for them, the whole action taking
the form of a "solemn prayer" or grace.

The Geneva version agrees with Tyndale in harmonizing
εὐχαριστειν in v. 27 with v. 26 and thus reads "gave thanks".
Tomson follows Beza and translates "blessed". The Bishops'
Bible has "given thanks" which is corrected to "blessed" in
the Bodleian copy. An annotation is added in the margin, in
italics, "Many Greek copies have gave thanks." This seems to
be derived from Beza's 1598 annotation. The AV reads "blessed" agreeing with Beza and the Vulgate.

St. Mark

At Mark I.34 Beza has "quod ipsum nossent" in all his
versions, whereas the Vulgate reads "quoniam sciebant eum".
In his 1598 N.T. Beza suggests that both the interpretations
are possible. Either Jesus did not allow them to say *that*
they recognized him to be the Lord, or he did not allow them
to speak *because* they knew him to be the Messiah. In support
of this latter interpretation he mentions that "quatuor codices addunt Χριστον ειναι sicut scribit Luc IV.41".[48] According to Erasmus, Beza claims, the reason for the command is to
prevent the daemons from revealing the fact too soon. But he
himself thinks it more likely that Jesus ordered the daemons
to keep silent "quod videlicet diaboli munus non sit praedi-
care Evangelium". Otherwise it might have seemed as if Jesus
was in collusion with Satan. Whichever of the two interpretations we adopt the sense of the passage is not noticeably altered. Beza presumably preferred to say "quod nossent" because λαλειν is used in the N.T. with direct object but not

with ὅτι (cf. Matthew XXIII.1, Mark VI.50, Luke XXIV.6).
Where ὅτι is used without any intervening word it is causal.[49]
Beza puts the clause governed by ὅτι into direct speech.

Of the English versions Geneva and Tomson follow Beza reading "to say that they knew him".[50] Bishops' agrees with the Tyndale/Vulgate reading "because they knew him". In the Bodleian Bishops' the marginal alternative "to say that they knew him" is inserted after Beza. The AV retains the Bishops' text keeping the Beza/Geneva reading as marginal alternative. This was presumably for mainly syntactical reasons; it would be much easier to treat ὅτι causally, rather than making it introduce indirect speech.

At Mark II.23 Beza has "iter faciendo" for ὁδον ποιειν in all his versions where the Vulgate reads "progredi". In his 1598 N.T. Beza points out the obvious syntactical difficulty: "Videtur autem permutata verborum collocatio; nam planior erit oratio si dicas, *iter faciendo vellere spicas* quam si ad verbum interpreteris *iter facere vellendo spicas*." He goes on to say that the Vulgate "progredi" is really a translation of περιβαινειν and that Erasmus' "inter viam" translates ἐν τῃ ὁδῳ. The syntax suggested by Beza was adopted by the English versions as early as Tyndale's time. His version read "as they went on their way" and Geneva and Tomson agreed with this (presumably after consulting Beza). Bishops' Bible reads "by the way" agreeing with the Erasmus/Great version. This is corrected in the Bodleian copy to "as they went" reading adopted by the AV. The syntactical order of Tyndale/Geneva/Beza has been partly confirmed by modern theologians. Gould in his commentary on St. Mark points out "And as for making the principal and subordinate clauses exchange places, in this case the peculiarity is not so great. *They began to go along plucking...* is not so very different from *they began, going along, to pluck...*".[51]

At Mark IV.40 Beza translates οὕτως in all his versions. Thus in his earlier editions he has "Quid ita timidi estis" which by 1598 he changes to "Quid ita formidolosi estis". τι δειλοι ἐστε οὕτως is the Textus Receptus reading and occurs in most Koine MSS.[52] Beza explains in his 1598 annotations that he interpreted the passage as rebuke to the disciples but rebuke mixed with amazement. He turns down the Vulgate reading: "Quid timidi estis?" which is backed by two MSS[53] as conveying mere surprise without the notion of reproach.

Of the English versions Tyndale agrees with Beza/TR reading "Why are ye so fearfull". This reading is also adopted by Geneva, Tomson and Great Bible. The Bishops' Bible here proves to be the most conservative agreeing with the Vulgate and reading "Why are ye fearfull". In the Bodleian copy the annotator inserts in the margin "or, in this sort". Evidently he had read Beza's note and wanted to stress the idea of rebuke. The AV, however, returns to the previous "majority" reading "Why are ye so fearfull".

At Mark V.23 Beza throughout has "rogo ut venias" for ἵνα ἐλθών as opposed to the Vulgate "veni". In the 1598 N.T. Beza mentions that Codex Bezae ("meus vetustissimus exemplar") and the Syriac N.T. both read ἐλθὲ ἵνα ἐλθών. (It is interesting to see that Beza refers to D here but does not quote it as omitting τι δειλοι ἐστε οὕτως at IV.40.) He goes on to say that if we agree with Vetus in following the Syriac/D interpretation, there is no need for an ellipsis which is otherwise absolutely necessary. *All* the English versions from Tyndale to AV insert the ellipsis. This would suggest that Beza's remark here is a comment on consistent practice, rather than a proposal for a new interpretation.

At Mark VI.10 Beza has "illinc" for ἐκεῖθεν in all his versions (Vulgate "inde"). In the 1598 N.T. Beza explains that ἐκεῖθεν refers to ὅπου not to οἰκίαν. "Vetat enim hospitium mutare in ista veluti pervolitatione. Nonnulli referunt non ad ὅπου sed ad οἰκιαν sensu prorsus inepto." Tyndale, Geneva, Tomson and Bishops' all read "thence" for ἐκεῖθεν thus not making it clear whether they are referring to "house" or "place". The AV evidently follows Beza's annotation and makes clear the reference to ὅπου by repeating "from that place".

At Mark VI.19 Beza has "imminebat ei" for ἐνεῖχεν αὐτῷ in all his versions. In the 1598 N.T. he suggests that the Vulgate/Erasmus "insidiabatur ei" is too loose a translation. "Ego vero nusquam memini legere ἐνεχεῖν pro Insidiari." Hesychius' interpretation ὠργίζετο (was angry with) also seems unsatisfactory to Beza, "aliquid etiam amplius videtur significare nempe summam offensionem quae facit ut omnes captentur occasiones quibus cuipiam noceatur...quod Latini translatitiem declarant verbo 'Imminere'". As illustration of this interpretation he refers to John Apocalypse II.4, XIV.20 and quotes the parallel French expression "en avoir à quelcun".

Gould, in his commentary on St. Mark, although he does not refer to Beza, reaches the same conclusion as the Genevan scholar with regard to the meaning of ἐνεχεῖν. He points out that the rendering "had a quarrel against him" requires the ellipsis τον χολον, and therefore it seems most plausible to take ἐνεῖχεν in the same way as Latin *insto/immineo* and thus translate "she followed him up, did not relax hostility against him" (cf. mn. colloquial English "had it in for him"). None of the English versions, except Tomson, follows Beza here. Bishops' Bible agrees with Tyndale and Great, reading "layd waite for him". Geneva has "had a quarrel against him" and Tomson reads "sought occasion against him" thus conveying the idea of hostility maintained over a period of time. In the Bodleian Bishops' "had a quarrel to" is suggested as marginal alternative. The AV has the Genevan "had a quarrel against" in its

text suggesting "or, an inward grudge" in the margin. The
latter is probably closer to Beza's intended meaning of
ἐνεχειν.

At Mark VI.52 Beza has in all his versions "Non enim
attenderant *quod factum fuerat* illis panibus" for οὐ γαρ
συνηκαν ἐπι τοις ἀρτοις. Thus, according to him, ἐπι τοις
ἀρτοις does not denote the object of the verb "concerning the
loaves", but the ground of understanding, on the grounds of
the (miracle of the) loaves. Beza explains this in his 1598
N.T. "Miraculum illud quinque pannum non satis considerave-
runt...." He disagrees with the Vulgate/Erasmus reading "Non
enim intellexerant de panibus" which makes "concerning the
loaves" the object of συνηκαν. He claims that if that were
the case the construction περι των ἀρτων would be used. Tyndale, Great and Whittingham agree with Vulgate/Erasmus version
and read "they understode not of the loves". All the other
English versions, however, appear to agree with Beza, in supplying an ellipsis of some sort. Thus Geneva, Tomson: *the
matter of* the loaves, Bishops': *what was done* of the loaves.
The AV, under the influence of Beza's 1598 annotation is even
more explicit, "the miracle of the loaves".

At Mark VI.56 Beza and the Vulgate have "tangebant eum"
for ἡψαντο αὐτου. But in the 1598 N.T. Beza explains that
αὐτου here could refer either to the κρασπεδον or to Christ
himself. "Nam de ea quae vestimentum illius tetigerit, dicit
Dominus, Quis *me* tetigit?" Of the English versions Tyndale,
Great, Geneva and Tomson read "him". The Bishops' Bible has
"it" which is corrected to "him" in Bodleian Bishops' with
"it" as marginal alternative. This, in fact, is the reading
as adopted by AV.

At Mark VII.2 Beza has "pollutis" for κοιναις as opposed
to the Vulgate/Erasmus "communibus". However, he does not reject the latter translation out of hand explaining that "com-

mon" here means "dirty". Beza goes on to explain that the Pharisees forbade food taken with dirty hands in case the hands had touched forbidden things and would thus pollute or defile the food. Beza's translation is more explicit in indicating the notion of the "ceremonially unclean", although "common" in late Greek did denote what is ordinary or vulgar or profane, as distinguished from select or sacred things.

English versions from Tyndale to Tomson all read "common" in agreement with the Vulgate/Erasmus version. The Bishops' Bible has "defiled" which is very close to Beza's rendition "pollutis" and possibly influenced by it. This is corrected in the Bodleian Bishops' to "common" (from Geneva Bible). The AV, however, keeps to "defiled" and inserts the less explicit "common" as a marginal alternative (cf. Matthew XV.11, Acts X.14).

At Mark VII.3 Beza adheres to the original πυγμῃ and so translates "pugno laverint manus" throughout, after Epiphanius.[54] He explains the Vulgate/Erasmus reading "crebro" by the fact that Vulgate, Vetus (also Syriac MSS) have πυκνα. Codex Bezae (referred to as "meus vetustissimus exemplar") has πυκμη which was possibly intended to read πυκνα.[55] Beza also quotes Theophylactus' interpretation[56] here suggesting that the phrase means "ad cubitum usque; quasi cubitaliter dicas". Beza himself prefers to follow the simplest reading i.e. that the Jews take great care in washing their hands "ut facere solent qui manum manui affricant et pugnum inferunt alterius palmae". Thus πυγμῃ, according to Beza, refers simply to the manner in which hands are washed not to any prescribed method of washing them. Beza quotes the Syriac version in support of this hypothesis; the Syriac N.T. translates πυγμῃ as (dabbetilaith) i.e. "sedulo et accurate" (cf. Luke I.39).

None of the English versions follow Beza here. Tyndale,

Tomson, Geneva and Bishops' all read "oft" agreeing with the Vulgate/Erasmus version. In the Bodleian Bishops' a marginal note is added in italics, "Or, diligently, in the Originall with the fist; Theophy. up to the elbow". This would suggest that the annotator had read Beza's comments and picked out the three readings suggested by Beza including his own "original" "with the fist". The AV reads "oft" in the text but repeats the marginal note as in Bodleian Bishops'. It is interesting to note that Gould in his commentary on St. Mark agrees with both Beza's reading and his interpretation of it, as against AV and others.

At Mark VII.15 Beza reads τα ἐκπορευομενα ἀπ' αὐτου "quae expediuntur ex eo" in all his versions. Vulgate and Erasmus read τα ἐκ του ἀνθρωπου ἐκπορευομενα which, according to Beza, occurs in one MS.[57] Tyndale, Geneva and Tomson agree with Beza reading "out of him". The Bishops' version agrees with the Vulgate/Erasmus/Great reading "proceed out of a man". This is corrected in the Bodleian copy to the Bezan reading "come out of him" which is also adopted by the AV.

At Mark VIII.24 Beza's early translation for βλεπω τους ἀνθρωπους ὁτι ὡς δενδρα ὁρω περιπατουντας was "video homines; nam cerno instar arborum ambulantes". From 1589 onwards, however, Beza adopts the textual reading ὡς δενδρα περιπατουντας (omitting ὁρω),[58] quoting as his support for this Vetus, Complutensian Polyglot and "Codex Bezae". The same reading was evidently the source for the Vulgate "Video homines velut arbores ambulantes". Erasmus follows the ὁρω reading and translates "Quoniam velut arbores cerno ambulantes". Beza criticizes this on the grounds that the participle "ambulantes" appears to refer to "arbores". Beza wants to stress that the blind man sees men moving *as tall as trees* (not, sees men moving *like* trees) and to avoid Erasmus' ambiguity he translates ὡς δενδρα as "instar arborum" (in the likeness of trees).

Tyndale agrees with the Erasmus reading and has "For I see them walke as they were trees". The Bishops' Bible agrees with this substituting "perceive" for "see" (after the Great Bible), Geneva and Tomson read "for I see them walking like trees" which seems to be based on Erasmus. The AV however, seems to base its readings on Beza 1598. It omits ὁρῶ and, in order to avoid the ambiguity of connecting "trees" with "walking", it follows Beza's syntactical order reading "I see men as trees walking". This correction does not appear in Bodleian Bishops'.

At Mark IX.16 Beza although he has πρὸς αὐτούς in his *Greek* text (1589/98) reads "inter vos" in his Latin text, translating ἐν ὑμεῖν from the Vulgate and Codex Bezae.[59] He mentions (1598) that "Frobeniana editio habet πρὸς αὐτούς -- adversus eos". Tyndale reads "with them" but all the other English versions have "among yourselves" presumably under the combined influence of Beza and the Vulgate. Bishops' suggests "with them" as marginal alternative but AV prefers to adopt this TR reading in its text, retaining the Vulgate/Beza "among yourselves" as marginal alternative.

At Mark X.42 Beza in his early versions had "Scitis eos quibus placet imperare Gentibus" (them to whom it seems good to rule the Gentiles). But from 1589 onwards he reads "Scitis eos qui censentur imperare Gentibus" where the Vulgate has "Scitis quia ii qui videntur principari Gentibus". He justifies his reading saying that οἱ δοκοῦντες here refers to those whose rule the people acknowledge and thus signifies the same as οἷς δέδοκται,[60] (thought by them i.e. the people, to rule). Beza rejects the Vulgate/Erasmus translation on the grounds that "videntur...dici solet de iis qui reipsa non sint id quod esse videntur" which he does not think appropriate here even though δοκεῖν may be used in this sense (Matthew III.9). Beza's view on this would seem to be confirmed by that of the

modern theologians.[61] Jesus here has in mind the difference
not between real and apparent rule but between the ideal and
the practice of ruling. People often rule because of force,
heredity, flattery, etc. not because they are *ideally* suited
for leadership.

Of the English versions Geneva follows early Beza but
appears to misinterpret in taking Beza's "placet" to mean
"those to whom it is *pleasing* etc.". Tomson omits the entire
"thinking" or "seeming" aspect of the passage reading simply
"they which are princes among the Gentiles". Tyndale and
Bishops' agree with each other and with the Vulgate/Erasmus
version reading "seem". In the Bodleian copy this is corrected to "they which are accompted" after Beza's passive sense.
This is the reading adopted by the Revisers who also retain
Beza's early reading in the margin "they which thinke good to
rule over Gentiles".

At Mark XIV.3 Beza has "nardi liquidae" throughout whereas the Vulgate reads "nardi spicati". In the 1598 N.T. Beza
assesses his own and the Vulgate reading. He justifies his
own rendering "liquid" by saying that πιστικης comes from πινω
"quasi potabilem dicas". He goes on to say that "Vulgata, ut
habent multi vetusti codices πιστικης hoc loco vertit 'Spicati'; quasi corrupta Latina vox pro σπικατης scripta sit...."
But he also mentions that Pliny[62] refers to a very precious
ointment which he calls "Nardi spicam", "Spicam nardi" and
"Spicam". Moreover, Galenus and Aegineta both adopt the Latin
terms φολιατον and σπικατον without mentioning explicitly any
word for "nard", "quasi satis id per se intelligatur". Moreover Codex Bezae[63] has πιστικης μυρον i.e. "unguenti ex Spi-
cata" under "Nard". The Vulgate translation thus has too much
Classical and Mediaeval support to be dismissed out of hand,
concludes Beza. Tyndale has "...narde, that was pure". Geneva and Tomson appear to agree with the Vulgate and read "Spike

narde". The Bishops' Bible has "very precious ointment nard". This is left uncorrected in the Bodleian copy, but the annotator suggests marginal alternatives "or, pure nard, or liquid nard". The AV reads "Spikenard" after Geneva/Vulgate in the text but adopts the Bezan suggestions (as put forward in Bodleian Bishops') in the margin.

Moulton,[64] in *Grammar of N.T. Greek*, suggests the following possibilities for πιστικος. The word is either Greek from πιστος "fit to be trusted, genuine", or from πιστος "liquid" (as Beza). It could also be a loan-word, transliterated from the Aramaic (pistaca). The Vulgate version, as well as the Classical/Mediaeval references suggest σπικατον as name of an ointment. This was "played upon" by an early Galilean tradition thus becoming πιστικον.

At Mark XIV.31 Beza reads ἐκ περισσου μαλλον and translates "multo magis dicebat" in all his versions. He points out that neither the Vulgate nor Codex Bezae read μαλλον but he agrees with Erasmus on the point that μαλλον emphasizes Peter's vehemence.[65] He departs from Erasmus' punctuation however (Erasmus punctuates after ἐλαλει and joins μαλλον onto the next sentence thus reading "Most certainly, if I should die with thee") for two reasons; firstly this punctuation does not occur in any MSS, secondly it is most unusual to find μαλλον at the beginning of a sentence without the addition of the particle δε when μαλλον is intended to mean "indeed" etc. Beza thus inserts μαλλον after περισσου without punctuation and treats the whole phrase as if it were πολλῳ μαλλον or πολλῳ περισσοτερως. Of the English versions Tyndale reads "he spake boldlyer" (no μαλλον). Geneva and Tomson also omit μαλλον, having simply "he said more earnestly". The Bishops' Bible agrees with previous versions in this and has "more vehemently". In the Bodleian copy, however, this is corrected to "he spoke the more vehemently" i.e. ἐκ περισσου μαλλον and this reading is adopted by AV.

At Mark XIV.49 Beza reads "Sed oportet ut impleantur Scripturae" for ἀλλ' ἵνα πληρωθωσιν αἱ γραφαι. He supplies 'oportet' on the authority of the Syriac N.T. from Matthew XXVI.56. The Vulgate has no ellipsis and reads simply "Sed ut impleantur Scripturae". Tyndale agrees with this having "that the scriptures should be fulfilled". Geneva and Tomson insert *"this is done* that the Scripture..." and Bishops' Bible agrees with Great in reading *"these things come to pass..."*. The AV appears to adopt the Beza/Syriac ellipsis reading "but the Scriptures must be fulfilled". This is probably the simplest way of supplying the idea of inevitable fulfillment.

At Mark XIV.72 Beza reads ἐπιβαλων ἐκλαιε(ν) with the TR.[66] The Vulgate reads ἠρξατο κλαιειν with Codex Bezae and the Syriac version. Erasmus has "Prorupit in fletum" i.e. ἐπιβαλε τῳ κλαιειν. Beza points out here "Possit etiam aliquis interpretari ἐπιβαλων. Quum hoc animadvertisset i.e. re animadversa."

Tyndale, Great and Bishops' agree with the Vulgate reading "beganne to weepe". Geneva and Tomson follow the Beza/Stephanus reading "wayinge that with himselfe, he wept". In Bodleian Bishops' "he begane to weepe" is corrected to "he fell a weeping" i.e. ἐπιβαλε τῳ κλαιειν.

The AV, however, adopts the Stephanus/Beza reading in the text "and when he thought thereon he wept". The Vulgate reading "he began to weep" is suggested as a marginal alternative along with "he wept abundantly" after Erasmus.

At Mark XV.3 Beza does not insert αὐτος δε οὐδεν ἀπεκρινατο which appears in the Complutensian Polyglot,[67] in any of his editions. However, in the 1598 N.T. he *quotes* the Complutensian reading and points out that "idque videtur optime convenire cum iis quae subiiciuntur". Tyndale, Great, Tomson and Geneva agree with the Beza/Vulgate reading. Bishops' inserts "but he answered nothing" after the Complutensian. This is crossed out in the Bodleian Bishops' but the AV reverts to the Complutensian reading, perhaps partly on the authority of Beza's recommendation of it.

At Mark XV.28 Beza has "Cum sceleratis numeratus est" for μετα ανομων ελογισθη[68] as opposed to the Vulgate "Cum iniquis reputatus est". Beza finds the Vulgate version too weak and points out that "vocabulum ipsum της λογιστικης quae species est Arithmetices, indicat interdum pro αριθμεισθαι usurpari, quam significationem hinc servandam fuisse inde apparet quod respondet verbo (manah) quo utitur Esaias capite LIII.2...". It might be added that the verb "numeratus" is borne out by the facts of the case. Jesus was crucified with *two* thieves and was thus taken for the *third* thief.

No English version from Tyndale to AV omits v. 28 and all versions up to Bishops' read "counted". The corrected "was reputed" in the Bodleian copy is not taken up by the Revisers, who have "numbered", a literal translation of Beza.

St. Luke

At Luke I.4 Beza translates επιγνως as "agnoscas" in all his versions on the authority of Erasmus and Theophylactus. The latter had interpreted επιγνως to signify "a greater knowledge of something which had *already* been recognized". Thus the Vulgate "cognoscas" is inadequate in the view of Erasmus and Beza.

The Erasmus/Beza reading is borne out by modern interpretations of επιγνωσκω. Thus Cremer "to give heed, to notice attentively...then, generally = to know". In later Greek the word was used in its primary strong sense and also in the secondary weaker sense (cf. Rom. I.21 and Rom. I.32) so that the Vulgate cannot be said to be wrong here, although possibly mistaken in the context.

This distinction between γνωσις and ἐπιγνωσις apparently breaks down when it comes to the English versions. Geneva and Tomson seem to translate Beza's "agnoscas" literally as "acknowledge". The Bishops' Bible reads "know" (in agreement with Tyndale) which is corrected to "acknowledge" in the Bodleian copy. The AV, however, does not take this up, preferring "know". Instances of the 16th century English usage of it would suggest that "know" did not mean the same as "cognosco". Coverdale in his version of the Psalms (XXXI.7) read "thou has *knowen* my soule in adversitie". On the other hand Shakespeare had "the kingdomes that *acknowledge* Christ"[69] (1. Henry IV.III.11). Both the words are used in the intensive sense of knowledge implied by ἐπιγνωσκω. However, if "know" and "acknowledge" were indiscriminate, the correction in Bodleian Bishops' would appear to be (a) either gratuitous or (b) an instance of blind copying of the Geneva version. Perhaps we may conclude that "acknowledge" in 16th century English was slightly more emphatic than "know" and that the Revisers preferred "know" since it could be conveniently ambivalent.

At Luke I.17 both Beza and the Vulgate read "ad prudentiam iustorum" for ἐν φρονησει δικαιων. Beza explains in the 1598 edition that the reading "prudentia iustorum" (i.e. by means of wisdom as opposed to force) is not admissible firstly because it does not appear in Malachi III.1 and IV.4.5 from where the words are taken; secondly, the construction of this phrase ought to parallel the construction καρδιας πατερων ἐπι τεκνα (hearts of fathers *to* children) and thus ἐν ought to be taken in the sense of εἰς (cf. Luke XXIII.42). This gives the sense that John would make fathers wise and good, in recognition of this children would draw closer to their fathers, just as soon afterwards, the faithful would draw to Christ in recognition of his wisdom and justice.

Tyndale, Geneva and Tomson all read "to the wisdome". Bishops' agrees with this, but the Bodleian annotator inserts "or, by the wisdome". The AV adopts "to the wisdome" in the text, but keeps the marginal alternative "or, by".[70]

For λαον κατεσκευασμενον Beza has "populum instructum" in his earlier versions which becomes "populum apparatum" by 1598. The Vulgate reads "plebem perfectam" which, Beza points out, is a translation of δημον κατηρτισμενον "quod neque usquam legi neque puto convenire". His main objection to it is doctrinal; John's baptism was not merely a baptism of repentance, it also implied remission of sins[71] in view of the impending death of Christ. Beza leaves open the question of whether John's baptism is a gift of the Spirit but does say that it leads to "regenerationis beneficium". However, John's *ministry* was no more than a beginning of the teaching of the Gospel. Tyndale has "to make redy the people" which expresses no idea of perfection but omits the translation of κατεσκευασμενον. Geneva and Tomson read "prepared" after Beza. Bishops' reads "perfect" in agreement with Great Bible, but this is corrected to the Beza/Geneva "prepared" in Bodleian Bishops'. The AV also reads "prepared".

At Luke I.28 Beza has "gratis dilecta" for κεχαριτωμενη[72] in all his versions. He construes the word, apparently coined by Luke to mean the same as the Hebrew (nirtsah), "quam Deus pro sua gratuita bonitate gratam et acceptam habet", or literally "graced" (cf. Eph. I.6). Erasmus here has "gratiosa" which, according to Beza, does not convey that the grace was bestowed solely by God and consisted in Christ himself. The Vulgate and the Syriac versions read "Gratia plena". This Beza considers to be too far removed from the Original, and thus giving rise to misinterpretations of the passage. Tyndale agrees with the Vulgate/Syriac versions and reads "full of grace". Geneva and Tomson translate Beza and have "*thou that art* freely beloved". The Bishops' Bible reads "*thou that art* in high favour" (after Erasmus) which is corrected in the Bodleian copy to the Vulgate reading "full of grace". However, a marginal insertion in secretary hand suggests: "favourably accepted". The AV retains the original Bishops' reading but inserts in the margin "or, graciously accepted".

The Revisers thus choose the classical, neutral interpretation of Χαρις (N.T. equivalent: δεκτος) in both their reading and their marginal suggestion. This has the merit of leaving open the theological side of the question. The AV appears neither to impute inherent grace to Mary, nor explicitly to say that her grace came solely from God. We can suggest that the Revisers inclined to the latter viewpoint, if we consider the AV insistence on the *passive*.[73]

At Luke I.45 Beza in all his versions reads "Et beata *est* quae credidit; nam etc.". He mentions that some versions of the Vulgate have "Quae credidisti" and "Fient tibi" which suggests a MS σοι for αὐτῃ. Most versions, however, read "Et beata quae credidit, quoniam". Both Beza and the Vulgate interpret ὁτι here as introducing the grounds for Mary's blessedness. The other possibility is to take ὁτι in the sense of "that" in which case the subordinate clause explains the content of Mary's beliefs.[74] Beza (1598) admits this as a possible reading "ut post πιστευσασα non adscribitur distinctio et ὁτι non αἰτιολογικως sed εἰδικως accipiatur" (after Theophylactus). Geneva, Tyndale and Tomson read "for". Bishops' omits the comma and reads "that".[75] The AV reverts to the reading "for" retaining "that there" as a marginal alternative.

At Luke I.77 Beza has "per remissionem" for ἐν ἀφεσει as opposed to the Vulgate "in remissionem". In the 1598 N.T. he comments that ἐν here should be taken in the sense of δια even though such construction is rare in Greek. He justifies this reading saying that remission of sins is the way in which God the Father saves us through the Son (cf. Rom. IV.7). Thus he does not differentiate (as above I.17) between John's and the Christian baptism.[76] Of the English versions Geneva and Tomson agree with Beza reading "by the remission". Bishops' in agreement with Tyndale and Great has "for the remission". The AV agrees with Beza/Geneva reading "by" but inserts "or, for" in the margin.

At Luke I.78 Beza reads "propter viscera misericordiae Dei" in his early versions which, from 1589 onwards he changes to "Ex intima misericordia Dei". In the 1598 version he points out that δια σπλαγχνα ελεους is equivalent to the Hebrew (berachanim chesdo) "id est ex ipsis visceribus sese exercentem misericordiam". He thinks that the Hebraism partly expresses Christ's taking on a fleshly form, and does not convey (as some have thought) that God feels the same kind of love for Christ as mothers do for their children. All English versions have read "tender mercy". The AV inserts "or, bowels of mercie" in the margin, reading which agrees with early Beza, Vulgate, Erasmus and Rheims.

At Luke II.9 Beza has "supervenit" in all versions as opposed to the Vulgate "stetit iuxta illos" and Erasmus "adstitit". In the 1598 N.T. Beza adds the gloss "i.e. repente venit quum nihil minus expectarent. Nam inter omnes verbi εφισταναι significationes haec mihi visa est hoc loco maxime accommodata".

Geneva and Tomson both agree with Beza reading "came upon". The Bishops' Bible, agreeing with Tyndale and Great, has "stood hard by them" but this is corrected in the Bodleian copy to "came upon" reading also adopted by the AV.

At Luke III.15 Beza in all his versions has "Expectante autem populo" for προσδοκωντος as opposed to the Vulgate "existimante". In his annotations to the 1598 N.T. Beza explains that the Greek phrase literally means "quum populus in expectatione esset, animis videlicet magnae spei plenis in Joannem respiciens". He compares the idiom to the French expression "Il s'attendait a Jehan" and points out that the Syriac version translates προσδοκωντος by (sebar) "quod significat etiam *sperare*". In view of this he rejects the Vulgate rendering, as it does not suit the context here.

Geneva, Tomson and Bishops' all read "people waited"--a more neutral rendering of προσδοκωντος which does not really convey the idea of hope (Tyndale and Great: "were in a doute"). In the Bodleian Bishops' "people waited" is corrected to "people were in expectation". This is the reading adopted by the AV after Beza. As marginal alternative, the Revisers supply "in suspense" which is slightly stronger than "expectation".

At Luke IV.29 Beza and the Vulgate both read "supercilium montis" for ἑως ὀφρυος. In the 1598 N.T. Beza explains that this is the name used metaphorically for that part of the hill which is closest to the summit. (This would accord with the geographical location of Nazareth--on the slope of a hill.) Geneva here agrees with Tyndale's translation "edge of the hill" and Tomson adopts that in preference to the Bezan reading. The Bishops' Bible has "top of the hill" which could be an inaccurate translation of "supercilium". This is corrected to "brow" in the Bodleian copy. The AV reads "brow" but keeps the Tyndale/Geneva reading as a marginal alternative.

At Luke VI.7 Beza reads κατηγοριαν αὐτου[77] in all versions and inserts the preposition κατα - adversus into his *Latin* text on the analogy of Matthew X.1.[78] In support of the insertion he quotes Theophylactus, Froben[79] and "three old codices". Beza grants, however, that the Vulgate reading "unde accusarent eum" expresses the correct sense of the passage.

The reading suggested by Beza had occurred in the English versions as early as Tyndale who read "that they might find an accusation against him". Geneva and Tomson agree with this reading but it is difficult to say on whose authority. The Bishops' Bible agrees with the Vulgate/Great version and has "that they might find how to accuse him". In the Bodleian copy this is corrected to "that they might find an accusation against him" which is also the reading adopted by the AV.

At Luke VI.40 Beza reads "sed quisquis erit perfectus discipulus, erit ut magister" for κατηρτισμενος δε πας εσται ὡς ὁ διδασκαλος αὐτου whereas the Vulgate has "perfectus autem omnis erit si sit sicut magister eius". Erasmus, too, on the authority of the Vulgate and Theophylactus, takes εσται in the sense of εστω thus interpreting the passage as prohibiting the disciple from taking on those responsibilities which the teacher himself does not have (cf. Rom. VII.29) i.e. the disciple will be perfect if he imitates his teacher in every way. Beza disagrees; Jesus is not merely asking his disciples to act like Him; He is speaking against the critics of the master who cause positive harm. κατηρτισμενος...αὐτου is thus a definition of a perfect disciple, not a promise. Whittingham, Geneva, Tomson translate Beza verbatim reading "whosoever will be a perfect disciple shall be as his master". The Bishops' Bible also agrees with this reading,[80] but the Bodleian annotator inserts a correction "everyone shall be perfected as his master is", (i.e. everyone will be like the master when they become perfected). The AV appears to insert a modified version of the Beza/Geneva reading "everyone that is perfect shall be as his master", probably omitting the ellipsis on grounds of accuracy. The more conservative reading "everyone shall be perfected as his master" is inserted in the margin.

At Luke VII.30 Beza has "consilium Dei abrogarunt adversus semetipsos" in the 1598 N.T. (Previous versions: consilium Dei reiecerunt adversus semetipsos.) The Vulgate has "consilium Dei spreverunt in semetipsos". Beza claims that the preposition is understood here and so he inserts it into his *Latin* text on the authority of Theophylactus, Froben and three old codices.[81] Thus the phrase means "suo maximo damno". He admits the Vulgate reading as a possibility--"apud se" (εἰς in the sense of ἐν) which suggests that they were afraid to reject John's teaching *openly*, on account of the people (cf. Matthew XXI.26). Beza does not mention the possibility of interpreting εἰς ἑαυτους as "with regard to themselves".[82]

As for "abrogarunt", Beza justifies his use of it by saying that the Greek verb ἀθετειν refers to the final result of the Pharisees not being baptized[83] (so in Gal. II.21). He points out, however, that, as Paul says, the counsel of God cannot be rescinded, since the very rejection of it is the execution of God's counsel against the repudiator (cf. Mark VI.26, Rom. I.21).

Tyndale here agrees with early Beza reading "despised the counsell of God against themselves". This reading was adopted also by Whittingham, Geneva, Tomson and Bishops'. The Bodleian annotator inserts a correction "rejected" for "despised", and this is adopted by the AV. This gives the rendering: they rejected the counsel of God, but the counsel of God was against themselves. The AV inserts the more neutral Vulgate reading "frustrated in themselves" in the margin. This gives the meaning "they rendered null the counsel of God *privately*, by not wanting to be baptized, but made no open objection".

At Luke VIII.14 Beza has "ne fructum perferunt" in all his versions as opposed to the Vulgate "non referunt fructum". In the 1598 N.T. he suggests, rightly, that the word is not derived from τελος as Erasmus supposed but from τελεος (perfect) and φερω (to bear). Thus the idea expressed is one of "bringing to perfection" rather than "finishing" or "bringing forth". All the English versions from Tyndale up to and including Bishops' read "bring forth" here. In the Bodleian Bishops' however, "bring forth" is corrected to "bring to perfection" and this Bezan reading is also adopted by the AV.

At Luke VIII.18 Beza has "quod videtur habere" in all his versions for ὁ δοκει ἐχειν whereas the Vulgate reads "quod putat se habere". The original correction of "putat" to "videtur" was done by Erasmus. Beza approves and follows it specifying "quod videtur habere et *sibi* et aliis". He goes on to say that this applies to a man who acts under false pretences with regard to himself and others, not, as the Vulgate suggests, with regard only to himself.

Of the English versions Whittingham, Geneva and Tomson agree with Beza/Erasmus reading "it seemeth that he hath". Tyndale, Great Bible and Bishops' follow the Vulgate reading "which he supposeth that he hath". The Bodleian annotator corrects this to "which he seemeth to have". This reading (which seems to be a literal translation of Beza) is adopted by the AV text, the Vulgate reading "thinking that he hath" being retained in the margin.

At Luke VIII.29 Beza has "agitabatur" for ἠλαυνετο as opposed to the Vulgate/Erasmus "agebatur". He explains in the 1598 N.T. that ἠλαυνετο means "cum impetu impellebatur ut eques calcaribus equum agitat", on the authority of Plautus. He suggests that the Vulgate/Erasmus "agebatur" is a translation of ἠγετο which is too weak in the context. All the English versions up to and including Bishops' follow the Erasmus/Vulgate version and read "was carried". In the Bodleian copy this is corrected to "was driven", which is the reading adopted by the AV.

At Luke IX.22 Beza has "excitari" for ἐγερθηναι in his earlier versions which by 1598 he has corrected to "suscitari". He does, however, translate the Infinitive Passive throughout. The Vulgate has "resurgere" which is followed by all the English versions from Tyndale up to and including Bishops'. In the Bodleian copy this is corrected to the passive "be raised" which is also adopted by the AV.[85]

At Luke IX.46 Beza has "disceptatio" for διαλογισμος as against the Vulgate/Erasmus "cogitatio". Διαλογισμος in the N.T. has two meanings; firstly, objectionable thoughts (Luke II.35, Rom. I.21, 1 Cor. III.20), secondly, "suspicions or doubt proceeding from the state of indecision" (Rom. XIV.1, Phil. II.14). Beza goes beyond either of the two basic meanings on the authority of Mark IX.33 which suggests that there was a *dispute* between the disciples and that the dispute was spoken.

Beza seems to be confusing διαλεγεσθαι and διαλογιζεσθαι. The former tends to denote discussion, the latter inner doubt.[86] In any case it is more appropriate at this stage that the disciples should have serious doubts about who should be the best as opposed to just having a petulant quarrel about it. Tyndale, Geneva, Tomson and Bishops' agree with Beza reading "disputacion". In the Bodleian copy this is corrected to "reasoning" which is adopted by the AV. This conveys the meaning of διαλογισμος more accurately than "disputacion".[87]

At Luke X.22 Beza, Vulgate and all the English versions with the exception of Geneva 1560 omit και στραφεις προς τους μαθητας ἐιπε. Beza, in his 1598 N.T. remarks that the phrase appears in many ancient MSS.[88] But, he says, "quae verba non legit Vetus interpres et sane puto hinc redundare, quamvis aliter sentiat Valla".[89] The Bodleian copy of the Bishops' Bible inserts a marginal comment in italics "many ancient copies add these words 'and turning to his Disciples he said'". This marginal comment also appears in the AV. Possibly it is a translation of Beza's 1598 annotation.

At Luke XI.3 Beza reads "in diem" for το καθ' ἡμεραν in all his versions. In the 1598 N.T. he explains that he takes the expression to mean "quanto in hunc diem opus est" after Quintilian's[90] thirteenth "declamatio" where beasts and birds are said to live from day to day. Christ here reminds us of this example so that we do not wear out our days in unnecessary anxiety. Interpreted in this way το καθ' ἡμεραν will mean the same as σημερον in Matthew VI.11.[91] The Vulgate version has "hodie" which Beza finds too weak, especially as το καθ' ἡμεραν can also be translated by "in singulos dies" as in some Vetus codices and Erasmus' Latin text. Although Beza approves of this translation, he nonetheless disagrees with Erasmus' interpretation of it. Erasmus claims that tomorrow's bread is being asked for and assumes that the prayer takes place in the evening. Beza points out that there are no good grounds for thinking that; Syriac version has ('cul-iom') "omni die".

Tyndale reads "evermore". Bishops' Bible agrees with the Vulgate/Great version and has "this day". Whittingham, Geneva and Tomson all agree with Beza reading "for the day". In the Bodleian Bishops' "this day" is corrected to "day by day" (after Erasmus). This reading is adopted by the AV text with the Beza/Geneva reading in the margin.

At Luke XVII.20 Beza has "ita ut observari possit" for μετα παρατηρησεως in all his versions. In the 1598 N.T. he paraphrases the expression as "cum externo quopiam maiestatis splendore ex quo possit agnosci". He goes on to say that there were signs announcing Christ as the Messiah, but the Pharisees were expecting an earthly kingdom and thus wanted more positive signs. Theophylactus relates μετα παρατηρησεως to time rather than space explaining that the kingdom of God is not decided for any definite period "sed semper est praesens ei qui velit credere et vivere ut fidelem decet". Other commentators (Beza does not specify) take this a stage further and equate παρατηρησεως with παραδοσις. Beza objects to this since Christ does not say that the kingdom is a purely internal experience "in animo per fidem purgato".

Tyndale and Great Bible read "with waytinge for". Whittingham, Geneva, Tomson and Bishops' all read "with observation" (after the Vulgate--dismissed by Beza as "too obscure"). The Bodleian copy suggests "with outward show" (after Beza) as marginal alternative. This is retained in the AV margin (text "with observation").

The same theological point is made at Luke XVII.21 where for ἐντος ὑμων Beza has "intus habetis" in all his versions as opposed to the Vulgate "intra vos est". In the 1598 N.T. Beza justifies his reading. The Hebrew expression (beker-bechem) means literally "in medio vestri". This suggests that the Messiah is openly among them. Were it not for the perverted opinion regarding the terrestrial kingdom of God, they would have recognized him (cf. John I.11). Beza then explains that he objects to the literal interpretation "in vobis", "inter vos" or "apud vos" since that would suggest that the kingdom of God is a purely spiritual matter. Such an interpretation is too extreme and unconfirmed by any other mention of the kingdom in the Bible.

Creed in his commentary on St. Luke (p. 219) agrees with Beza. However, all the English versions from Tyndale to AV prefer to follow the Vulgate and read "within you". The AV, however, inserts the Bezan reading "among you" as marginal alternative. This conservatism on the part of the English versions, however, need not be more than apparent when we remember that "within" can mean both "in the mind" and "within your boundary", i.e. "in the midst of you". The ambiguity on the part of the English versions is thus most likely intended to reflect the ambiguity of the Greek.

At Luke XVII.36 Beza and the Vulgate both insert δυο ἐσονται ἐν τῳ ἀγρω.[92] Beza points out that this verse is omitted by Erasmus who thinks it is an interpolation from Matthew. The verse does, however, occur in the Syriac N.T., in the Complutensian Polyglot and "aliquot vetustis codicibus" including Codex Bezae.

Of the English versions Tyndale does not insert v. 36. The Great Bible inserts it in italics, Whittingham and Geneva omit it, Tomson inserts it (evidently under Beza's influence) and so does Bishops' 1602. The Bodleian annotator adds a marginal comment in italics, "The 36 verse is wanting here in the most of the Greeke copyes." The AV reproduces the verse *with* the comment.

At Luke XVIII.7 Beza reads και μακροθυμων ἐπ' αὐτοις which, in the 1598 version he translates "etiamsi patiente sit animo super ipsis". (Earlier versions: etiamsi iram differat super ipsis.) After Theophylactus he takes και in the sense of καν (although) and interprets the Greek as meaning literally "quantumvis tardus videatur in ulciscendis ipsorum iniuriis". But, Beza goes on to say, Chrysostom reads και μακροθυμει ἐπ' αὐτοις "et iram cohibebit super ipsis".[93] This reading is also adopted by Codex Bezae, Vetus and the Vulgate. Beza suggests that one reason for preferring the μακροθυμει reading is the mention of vindication ἐν ταχει at Luke VIII.7. This is contradicted if we then read "although being long-suffering over them". In spite of that Beza says that he could not adopt the μακροθυμει reading "quum et universa Scriptura et sanctorum innumerabiles historiae testantur a Domino interdum diu differri supplicium in impios et Ecclesiae adversarios constitutum". None of the English versions adopts the μακροθυμει reading here. Tyndale, Great, Whittingham and Bishops' all read "though he deferre them". Geneva and Tomson read "though he suffer long for them". The Bodleian annotator inserts, as correction, Beza's early reading "though he deferre his anger long concerning them". The AV reads "though he bear long with them". Modern theologians prefer the μακροθυμει reading here in view of MS attestation.

Creed in *St. Luke*[94] comments that "the meaning and grammar are alike obscure" here but he prefers the translation "Does God restrain his anger?" i.e. "Is God patient at the misdoings of those who ill-treat the elect?"

We have not examined all the annotations in the Synoptic Gospels of the Bodleian Bishops' but we have chosen instances which deal explicitly with a point of text, doctrine or style. Those notes which deal only with a point of punctuation or phrasing (e.g. insertion of "And" at the beginning of a verse) have not been considered. So far as text goes,[95] in three cases of those examined a Bezan reading appears as annotation in Bodleian Bishops' but is not then adopted by the AV. At Matthew II.11 the Revisers insert the better attested reading ειδον, at Matthew X.18 they dispense with Beza's ellipsis "ut hoc sit" since the sense in English is quite clear without it. At Mark XV.3 they restore the Complutensian reading which occurred in the Bishops' Bible but which was crossed out in the Bodleian copy in agreement with TR.

In two cases a Bezan reading occurs in the AV but not in the Bodleian Bishops'. At Matthew XIX.28 the AV is the only English version to follow the TR punctuation. The other punctuation remains uncorrected in the Bodleian copy. At Matthew XX.23 Beza's ellipsis which was followed by Geneva and Tomson is inserted in the AV but not in the Bodleian copy.

In two cases the AV inserts a more conservative non-Bezan reading in the margin which did not occur in the Bodleian copy. At Matthew I.11 the "Jakim" reading is inserted in AV margin; at Matthew VII.14 the "how" reading occurs in AV margin (after the Vulgate). There is one case where the Bodleian copy suggests a marginal alternative which is not taken up by the AV. This occurs at Matthew V.47 where the Bodleian copy has "or, friends" in the margin, possibly under the influence of Beza's "annotatio".

In other cases, however, a textual emendation in Bodleian Bishops' tends to correspond to the AV reading, for instance Matthew VI.34, Mark VII.3 (margin), Mark XIV.31, Luke XVII.36 (margin).

In matters of doctrine the most noteworthy passages are at Matthew III.8, Matthew V.18, Matthew VI.7, Luke I.17, Luke I.28, Luke I.77, and Luke XVII.20.21. In the first of these there is slight disagreement between Bodleian Bishops' and AV as regards the translation of ἄξιος[96] but both have "repentance" for μετανοια thus avoiding the notion of penance, but being less extreme than the Geneva/Tomson "amendment of life" which both versions insert in the margin. The disagreement in the matter of ἄξιος could possibly be due to two different versions of Beza being consulted.

At Matthew V.18 there is full agreement between Beza, the Bodleian annotator and the AV in emphasizing that the O.T. Law still stands, although subordinate to the Gospel. At Matthew V.21, however, the AV is in agreement with Beza that Christ is denouncing the corruptions of the Law rather than the Law itself, but goes further than Bodleian Bishops' by inserting the Bezan reading in the text rather than in the margin.

At Luke I.17 AV agrees with Beza and the Bodleian version in emphasizing that John's ministry was only preliminary to that of Jesus, but at I.77 the Revisers compromise and although they have the Bezan reading (suggesting that John's baptism was equivalent to Christian baptism) in the text, they nonetheless insert the conservative interpretation in the margin.

At Luke I.28 the Bodleian annotator is seen to be more conservative than the AV in attributing intrinsic grace to Mary; the AV (retaining the original Bishops' reading) is closer to Beza but leaves the question of bestowed or intrinsic grace open.

At Luke XVII.20.21 AV, Bodleian Bishops' and Beza all agree in stating that the kingdom of God cannot be seen in terms of earthly *glory* but is not a purely spiritual experience.

As regards phrasing and style we would expect most of the "Bezan" passages in the AV to be derived from Geneva via the Bodleian Bishops'. This, however, is not the case. In nine instances out of those examined, the AV does adopt a Bezan reading via Bodleian Bishops' and Geneva.[97] In eight cases a Bezan reading in the AV is accounted for by the Bodleian Bishops' only (Matthew XVIII.26 and XXV.26--also Tomson).[98] In two cases an AV Bezan reading is accounted for by Geneva but not by Bodleian Bishops'.[99] At Matthew V.47 the Bodleian annotator has inserted the correction "greete with embracing" which could only be derived from Beza's "complexi", but the AV restores the more conservative reading "salute". In the same place the AV adopts Beza's interpretation of περισσον without the precedent of any English version or of a correction in Bodleian Bishops'. There are four other cases where a Bezan reading appears in the AV with no precedent.[100] At Matthew IV.12 the Bodleian Bishops' inserts a Bezan reading in the margin, which the AV adopts in its text.

We have examined all the crucial Bodleian annotations so that these results can give us a good idea of the relationship between Bodleian Bishops' and the AV, and of Beza's influence upon both. It seems that the divergencies of content between the Bodleian Bishops' annotations and the text and marginal notes in the AV are too numerous to warrant identifying Bodleian Bishops' as a later collation of King James' and Bishops' text. At the same time the differences between the two sets of readings are not great enough to preclude some relationship between the annotations and the AV text. Some clue to this relationship may be obtained by reviewing the influence of Beza upon each text. Here it must be borne in mind that during the making of the AV, Beza's 1589 and 1598 editions of the New Testament provided the latest and the most authoritative version of the Textus Receptus. That they *influenced* the Revisers has been proved beyond doubt by Scrivener; we are here considering primarily the nature of this influence. Bodleian annotations apart, it appears from the other evidence considered in this chapter that (a) the Revisers paid attention to Beza's text and annotations throughout, even to the extent of inserting abbreviated versions of his annotations into their margin (Matthew XV.5/6), (b) that Beza not only influenced the *text* and doctrine of the AV but also their phrasing to a much greater extent than might be suspected, (c) that, in spite of this, the Revisers did not abandon their general policy of compromise and tended to moderate or even eschew some of his more extreme pronouncements. The best instances of this in the Synoptic Gospels are Matthew II.11 where the Revisers restore the better attested reading εἴδον and Luke I.77 where the more conservative interpretation of John's baptism is inserted in the margin. There are, however, cases where the AV appears to be more "pro-Bezan" than the Geneva Bible, as regards wording (Luke IV.29, III.15). From this we may assume that, so far as the Synoptic Gospels are concerned, the Revisers followed Beza in most cases, but tended to moderate any readings which seemed inadequately supported, or which seemed too extreme doctrinally. If we then turn to the Bodleian annotator's use of Beza we find that there are a very few occasions where he is more conservative than the AV but that there are also instances where he adopts Bezan readings which do not occur in the AV. Best instances of this are at Matthew V.47, II.11, X.18 (crossed out). At Matthew XXIII.2 the annotator puts in an explicit note "Beza readeth 'sit'". On the other hand at Matthew II.6 (margin), Luke I.28, Matthew V.21, the Bodleian annotator is more conservative with regard to Beza than the AV.

Thus on the AV principles established above there can be little doubt that the Bodleian Bishops' annotations represent a stage in the making of the AV. The annotations show that Beza was referred to throughout and that the Revisers at this stage were less reluctant to accept some of Beza's doctrinal points than at other stages. This conclusion will emerge more clearly when we come to consider the work of the Final Revision Committee and Beza's influence on the Epistles.

Altogether we can say at this stage that, unlike the translators of the Geneva Bible and Tomson, the Revisers were not interested in Beza from the point of view of doctrine but from the point of view of an authoritative edition of the TR with a critical apparatus and exegetical material.

Relationship Between Bodleian Bishops' and the Theology of Two Members of the Oxford Company

Thus on the basis of internal evidence we have been able to establish that the Bodleian Bishops' directly precedes the AV. Our further task--that of examining the external evidence in order to see whether and how it can be related to our textual findings--proved to be a difficult one. As has already been pointed out, the handwriting of the marginal annotations gives no clue as to the identity of their executor. We know, however, that about forty folio copies of the Bishops' Bible printed by Robert Barker in 1602 were issued to the various companies of Revisers. Thus it seemed reasonable to make an attempt to discover whether any member of the Oxford Company *might* have owned the Bodleian copy. This line of approach did not produce very satisfactory results since very few of the works of the Oxford Company members seem to have survived in either MS or printed form. Only two of their extant works were found to be relevant to this enquiry: John Harmar's translation of *Master Bezaes Sermons upon the three first chapters of the Canticle of Canticles*, (Joseph Barnes, Oxford, 1587) and George Abbot's *An Exposition upon the Prophet Jonah contained in certaine sermons preached at S. Maries Church in Oxford*, (Richard Fell, London, 1600). Although both are Old Testament commentaries they nonetheless do contain much New Testament material as well as general comments on Church Government.

We shall here examine the theology of both commentaries in order to see how it compares with the theological outlook of the Bodleian Bishops'. Harmar's translation was dedicated to the Earl of Leicester. In the dedicatory epistle he points out that "Some fewe thinges being personal matters I must confesse unto your lordship, I have omitted in the printed translation which are pointed unto by a little star that who so list to see them maie by that meanes consult the autor himselfe." Harmar goes on to say that he and many others thought it better, in view of the general wisdom and value of Beza's work, to remove the few phrases which might cause contention.

Our intention was to compare Harmar's abbreviated sentences with Beza's full pronouncements on the various matters. Unfortunately the French original of Beza's sermons proved to be unavailable.[101] We have thus attempted to compare Harmar's translation with Beza's pronouncements on the same matters in the *Annotationes Majores*, 1598.

Only seven asterisks occur in Harmar's translation of Beza's *sermons*: two in the sixth sermon on Chapter I, one in the eighth sermon on Chapter I, and four in the tenth sermon on Chapter I. One of those (eighth sermon on Chapter I) abbreviates Beza's original statement on vestments; the others all abbreviate Beza's pronouncements on Church Government. A good example of Harmar's editing of Beza occurs in the tenth sermon on Chapter I.

> "Such are the reverend names of Bishop, Pastor, Elder or Ancient, Doctor and Deacon* which they afterwards by little and little divided into many other degrees* to hatch at the length an Oecumenicall Bishop, that is to say, a Bishop of the universal worlde."

We can see that Harmar's text, although it does not condone, nonetheless does not explicitly condemn the hierarchical system of Church Government. A similar comment is made by Beza in the *Annotationes Majores* at Phil. I.1. Beza specifies that there are two ranks in the Church "nempe episcopi ac diaconi". "Episcopi" is a general term for those in charge of preaching and government; they could also be called pastors, doctors or elders (presbyteri). Deacons are those in charge of alms, etc. Beza then goes on to say that it was later that the name of "Bishop" was adopted for him "qui politiae causa reliquis fratribus in coetu praeerat". It was then, according to Beza, that "coepit diabolus prima tyrannidis fundamenta iacere in Dei Ecclesia". From this arose Archbishops, the four Patriarchs and finally an Oecumenical Bishop.

From this example we see the difference between Beza's and Harmar's views; both are Puritan but Beza is expressly presbyterian. Harmar does not specify the original function of a Bishop and does not differentiate between that and his subsequent functions; nor does he attribute the division into degrees to the work of the devil.

Although this example of Harmar's editing of Beza has no exact parallel in the Bodleian Bishops', it nonetheless confirms what we already know of the Church of England at the end of the sixteenth century,[102] and also of the Revisers' general attitude to Beza. We have already seen that (pp. 90-91 above) the Revisers tended to moderate Beza's more extreme pronouncements on the questions of John's Baptism and Mary's grace and we further notice that Harmar's tendency to edit Beza's pronouncements on Church Government is in accord with the Revisers' overall policies.[103]

We shall now consider the tripartite relationship between Beza, Abbot's Theology in his *Lectures on Jonah* and the Theology in the Bodleian Bishops' and the AV. In order to obtain a clear idea of this, we shall compare Abbot's work with Nathaniel Baxter's translation of Calvin's *Lecture on Jonah* which was dedicated to Sir Francis Walsingham and printed by Edward White, London, 1580. We have already remarked above (p. 90) that both the Revisers and the Bodleian Bishops' annotator agreed with Beza in emphasizing a close relationship between the Old and the New Testament (Matth. V.18, Matth. V.21). We shall now compare this outlook with Abbot's and Calvin's attitudes as expressed in their respective *Lectures on Jonah*. For the purposes of this discussion we shall confine ourselves to statements made by the two scholars in the first lecture, "And the worde of the Lorde came to Jonah".

Calvin does not ignore the parallel between the Old and the New Testament here. He comments: "They say that the Gospell should be transported unto the Gentiles, even as Jonah was ledde awaie from his owne Nation and given a teacher unto

forraine and prophane." However, he goes on to say that the
reader should not make too much of the parallels between
Christ and Jonah. The only explicit parallel in the Scriptures is between Jonah spending three days in the belly of
the whale and Christ spending three days in the bowels of the
earth. In Jonah's time God had not yet shown what he would
do by the coming of Christ. Moreover, it was only after the
Resurrection that Christ's effect on the Jews and Gentiles
was made plain. Before that "God would have the adoption of
the generation of Abraham continue firme and sure that the
Jewes might excel, above al other people...".

Abbott takes a different view. He claims that the prophet "was a figure of the Redeemer of the world and in that did
lively express him". This was for two reasons, firstly because he was God's messenger, secondly because the period of
"death" in the case of both Christ and Jonah was three days.
He then adds it "may be deduced not unfitly out of the text"
that there is a parallel between Jonah's mission to the Ni-
nivehites and Christ's mission to the Gentiles. He then
elaborates, saying that in both cases God's purpose was "to
take away his word together with his Prophet from those who
long had it and brought forth no fruites accordingly". He
then makes a general point that if the word of God is neglect-
ed by the Christian nations then it will be taken away from
them.[104]

We see from this that Abbot's commentary on Jonah is in
accord with the tendency to establish close links between the
Old and the New Testament, a tendency which is also manifested
by both the Bodleian Bishops' and the AV.

This investigation did not aim to be a conclusive study
of the Revisers and their views. Such a work would, in any
case, fall outside the scope of this enquiry. We have, however, adduced two clear instances where the Theology of the

Revisers' works is in accord with the principles of Revision adopted by the Bodleian Bishops' and the AV, and with their attitude to Beza.

NOTES

1. Scrivener examines the influence of Beza on AV in his *Authorized Version*. His enquiry establishes Beza as the main influence on the AV New Testament. See esp. Scrivener's appendix E. pp. 244-263.

2. For identification of first and second issue of AV see Scrivener, *Authorized Version*, pp. 1ff. He concludes that the issue with the misprint at Ex. XIV.10 is the second 1611 issue. This would suggest that the copy of the 1611 AV in the Bodleian is mistakenly catalogued as the "first issue". I have used this Bodleian copy here but have followed Scrivener in referring to it as the *second issue*.

3. See Nestle & Aland, and Souter.

4. Geneva 1560 has "feede".

5. Cf. Ch. I, p. 36 n. 15 above.

6. The *fruit(s)* variants in the versions seem to be merely stylistic. Neither Nestle & Aland, nor Souter give any variants for καρπον.

7. See Ch. I, pp. 36-37 n. 16 above.

8. No real difference of meaning between 'Avoid' and 'Get (thee) hence' in 16th Century English usage. See S.O.E.D. (1970).

9. παραδιδωμι was used in classical Greek with the connotation "to give up to justice". See Liddell & Scott, p. 1308.

10. See also Ch. I, p. 37 n. 17 above.

11. *Confessio Christianae Fidei et eiusdem collatio cum Papisticis Haeresibus*. Per Theodorum Bezam Vezelium, (Geneva, Eustathius Vignon, 1587).

12. For discussion of Beza's MS sources see p. 5 above. Erasmus in his 1535 edition reads ἀδελφους and comments "Plerique Graeci codices habent τους φιλους i.e. Amicos. Verum Iudaei fratres appellant quomodo libet cognatos atque ita legit Hieronymus." (*Omnes quae extant D. Hieronymi Stridonensis lucubrationes*...per Des. Erasmum digestae...in novum tomos; Froben, Basle, 1535.)

13. This construction probably is theologically more accurate; Jesus is still emphasizing the difference between the Old and the New.

14. The Great Bible has "let not trumpetes be blowen before thee". Bishops' seems to have as its source here the Vulgate "noli tuba canere". Erasmus (1535) had "Ne tubis canatur" which presumably influenced Great Bible.

15. "δοξα...tum opinionem significat et existimationem tum etiam gloriam. Itaque interpretatus est *Glorificentur*... quo modo etiam nos, quoties quidem agitur de Dei laude et gloria" (Beza, 1598).

16. Tyndale and Great read "bable not much".

17. He quotes as best example of redundant prayers "Romanensum breviaria et horas quas vocent Canonicas, Rosaria et infinita huiusmodi, quorum vel Satanam ipsum pudeat" (N.T. 1598).

18. Legg cites the following Greek variants: αὐτης B* L: εαυτης ℵ B² G S V W 245. 258. 349. 475. 478. 487. 892: εαυτην *sic* 59. 700; εαυτη 485: τα εαυτης E K M N U Π Σ Φ fam¹. 1582. 22. 124. 346. 28. 33. 157. 565. 892(?) al pler., item et add. εις την αυριον 543. 826: το εαυτης θ: τα περι αθτης Δ.

19. In earlier versions Beza has "spectas" adding a note: "Aspicis, quod studium verbo spectandi potius quam videndi declaratur."

20. See Liddell & Scott, pp. 318, 1244.

21. Acc. Legg οτι ℵ* B* X (ὅτι *sic*) 1**. 118². 157. 372. 477*. 1365 *item* quoniam *vg*. (1MS) quia *m* (semel) Cop.^sa. bo. Arm. (cdd.) Geo¹. Or.: τι ℵᵇ et ᶜ B** Uncs. rell. 1*. 1582. 22. fam¹³. 543. 71. 349. 517. 565. 700* 892 al. pler. cf. quam *it* (pler) vg. (pler) Sy ^pesh hl. hier Aeth. Arm. (edd.) Faust, quae k: etc.

22. See Ch. I, p. 36 n. 15 above.

23. Also Great Bible (1539).

24. Cf. "They knowledge thee to be the Father of an infinite majesty" (1535), S.O.E.D.

25. Great: he commanded that they should go unto the other syde of the water.

26. See also Liddell & Scott, p. 883.

27. "Was caryed" also adopted by Geneva 1560 and Great Bible in preference to "ranne" or "rushed" agrees with Erasmus' translation "ferebatur" for ὥρμησεν.

28. In support of "comparate" he quotes Aristotle's κτητικη "ars omnis qua sibi unusquisquam victum parat". For list of volumes of Aristotle in the Geneva Academy c. 1572 see Ganoczy, *Bibliothèque*.

29. Erasmus (1535) as quoted by Beza, mentions *Libellum adversus Judaeos* then attributed to Cyprian. There the Greek παις is interpreted as both 'child' and 'son' but not 'servant'. But Beza (1598) points out, Cyprian disregards the Evangelists' tendency to draw upon O.T. prophets in order to show the fulfillment of the promise in Jesus and his Church (cf. Isa. XLII.1-4). The *Hebrew* word (ébed) means 'servant' not 'son' or 'child' and is translated as παις in some places in the Septuagint e.g. Jer. XXXIV.11.16. *Divi Cypriani episcopi Carthaginiensis et martyris Opera*...repurgata per Des. Erasmum... (Hervagius, Basle, 1540).

30. ἀνθρωπων here is translated 'servant' by both Beza and AV. ἀνθρωπος when it emphasizes the sarcical nature of man, is synonymous to παις; man because he is carnal, finds himself in subordination to God, cf. Rom. III.5, Gal. III.15 (see H. Cremer, *Biblico-Theological Lexicon of N.T. Greek*, [Edinburgh, 1962]).

31. Tyndale 1525: 'sonne'.

32. Rheims version has "vertues work in him".

33. I.e. a man could set apart his property for God, preventing anybody else from using it but maintaining the right to use it himself.

34. But Tyndale 1525 has "whatsoever thyng I offer, that same doeth profit the, and so shal he not honoure...".

35. Acc. Legg τον πατερα αυτου (om. θ fam^1. 1582. 22. 16. 349. 472. 517. 659. 1279. 1295. 1402. 1424. 1579 Or). + η την μητερα αυτου (om. 084 fam^{13}. 543. 4. 33. 251. 544. 700. 892. 1093. 1396. 1574). Uncs. rell. Minusc. pler. *b c f ff*$^{1.2}$ *g*^{1} *1 q* aur. vg. Sy. etc.

36. Acc. Legg αμην B X θ Π Φ 078 $^{vid.}$ ⸔ (exc. M) 118. 209. 22. fam^{13}. 543. 33. 700 al. plur. *a b c f ff*^{1} *g*$^{1.2}$ *h n q r*^{1} *vg* (2 MSS) etc.

37. Also Whittingham (1557).

38. Acc. Legg orabat a b ff^2 g^1 h l r^1 aur vg. (plur).

39. Nestle & Aland, Souter and Legg have the comma after μου thus agreeing with Beza/Vulgate/AV punctuation.

40. Cf. Tyndale (1534): "feare" and the Vulgate "verebuntur".

41. Neither Nestle & Aland nor Souter supply any variants, but acc. Legg + ισως 61. 1473 item + forsitan (forte h vg edd. Iren^{int}) b c e ff^2 (h) vg (2 MSS et edd) Sy $^{c.s.}$ pesh Arm. Iren^{int}, + forsitan (utique ff^1) post verebuntur (ff^1) vg. (tol.).

42. Erasmus' 1535 edition of the New Testament (Froben).

43. Cf. J. H. Moulton, *A Grammar of New Testament Greek*, (Edinburgh, T. & T. Clark, 1968), vol. II, p. 458.

44. Cf. Thomas Cartwright, *A Commentary upon the Epistle of Saint Paule written to the Colossians*, (London, Nicholas Okes, 1612). In the fourth of the sermons on Colossians I.5, Cartwright comments, "The Ministers ought to inveigh the more vehemently against sinne and to reprove it out of the word of God, and the Magistrates to see it more severely punished."

45. N.T. Tyndale (1534) "with the great voyce of a trompe"--even closer to Beza's Latin.

46. Souter accepts φωνης in his text giving the following variants which omit it: X L Δ θ 1 etc. 700 λ (vt.^{e}) ʃ(vt.^{s} vg) Σ (boh) ℟ Eus. Cypr. al. Nestle and Aland reject φωνης but quote it as appearing in D al lat. Legg omits φωνης but cites foll. variants: σαλπιγ. φωνης μεγαλης B X Γ Π Σ Φ ? minusc. pler...: σαλπιγ. και φωνης μεγαλης D. 476. 477. 482. etc.

47. Nestle and Aland quote ευχαριστησας as appearing in ℛ pm. Ju. Ir. Cl. Acc. Legg: ευλογησας ℵ B C D G L Z θ Φ Ω 074. 0160 ⲣ 37 ^{vid} ⲣ 45. 33. 157. 700. 892 al plur. *it*. *vg*. Sy ^{s}. pesh. hl. mg. Cop. Aeth. Arm. Geo^1. Tat. diat. Aph.: ευχαριστησας A W Γ Δ Π Σ ? (exc. GΩ) fam^1. 1582. 22. fam^{13}. 543. 28. 565 al. plur. Sy^{hl} *txt* Geo^2. Bas. Or^{mt}.

48. Neither Souter nor Nestle & Aland accept Χριστον ειναι in their text. Souter quotes the following variants with it: ℵ^c B C L W θ 1 etc. 13 etc. 28. 33. 700 al. Nestle & Aland mention B(Cal)W θ pm.

49. See Nigel Turner, *A Grammar of New Testament Greek*, (Edinburgh, T. & T. Clark, 1963), vol. III, p. 319.

50. Whittingham (1557): "because they knew him".

51. E. P. Gould, *A Critical and Exegetical Commentary on the Gospel According to St. Mark* (Edinburgh, T. & T. Clark, 1896), (I.C.C.), p. 48.

52. Nestle & Aland include τι δειλοι εστε ούτως in their text after C ℜ W al. Cf. Legg δειλοι εστε ℵ B D L Δ θ 565. 579. ...700 it. vg. Cop.$^{sa.}$ ^{bo}: δειλοι εστε ουτως A C W Π Σ Φ ⸓. 118. 22. 124. 33. 157. 1071 al pler. Sy $^{pesh.}$ $^{hl.}$ Geo. Aeth.

53. Minuscules of the ℜ type (see Ch. I, pt. 1 above).

54. Ganoczy lists two editions of Epiphanius, one Greek and one Latin, that would have been available to Beza. (1) *D. Epiphanii episcopi Constantiae Cypri octoginta haereses opus eximium*, Panarium... (Hervagius, Basle, 1544). (2) *D. Epiphanii episcopi Constantiae Cypri, Contra octoginta haereses opus*, Panarium sive Arcala aut Capsula Medica appellatum Iano Cornario medico physico interprete... (Winter, Basle, 1545). (Ganoczy, *Bibliothèque*)

55. Acc. Legg. πυγμη (πυκμη D, primo d...) A B (D) L N X Γ θ Π Σ Φ 0131 ⸓ Minusc. omn. Or. Epiph., item Sy. $^{hl.}$ $^{mg.}$; cf. pugillo *c ff i q r*^{1}: πυκνα ℵ W; cf. crebro *f g*^{2} *l r*^{2} vg. aur. (crebro pugillo) Geo. momento *a*, sub inde *b*; = diligenter Sy. $^{pesh.}$ $^{hl.}$ $^{txt.}$ Cop.$^{bo.}$ Aeth.; om. Δ Sy. $^{s.}$ Cop $^{sa.}$

56. For *Theophylacti Codex Romae impressus* see above. Also available to Beza, *Theophylacti, Bulgarie archiepiscopi, In quatuor Evangelia enarrationes* per Phil. Montanum Armentarianum denuo recognitae... (Hervagius, Basle, 1554) (in Latin).

57. Souter and Nestle & Aland have τα ἐκ του ἀνθρωπου ἐκπορευομενα. Neither quotes any variants but cf. Legg τα εκπορευομενα απ αυτου A X Γ Π Σ Φ ⸓ fam^1. 22. fam^{13}. 543. 28. 157. 1071 al pler....

58. Souter and Nestle & Aland insert ὁρω and mention no variants without it but cf. Legg ως δενδρα (+ ορω 238. 330) περιπατουντας (-τουντα 225) C^2 D M $^{mg.}$ W θ fam^1. 22. 28. 225. (238). (330). 349. 517. 472. 565. 892 etc....it. vg. Sy $^{s.}$ pesh. hl. Cop $^{sa.}$ $^{bo.}$ Geo. Aeth. Aug. (Legg also inserts ὁρω in his text.)

59. Cf. Legg εν υμειν D, cf. inter vos *it* (exc. *k*) vg.

60. Beza points out here "...unde δοξα pro opinione et Haeretici appellati δοκηται qui carnem Christi non reipsa extitisse, sed talem visam fuisse docuerunt" (1598).

61. See Gould, *St. Mark*, p. 202.

62. *Galeni Pergameni...Opera omnia...*, (Cratander & Bebel, Basle, 1538). *C. Plinii Secundi Historiae mundi libri XXXVII...Sigismundi Galenii Annotationibus...*, (Froben, Basle, 1549).

63. According to Nestle & Aland D omits ναρδον πιστικης πολυτελους and substitutes nothing in its place.

64. For details see Moulton, *Grammar of N.T. Greek*, (Edinburgh, T. & T. Clark), 1968), vol. I, p. 379.

65. Souter and Nestle & Aland both read εκπερισσως and supply no variants with μαλλον but cf. Legg + μαλλον A N W X Y Γ Σ Φ 0116 ? fam^1. 22. fam^{13}. 543. 28. 157. 579. 1071 al pler. Sy ^{hl}.

66. Legg, Souter and Nestle & Aland all have επιβαλων εκλαιεν in the text but cf. Legg και ηρξατο κλαιειν D θ 565 it. vg. Sy s· pesh. hl. Cop. sa. bo. Geo. Arm. Aug.

67. Cf. Legg + αυτος δε ουδεν απεκρινατο N U W Δ Θ Σ Ψ fam^{13}. 543. 33. 106. 108. 127. 238. 247. etc.

68. Whole verse omitted in the text of Souter, Nestle & Aland and Legg. 28b represents a quotation from Is. LIII.12 which it is very unusual to find in Mark. However, the main sources for including 28 are ℵ θ pm lat sy ^{P} and some Patristic MSS. It is interesting to note that Beza makes no mention of the omission of 28 by D.

69. See S.O.E.D.

70. Modern scholarship suggests "in the wisdom" (J. M. Creed, *The Gospel According to St. Luke*, (London, Macmillan, 1930), p. 11.

71. Beza's views on John's baptism were criticized by Gregory Martin, especially the distinction between the baptism (equal to Christ's) and the doctrine (inferior to Christ's). Martin refers this to Acts XIX.3. His objections are answered by Fulke (*A defence of the sincere and true trans-*

lations of the Holy Scriptures..., by William Fulke, ed. by
C. H. Hartshorne [Cambridge, University Press, 1843], pp. 452-454, [Parker Society]). However, Beza in a note on Acts XIX.3 (1598) lists three types of Baptism: (1) literal immersion in water, (2) baptism whereby the Holy Spirit is given, (3) John's baptism i.e. the baptism of repentance (although it implies remission of sins).

72. Fulke supports Beza's translation of κεχαριτωμενη as against Martin's suggestion "full of grace". See *Defence*, ed. Hartshorne, pp. 469-70.

73. John Bois' note on Eph. I.6 would suggest a desire *not* to impute inherent grace to Mary, while at the same time, being less explicit about the *gift* of divine grace than Beza (see Ward-Allen, *op. cit.*, p. 59).

74. Nestle & Aland quote no variants without a comma, but Souter points out "virgula post πιστευσασα secundum sensum sive ponenda (ut θ and Egyptian versions) sive tollenda" (as some versions of Vetus and Vulgate).

75. Bodleian Bishops' has in italics, in the margin, "or, which beleaved that there".

76. For contemporary discussion of this see C. K. Barrett, *The Gospel According to St. John*, (London, SPCK, 1955), p. 174.

77. Acc. Tischendorf κατηγορειν cum ℵ* B S X (D - γορησαι) 1. 22. 28. 124. 131. al5 g¹...item *b c ff²* vg; κατηγοριαν cum ℵᶜ A E F W H K L M (R vid quia κατ sequitur) U V Γ Δ Λ H al pl....

78. According to Nestle & Aland κατ' occurs in KL pm (with κατηγοριαν).

79. All 16th century editions of Erasmus were printed by Froben. Beza refers throughout to the 1535 edition (Ganoczy, *Bibliothèque*, p. 108).

80. Tyndale and Great: "Every man shal be perfecte even as his master is."

81. Neither Souter nor Nestle & Aland quote any variants with κατα but Nestle & Aland mention that D omits εις εαυτους. Beza shows no knowledge of this.

82. See Creed, *St. Luke*, p. 108.

83. I.e. they denied that John had any significance in the purpose of God.

84. Rheims version also adopts the more emphatic reading "driven".

85. Beza shows no knowledge of the D reading μεθ' ἡμερας τρεις or of the reading ἀναστηναι (as in C ℵ D al) for ἐγερθηναι.

86. See Cremer, *Lexicon*. At Mark IX.33 Beza, after TR, reads διελογιζεσθε προς ἀλληλοις which would give the meaning "conferred among yourselves" but not, as he claims "argued among yourselves". In Luke IX.46 the vocal aspect is not mentioned.

87. Cf. Rheims version: cogitation. But at Mark IX.33 Revisers read "disputed".

88. Acc. Tischendorf και στραφ cum. A C* E G H K S U V W^a X Γ Δ al longe plu c ff^2 lq go Syr^{sch} et ^{p} Aeth $^{cod\ a}$ Pers^p... s^e Gb.

89. Laurentius Valla, *In Latinam Novi Testamenti interpretationem...*, edente Erasmo, (Basle, 1526).

90. *M. Fabii Quintiliani Oratorium Institutionum lib. XII...*, (Badius, Paris, 1519).

91. He points out that D, or, as he calls it "meus vetustissimus exemplar" actually reads σημερον. This is confirmed by the Nestle & Aland apparatus.

92. Nestle & Aland quote the following variants with v. 36 D (pm lat sy). See also Tischendorf, I, p. 637.

93. Nestle & Aland and Souter both have μακροθυμει in the text. Nestle & Aland mention the μακροθυμων variant as appearing in ℵ pm. Cf. Tischendorf, I, και μακροθυμων cum Γ Δ Λ R unc^8 al pler Syr$^{sch\ et\ p}$ Dam ^{par}.... (See also Ch. I, p. 12 above.)

94. See Creed, *St. Luke*, p. 223, cf. RVS, Luke XVIII.7, "And will not God vindicate his elect who cry to him day and night? Will he delay long over them?"
    N.E.B.: "And will not God vindicate his chosen, who cry out to him day and night, while^B he listens patiently to them?" (B) *Or* "delays to help them".

95. For instances where AV agrees with Beza *against* Stephanus see Scrivener, *Authorized Version*, Appendix E.

96. See Fulke's *Defence*, ed. Hartshorne, p. 345ff.

97. Matthew II.16, VII.23, VIII.32, XII.18, XXI.37, XXIII.2; Mark X.42; Luke II.9, VIII.18.

98. Matthew XI.28, XVIII.26, XXV.26; Mark VI.56, XIV.31; Luke III.15, IV.29, VIII.29.

99. Matthew III.9, XV.5/6.

100. Mark VI.10, VII.2, XIV.3; Luke VI.40.

101. No mention of it is made in either Bodley or Dr. Williams' library catalogues. The British Library copy was destroyed by bombing.

102. For full account of the drawing up and emendations of the Lambeth Articles see H. C. Porter, *Reformation and Reaction in Tudor Cambridge* (1958), pp. 364-375. The Articles were printed for the first time in 1613 "Ex Typographeo Henrici Gymnasii Typographi, Impensis Johannis Juniorii Amsterdamensis Librarii", i.e. eighteen years after they were first drawn up.

103. Cf. AV reading "Bishopricke" at Acts I.20 as against Geneva.

104. Beza has only linguistic comments to make at appropriate places in his New Testament (Matth. XII.40, Matth. XXI.43, Luke II.32).

CHAPTER III

The Influence of Beza
on the Pauline Epistles and Hebrews

We have considered the influence of Beza on the English Synoptic Gospels in general and on the AV Synoptic Gospels in particular. It was concluded that Beza had a considerable influence on AV with respect to phrasing and that, judging by the annotations in Bodleian Bishops', the Revisers were more reluctant to accept some points of Beza's doctrine at the earlier stages of the Revision (as illustrated by the Bodleian annotations), than the final version would suggest.

We are now going to consider Beza's influence on the Epistles. As all the Epistles cannot be examined here we have chosen those that were likely to cause the greatest problems from the point of view of doctrine and phrasing: Romans, 1 Corinthians, Galatians and Hebrews. Referring to Prof. Ward-Allen's edition of the Fulman MS (which represents a copy of the Final Revision Committee's proceedings as written down by John Bois[1]) we shall compare the most important of Bois' glosses on the stylistic, doctrinal and textual points in the four Epistles with Beza's 1589/98 glosses on the same points. We shall then examine the corresponding readings in Tyndale 1534, the Great Bible, Geneva 1560, Tomson 1576, Bishops' 1602 and the AV. In this way we hope to establish the relationship between the Final Revision Committee and the AV, the reliance of both those on Beza, on Continental sources other than Beza and on earlier English versions. We shall also consider the difference (if any) between the nature of Beza's influence on the AV, Final Revision Committee and the Geneva Bible. Lastly we shall compare the Revision Committee's attitude to Beza with

that of the Bodleian Bishops' annotator and attempt to give a
general outline of the influence of Beza on the English N.T.

Before proceeding with the enquiry proper, we can obtain
some idea of the Revision Committee's attitude to Beza by considering specific references made by them to his work. Bois
in his notes refers to a wide range of scholarship, Classical,
Patristic and Contemporary. Mostly the scholars in question
are referred to by name only with no mention of the work or
page number. The only work to receive precise references including page numbers is the first volume of Sir Henry Saville's
edition of Chrysostom. This came out in 1610, just before the
Committee assembled, and so would not have been familiar to the
Revisers, in the same way as, for example, the editions of Camerarius, Augustine or Hesychius which they were using. Beza
is probably mentioned more often than any other single scholar
but Bois does not say which edition of Beza is being used.
However, Bois' references at 1 Cor. X.30 ("This interpretation
rejected by Beza A.D. deemed worthy of his advocacy...."),
1 Tim. I.5 ("...not however of the Law in general as Beza has
annotated incorrectly in this place..."), James I.3 ("For what
the difference is, however, between δοκιμιον and δοκιμην, look
in the writings of Beza at Rom. V.4..."), show that Beza's annotations as well as his text were being consulted. Of the
instances where Beza is specifically referred to by the Committee (Rom. V.12, XI.31, XIII.1; 1 Cor. X.17, X.10; Eph. I.
13; 1 Tim. I.5; Heb. IV.1; James I.3, II.22; 1 Pet. I.20, II.
5), five (1 Cor. X.17, 1 Tim. I.5, Heb. IV.1, James II.22,
Rom. V.12) provide an occasion for either a rejection or a
criticism of Beza. In five cases (Rom. XI.31, 1 Cor. X.30,
Eph. I.13, 1 Pet. I.20, 1 Pet. II.5) Beza's opinion is merely
quoted and in two cases (Rom. XIII.1, James I.3) Bois approves
Beza's translation and explanation respectively.

In the case of the first five instances listed above, in

three cases (1 Cor. X.17, 1 Tim. I.5, Heb. IV.1) the final version of the AV agrees with Bois against Beza. However, it must be borne in mind that at 1 Cor. X.17 no other English version follows Beza's reading,[2] and at 1 Tim. I.5 the AV simply follows the earlier English readings thus avoiding commitment on whether της παραγγελιας refers to that particular charge or to Christian teaching in general. Only in the case of Heb. IV.1 does the AV agree with the Final Revision Committee against Beza and English versions from Tyndale to Bishops' 1602. In two cases (Rom. V.12 and James II.22) the AV agrees with Beza as against Bois. At Rom. V.12 the AV adopts the Bezan reading "in whom" in the margin even though the Final Revision Committee considered it "difficult and unnecessary". At James II.22 the AV reads "Seest thou...?" with Beza although Bois had suggested that the interrogative should not have been written.

In cases where Beza's opinion is simply quoted the AV is found to follow Beza without exception. Thus at Rom. XI.31 the AV is the only one of the English versions to adopt the Beza/Theophylactus punctuation. At 1 Cor. X.30 the Bezan interpretation is adopted into the AV text but with the backing of the Geneva and Bishops' versions. At Eph. I.13 where Bois suggests that either ἠλπικατε (after Beza) or ἐκληρωθητε from V.11 should be supplied, the AV chooses the former. At 1 Pet. I.20 the Bezan translation "foreordained" is adopted by the AV, though again with the backing of the previous English versions (e.g. "ordeyned before": Tyndale). At 1 Pet. II.5 where Bois suggests οἰκοδομεισθε can be taken *either* imperatively (after Beza and Downes) *or* indicatively the AV chooses the indicative reading keeping the Bezan variant as marginal alternative.

Finally in the two cases where the Bezan reading is actually commended by the Final Revision Committee, at Rom.

XIII.1 the AV inserts Beza's translation "ordered" for τεταγμέναι in the margin. And at James I.11 the AV, in agreement with most other English versions, reads "trying".

If we guide ourselves only by those annotations of Bois' in which Beza is specifically referred to, it might appear as if the Final Revision Committee was trying to reject some of the Bezan readings but was ultimately deflected in its purpose. However, in order to estimate accurately the scope of Beza's influence on the Committee the AV and the other English versions, we cannot limit ourselves to only those glosses which mention Beza.

It must be remembered that Beza's N.T. was the *latest* edition of the N.T. and so would have been considered the most authoritative. Independent evidence of this is provided by Fulke's *A defence of the sincere and true translations of the Holy Scriptures*... which deals almost exclusively with Beza's Greek Testament. We can also gather from other sources that Beza was not only extremely popular in late Elizabethan and early Jamesian England but also enjoyed a considerable eminence. His work would have been thus very well known to the Final Revision Committee and on some occasions there would have been no need to refer to the author. Added to this was the fact that John Bois was simply making a record of the Committee's *proceedings* and so probably had neither the time nor the need for precise references in every single case. And we will see from the detailed examination of Romans, 1 Corinthians, Galatians and Hebrews that quite often Bois' gloss shows the influence of Beza without there being a specific reference to the Genevan Scholar. Moreover, the AV quite often inserts Bezan readings which are completely unacknowledged by Bois. Some of those come from the Geneva Bible; others come into the English New Testament with the AV. The exact proportions of those will be estimated by the following enquiry.

Romans

At Rom. I.9 Bois comments that ἐν τῷ πνευματι μου is equivalent in meaning to ἀδολως (guilessly, without fraud) and suggests that if το πνευμα here meant "spirit" as opposed to "ceremonies" then "my" would not be added.

Beza in his 1589 and 1598 N.T. makes the point that the addition of μου in the text points to the meaning "spiritu meo i.e. plane volens et ex animo illi addictus". Beza thinks that although a tacit distinction is being made between spirit and ceremonies, this is not Paul's main concern here. Of the English versions Geneva and Tomson read "in my spirit" making clear by means of marginal notes that they adopt Beza's interpretation. The Bishops' Bible (1602) agrees with Tyndale's reading "with my spirit". This gives us no clue as to how "spirit" is being interpreted. The AV has "with my spirit" in the text and "in my spirit" in the margin. This could imply either two interpretations of "spirit" or two different ways of translating ἐν. Bois' note which is based on Beza's corresponding "annotatio" suggests the former possibility.

At Rom. I.20 Bois comments that ἀπο κτισεως κοσμου refers to time and means the same as ἀπο καταβολης κοσμου. It has been taken in this sense by Chrysostom, Hom. 6 in Gen. p. 37 line 2.[3] Beza (1589/98) at the same place has the translation "a creatione mundi" in agreement with the Syrus interpres. He considers both the Vulgate "a creatura mundi" and Erasmus' "ex creatione mundi" to be 'barbarous' since it is neither the created things that are discussed nor the actual construction of the world, but time from creation of the world as in Mark X.6. Beza, however, does not mention his own earlier translation here "ex creatione mundi".[4] This was followed by Geneva and Tomson who read "by the creation of the world". Bishops' has here "through the creation of the world".

It must be noted that the reading which is recommended by Bois with the support of Chrysostom and by Beza (1589/98) has already appeared in Tyndale's 1534 version ("from the creation of the world"). The AV also adopts this. The similarity between the wording of Bois' note and that of Beza would point to the conclusion that Bois referred to the 1589/98 edition and used Chrysostom to corroborate Beza's view.

At I.28 Bois glosses εἰς ἀδοκιμον νουν as μηδυναμενον δοκιμαζειν τα διαφεροντα and then comments on the ἀντανακλασις in ἐδοκιμασαν and ἀδοκιμον. In order to retain the balance between the two halves of the sentence the meaning should be: "and *as they judged it* not the best way to reteine God in knowledge: or, to have God in acknowledgement. God delivered them into a mind *void of judgement*". He then comments that the verse refers to those who obtained natural knowledge but not θεογνωσια.

Beza adopts the translation "mentem omnis iudicii expertem" in all his versions. He disagrees with Erasmus' interpretation of ἀδοκιμον νουν as "mentem quae propter scelera omnibus displiceat" (i.e. reprobate mind) considering it too weak. On the other hand, he thinks that those who interpret the Greek as meaning mind rejected by God in contrast to an elected one "videntur multo severiores quam par sit". He himself interprets the passage as saying that men are not perfect enough to rely solely on natural knowledge without being misled by it. Thus ἀδοκιμος νους is a mind deprived of proper powers of reasoning. Bois and Beza are in full agreement here with regard to both reading and its interpretation. The Bishops' Bible here agrees with Tyndale and Great, reading "lewd mind". Geneva and Tomson follow Erasmus/Vulgate in preference to Beza and read "reprobate mind". This is also the reading adopted by the AV text, although Revisers suggest the Bois/Beza reading as a marginal alternative.

At Rom. III.9 Bois takes προεχομεθα[5] as referring to the Jews either in the sense of "are we surpassed by the Greeks?" or in the sense of "are we preferred, are we God's darlings?". Beza in all his versions agrees with Bois in so far as the latter meaning of the passage is concerned. In the 1598 version he points out that the Apostle says "praecellimus" not "praecellitis" firstly because he is, in fact, one of the Jews and, secondly, he will not offend the Jews if he counts himself as one of them. However, Beza unlike Bois does *not* translate προεχομεθα by the grammatical passive. Geneva and Tomson here agree directly with Beza reading "What then? Are we more excellent?" Bishops' Bible and Tyndale agree with the Vulgate/Erasmus "Quid ergo? praecellimus eos?" which they translate as "What then? Are we better *than they*?" This reading is also adopted by the AV in preference to either the Beza/Geneva reading or to Bois' suggestions.

At Rom. III.25/26 the two parts of Bois' note are separated by other annotations on the Romans in the Fulman MS. It is clear, however, that the Final Committee was concerned with two problems at vv. 25/26. The first one is the problem of interpreting δικαιοσυνη. Bois takes this to mean "punitive justice". Secondly there is the problem of the theological significance of this justice. Bois comments that the whole passage demonstrates that God is simultaneously just and merciful with regard to both past and present sins. From this we can assume that Bois interprets παρεσις as remission of past sins in Christ and not as the overlooking of sins in the past so that they can be expiated through Christ's death.

Beza is much more explicit here and has a lengthy comment on these verses in his 1598 N.T. where he deals with both the concept of δικαιοσυνη and the concept of παρεσις. In relation to δικαιοσυνη he quotes Rom. III.21, "Nunc autem absque Lege Iustitia Dei per fidem Christi patefacta est." He is thus seen to agree with Bois in taking it as referring to punitive justice; in Christ God punished all sinners and at the same time justified them.[6] Beza then considers the question of παρεσις. The revelation of God's justice, he says, poses a two-fold question: (1) Why was Christ's coming delayed? (2) What happened to the O.T. Fathers who lived before the Redemption? They were undoubtedly sinners and it was necessary for them to expiate their sins before they could be remitted. According to Beza, the Apostle explains this considering Redemption in two periods of time: (1) period before the *actual* Redemption, (2) period after the Redemption which he calls τον νυν καιρον. God demonstrated his justice with regard to both. Thus He did not deal with the Ancients as they deserved but *overlooked* their sins and put off their punishment until their sins could be expiated through the death of Jesus together with the sins of those who lived after the moment of Redemption. Beza thus differs from Bois in taking παρεσις as referring to overlooking of sins *in* the past as opposed to remission of sins which took place in the past. Tyndale, Great, Geneva and Bishops' all render παρεσις as "forgiveness of sins that are past". The AV text "remission of sins that are past" agrees with the Vulgate, Erasmus and Rheims versions, and also with Bois' interpretation. However, the AV marginal reading "passing over of sins that are past" is derived from Beza. Δικαιοσυνη is translated as "righteousness" by all English versions except Rheims[7] ("justice").

At Rom. IV.17 Bois suggests that κατεναντι οὐ ἐπιστευσε should be taken in the sense of ὁμοιως after Chrysostom.

Beza here translates "coram eo cui credidit" which he interprets as "cognatione spirituali". We are Abraham's children not because of any human relationship, but because he was the *first* to be given eternal life through faith. He disagrees with Chrysostom's rendition ὁμοίως i.e. "ad exemplum vel similitudinem" finding the idea that Abraham should be *like* God "inanis".[8] It is interesting that Erasmus (1535) although having the same translation as Beza, nonetheless interprets it after Chrysostom (also Theophylactus and the Graeca Scholia) "sive ad exemplum Dei cui credidit". Bois in adopting the Chrysostom rendering is in agreement with Erasmus as against Beza.

Tyndale here agrees with Ambrose and reads "before God whom thou has believed".[9] Geneva and Tomson read "before God whom he believed" and Bishops' has "before God whom ye believed". The AV is seen to follow Beza in wording, if not necessarily in interpretation, by translating "before him whom he believed".

At Rom. V.12 Bois points out that Beza's reading "in quo" (i.e. Adam) for ἐφ' ᾧ is difficult nor is it necessary.[10] This suggests that he is more concerned with the grammar than with the theology of the passage.

Beza justifies his reading by saying that ἐπι is often taken in the sense of ἐν (cf. Mark II.4 and Heb. IX.17). Moreover, as ἁμαρτια is feminine the relative particle "quo" cannot refer to it as some have translated. This last statement is most probably based on Erasmus' 1535 discussion of Augustine's reading: "Augustinus putat referri posse ad peccatum, ut intelligamus uno Adae peccato quodammodo peccasse omnes; quae lectio non constitit quum ἁμαρτια apud Graecos est generis foemini."[11] The Vulgate also reads "in quo" probably with the same signification as Augustine. As we have seen above, most English versions agree with Erasmus' reading "quatenus" here except Tomson who reads "in whom" after Beza. None of the versions before AV takes ἐφ' ᾧ in its straightforward causal sense "in view of the fact that" or "because". The AV has in the text "for that all have sinned" keeping the

Bezan "in whom" in the margin. Bois' note would suggest that he considered the causal rendition of ἐφ' ᾧ to be the simplest here.

At Rom. VI.4 Bois paraphrases δια της δοξης του πατρος as δια της οἰκειας της θεοτητος. Beza here reads "in gloriam" taking δια in the sense of εἰς so that the purpose of the Resurrection is emphasized, i.e. "ut deposita carnis assumptae infirmitate, intrans in gloriam Patris gloriosus Deo vivat in aeternum". However, he makes no positive objection to the Vulgate/Erasmus reading "per gloriam Patris" i.e. "gloriosi Patris virtute ac potestate". Bois inclines to the latter interpretation as do all the English versions including the AV. Only Tomson agrees with Beza's version "to the glory". It is interesting to note, however, that Barrett in commentary on the Romans translates "in manifestation of the glory" which is much closer to Beza's than to the Vulgate/Erasmus reading.[12]

At Rom. VII.22 Bois suggests "that all the whole world" and "that every creature" as translation of πασα ἡ κτισις.

Beza in his 1565 version had "omnes res creatas" which by 1589 he changed to "totum mundum conditum" and by 1598 to "totum mundum creatum". Erasmus and the Vulgate both read "omnis creatura" which had the agreement of *all* the English versions from Tyndale to Bishops' 1602. The AV here is in agreement with Bois' suggestion and adopts the Bezan reading in the text and the Vulgate/Erasmus reading in the margin. The reason for this is a stylistic one; Paul is trying to stress that the whole universe rather than its individual members need redemption. However, no substantial change of meaning occurs if we take πασα ἡ κτισις as "every creature".

At Rom. IX.6 Bois comments that he takes Οὐχ' οἰον δε in the sense of οὐχ' ὡς δε ὁτι in agreement with "non quod" in the Vetus versions. The phrase thus represents a refutation or a solution of an objection. He then adds, "A.D. has denied that at any place in the writings of Paul there can be found οἷον or οἷον τε ἀντι του δυνατον" (i.e. οἷον instead of δυνατον). It seems as if Downes' statement here refers to Beza's 1565/74 translation of the phrase which the Revisers must have consulted, if only in the Geneva version. In his 1598 N.T. Beza himself rejects his earlier interpretation, saying that he had wrongly taken οἷον in the sense of δυνατον translating the phrase as "Fieri tamen non posset" even though οἷον had no particle τε added to it. However in his last edition Beza translates "Non quasi vero" and says that this phrase is clear although elliptical; the Apostle is denying that the word of God can be said to have failed just because his brothers are separated from Christ. Tyndale's version is in agreement with the reading arrived at by Beza in 1598, "as though the word of God had not". Geneva and Tomson agree with early Beza; "Notwithstanding it cannot be that". Bishops' has "And it cannot be" and Erasmus and Vulgate both have "non autem quod". Thus there is an agreement between Bois, Erasmus and the Vulgate with regard to translating οὐχ' οἷον δε. The AV, however, reading "Not as though" agrees with late Beza and (in interpretation) with Tyndale.

At Rom. XI.29 Bois glosses ἀμεταμελητα (lit. not to be taken back) as οὐ παλιναγρετα (irrevocable). He quotes Camerarius on 2 Cor. VII.10 here who defines ἀμεταμελητον as immutable and immoveable. Beza also stresses the notion of irrevocability commenting at Rom. XI.29 "eiusmodi sunt et eorum ipsum poenitere non possit". He considers the Vulgate translation "sine poenitentia" to be unclear and dangerous. He does not explain why but we can assume that he disapproves of the expression because it carries a connotation of doing penance.[13] Moreover, Beza considers Augustine's translation "impoenitenda" to be too ambiguous since, in Latin, "non poenitendum munus" can mean "a gift not to be ashamed of". On the other hand he approves of Erasmus' paraphrase[14] "quod a Graecis non discedat".

We find an agreement here between Beza, Tyndale and Great ("it cannot repent him of them"). This version is probably closest to the grammar of the Greek and it does not convey the idea of penance. All the other English versions, including the AV, adopt the translation "without repentance". This is slightly more ambiguous but still conveys the notion of complete unchangeability, as stressed by Bois and Beza.

At Rom. XI.31 Bois makes an explicit reference to Beza saying that the translation (i.e. AV) retains the comma after ἠπείθησαν in agreement with Theophylactus and "all the usual editions of Beza". Downes disagrees here, thinking that the usual punctuation (comma after ἐλέει) should be followed "because otherwise the transposition will be extremely harsh and that other punctuation rests upon the authority of the transcripts, and in order that the sense be complete he understands ἐπί (in reference to) before τῷ ὑμετέρῳ ἐλέει".[15] It seems that the problem as expounded by Downes is one of simply punctuation, rather than punctuation affecting the interpretation. In fact the interpretation which Downes proposes ("they did not believe in your mercy in order that they themselves might obtain mercy") is different from Beza's. Beza in his 1589/98 versions reads "Sic et isti non obedierunt, ut per vestri misericordiam et ipsi misericordia donentur" (1565 "paruerunt"). He comments that there have been "multae incommodae interpretationes" of this verse and that "Nempe unus (ni fallor) Theophylactus hinc vidit quod res est". He then says that the Vulgate reading "crediderunt in vestram misericordiam" points to ἐν τῷ ὑμετέρῳ ἐλέει being taken in the sense of εἰς τὸ ὑμέτερον ἔλεος. The meaning then becomes "In order that the Jews might obtain mercy, they disbelieved the mercy that was shown to the Gentiles." However, Beza says, this construction is impossible because of the verb ἀπειθειν. Alternately, he suggests the Vulgate reading could be taken to mean that the Jews did not believe that mercy would come to the Gentiles from that particular source ("ut inde ad vos deveniret misericordia"). But he finds that this reading would remove the antithesis between τη τουτων ἀπειθεια and τῳ ὑμετερῳ ἐλεει and the Apostle would have to supply "quemadmodum" or "ita" as Erasmus had pointed out. Beza's comment on the Vulgate rendering throws some light on the procedures of Downes. By inserting ἐπι Downes was clarifying the Greek construction to make it plain that the Jews did not believe *in* the mercy that was shown to the Gentiles. Beza also mentions Erasmus' interpretation here. Erasmus takes Paul's meaning to be that the mercy shown to the Gentiles was offensive to the Jews so that they became alienated from the Gospel. Beza, however, thinks that the Apostle means the very opposite of that, since Rom. V.11, 13, 14, 17 and XI.30 suggests that salvation was given to the Gentiles because of the obstinacy of the Jews. The faith (i.e. mercy) bestowed upon the Gentiles was not an obstacle to the Jews but an opportunity given by God that they too might embrace the Gospel.[16] Thus, in his *translation* Beza makes it quite explicit that the mercy shown to the Gentiles was a necessary condition for the Jews also obtaining mercy. He also mentions Ambrose's reading "In vestra miseratione" or "when you were called to mercy" which he finds unconfirmed by any other source.[17] None of the versions or commentators mentions the theological problem posed by νυν or any variants for it.[18]

Of the English versions Tyndale, Geneva, Tomson and Bishops' all agree with the Vulgate punctuation and interpretation. Whittingham and AV follow the Beza/Theophylactus version.

At Rom. XII.3 Bois suggests that λεγω here is used in the

sense of παραινω (I exhort, advise) on the authority of the Greek Scholia.

The only other contemporary N.T. to take λεγω in this sense is Beza's N.T. (1574-1598). The Vautrollier edition of Beza has "edico" in the text with the marginal gloss "praecipio". Tomson has "I say" in the text with "I charge" in the margin. *All* the other English versions read simply "I say". Bois most probably agreed with the Bezan interpretation of λεγω and was citing the Greek Scholia as additional support. The AV reading "I say" does not necessarily imply their rejection of Bois, since "say" in English can be used in the exhortative sense.

At Rom. XII.6 Bois defines κατα την αναλογιαν as "according to the standard and rule of faith, or, according to the proportion and measure of faith which we have". Beza's 1574 N.T. has "pro proportione fidei" with the marginal gloss "ut quisque teneat revelationis suae modum". This translation is followed by Geneva and Tomson (who also translate the gloss). Beza retains his translation in the 1598 N.T. but he points out that κατα την αναλογιαν can be *interpreted* in two ways. It can mean either "congruentia", or, what the Apostle elsewhere calls μετρον. If we accept the former interpretation, then Paul is distinguishing between the true and the false canon of prophecy and Scriptural exegesis. If we accept the latter interpretation, then Paul is recommending that Prophets should not go beyond their task. Beza, like Bois does not give explicit priority to either interpretation, although his own translation takes αναλογια to mean "reasonable limit". Tyndale here reads "according to the grace that is given unto us", Bishops' has "after the measure of faith" taking measure in the sense of 'canon' in agreement with the Vulgate/Erasmus "secundum rationem fidei". The AV follows the Beza/Geneva translation "according to the proportion of faith".

At Rom. XIV.5 Bois paraphrases "Let each man acquire for himself true knowledge from the word of God so that, without doubt, he may preserve what the will of God is."

Beza in his 1598 N.T., as in his previous versions, has "unusquisque in animo suo plene certioratus esto". He says that it is possible to take τον νουν in the sense of "sententia" or "consilium" but he preferred to interpret it as "conscientia". Thus the verb πληροφορεισθαι means "to see and to believe in Lord Jesus". Beza, tendentiously, is against the Vulgate translation "Unusquisque in suo sensu abundet".[19] He points out that the verb "abundare" can imply obstinacy which πληροφορεισθω does not signify, and thus the sentence ceases to have a Christian meaning. For Deut. XII.8 expressly prohibits men from following their own inclinations. The same point is made by Paul at Col. II.8. Beza also disagrees with those who say that Paul here is condemning those of weak or hesitant conscience. For the most important thing, he says, is not that our actions accord with our conscience but that our conscience be based on the word of God. We see here that Bois' paraphrase of the verse is in agreement with Beza's exposition of it. However, there is very little difference between the various English *translations.* Tyndale reads "Se that no man waver in his awne meanynge". Geneva, Tomson, Bishops' and AV all have "Let every man be fully persuaded in his mind".[20] This agrees with Beza's translation and, it could be argued, that the use of the passive voice by all the versions implies "knowledge from the word of God" as opposed to human reason.

1 Corinthians

At IV.6 Bois explains ὑπερ ὁ γεγραπται as referring to the beginning of this chapter and to the end of the preceding chapter. He says that Paul "returns the Corinthian people not to that which was written by others but by Paul himself" and that ὑπ' ἐμου should be supplied before ἵνα μη. He translates εἰς ὑπερ του ἑνος φυσιουσθε as "that for some one ye be not puffed up". The Revision Committee is concerned here with the interpretation of ὑπερ ὁ γεγραπται and no mention is made of the reading without φρονειν which occurred in the Vulgate.[21] Beza in his 1598 N.T. does not comment specifically on ὑπερ ὁ γεγραπται. He does, however, comment on μη φρονειν saying that such thinking is evil unless contained within the limits which are prescribed by the word of God. This would suggest that he takes ὑπερ ὁ γεγραπται to refer to Scripture generally.[22] (This is a possible interpretation, although the word is not used in this sense anywhere else.)

Beza mentions the Vulgate reading and objects to the reading of Erasmus ("ut nequis supra id quod scriptum est, de se sentiat") since φρονειν does not refer to the person but "ad rem ipsam" (i.e. ὁ γεγραπται). φρονειν does not seem to have caused any problem as a textual reading in the English versions, but the verse posed two main problems. Firstly (as pointed out by Bois) there was the difficulty of translating ὁ γεγραπται. Secondly (as Beza implicitly mentioned in his criticism of Erasmus) there was the question of the object of φρονειν. Tyndale agrees with Erasmus' translation ("that no man counte of himselfe beyond that which is above written") and takes φρονειν as reflexive. The phrase "above written" suggests that he assumes ὁ γεγραπται means Paul's actual words. Geneva and Tomson read "that no man presume above that which is written" agreeing with Beza in making ὁ γεγραπται the object of φρονειν and taking ὁ γεγραπται to mean "the writings" or the Scripture generally. The Bishops' Bible also adopts this interpretation, reading "not to be wise above that which is written". The AV reads "...

not to think *of men* above that which is written". The Revisers thus agree with Beza (as against Bois) on the intrepretation of ὁ γεγραπται, but they differ from *all* the other versions in supplying *men* as object for φρονειν (presumably on the basis of 1 Cor. IV.6b).

At 1 Cor. IV.9 Bois comments on the exact meaning of ἐσχατους and ἐπιθανατιους. As regards ἐσχατους Bois refers to Scaliger's *Manili Astronomicon*[23] and concludes that ἐσχατους means the same as ἐφεδρους. Therefore the construction should not be translated "the last Apostles" (which is against the canon of Greek anyway) but "(sent us) the Apostles last" i.e. "as substitute fighters with the beasts".

Ἐπιθανατιους, according to Bois, again after Scaliger, means not merely those who were ordered to be thrown to the lions, but those who volunteered to be thrown to the lions. Beza translates ἐσχατους as "ultimos". This is not too far removed from Bois' suggestion as "ultimus" in Latin has the connotation of providing a terminus. The Vulgate has "novissimos" here, which means simply "latest" and Erasmus agrees with this interpretation although he translates "nos qui sumus Apostoli postremi". English versions from Tyndale to Bishops' read "the last Apostles". The AV has "us the Apostles last" thus agreeing with Bois and the Rheims version.

Ἐπιθανατιους Beza translates as "morti addictos" in agreement with Erasmus (Vulgate: "morti destinatos"). Tyndale, Geneva, Tomson and Bishops' read "appointed to death". The AV, however, has "approved to death" (Rheims: "deputed to death"). This would suggest the Revisers' agreement with Beza rather than with Bois, or the other English versions. "Appointed" could suggest self-appointment or appointment by an outside authority. "Approved", however, like "deputed", implies the presence of an external authority.[24]

At 1 Cor. VII.26 Bois glosses ἀναγκην as θλιψιν, διωγμον

and quotes Photius' phrase δια την ενεστωσαν των πειρασμων φοραν which would suggest that he takes ἐνεστωσαν in its literal sense "the present necessity" as opposed to the eternal condition of the Church. Beza is against that interpretation but Erasmus (1535) approves it (quoting Ambrose) and saying that "Oportet enim huiusmodi consilia pro temporum ratione moderari". *All* the versions here translate "present necessity". The AV, however, has "present distresse" in accord with Bois' interpretation of ἀναγκην ("or, necessitie" in the margin). Neither translation gives us any clue as to the versions' attitude to την ἐνεστωσαν ἀναγκην.[25]

At 1 Cor. VII.29 Bois reads ὁτι ὁ καιρος in agreement with Beza. He elucidates the phrase as "now calamities draw nigh and threaten". Andrew Downes interprets the passage to mean ὁτι ὁ καιρος ἐστι δυσκολος και κινδυνων ἀναμεστος but Bois does not agree with this on the authority of the Greek Scholia. ὁτι is omitted from the TR and the Vulgate but Beza claims that it appears in *seventeen* old codices,[26] Graeca Scholia and Basil. Beza's punctuation το λοιπον ἐστιν; ἱνα agrees with that of L, some Vulgate MSS and Chrysostom. Vulgate and Erasmus punctuate after συνεσταλμενος, although Erasmus (1535) admits the possibility of punctuating as Beza did; "atque ita Graeci videntur legere nominatim Theophylactus". However, he does not mention the ὁτι reading. Beza's Latin N.T. (1574) reads "quoniam tempus contractum est in posterum" with the marginal note "in fines siquidam saeculorum pervenimus". In his 1598 N.T. Beza reads "quoniam opportunum tempus est angustum in posterum" and explains that the Apostle is not talking about the shortness of human life but about the imminent disasters and the end of the world. We thus see that Beza makes it much clearer than Bois that it is the eschatological καιρος which is being considered. Bois makes this point implicit in his rejection of Downes' interpretation. Of the

English versions Tyndale and Great omit ὅτι and read "The time is short. It remaineth...." Geneva, Tomson and Bishops' insert ὅτι and also agree with Beza's punctuation, "because the time is short hereafter". The AV, however, reverts to the reading without ὅτι and to the Erasmus/Vulgate punctuation ("...the time is short. It remaineth..."). In this, the Revisers agree with the Tyndale, Great and Rheims versions and also with Downes' interpretation of the passage, taking καιρος as referring to the shortness of human life.[27]

At 1 Cor. VII.35 Bois has "but that you may decently and without distraction wait upon the Lord" for the Greek προς το εὐσχημον και εὐπαρεδρον τῳ κυριῳ ἀπερισπαστως. Bois' translation reproduces word for word Beza's 1598 version "ut decenter et apte adhaerescatis Domino absque ulla distractione" (1574: distinctione).

In his 1598 version Beza also mentions the reading εὐπροσδεκτον which he found in some copies but which he suspects of being corrupt.[28] In the Vulgate translation ("sed ad id quod honestum est et quod facultatem praebeat sine impedimento Dominum observandi") he objects, firstly, to the use of "honestum" for εὐσχημον since the Greek word is being used here to mean "quod est conveniens et accomodatum" (cf. Rom. XIII.3 and 1 Cor. XIV.40). Beza is making the point that marriage may be *honest* but the Apostle is urging us to do what is *proper* and not marry. Secondly Beza objects to "sine impedimento" for ἀπερισπαστως. Strictly the Vulgate phrase means ἀνεμποδιστως and so it weakens the marriage metaphor.

Tyndale and Great read "honest and comely...without separacion" (after Erasmus). Geneva and Tomson agree with this. Bishops' has "for comeliness' sake". The AV reads "but for that which is comely, and that you may attend upon the Lord without distraction". There is a substantial agreement here between Bois, Beza and the AV. The Revisers, however, are probably closer to the Greek syntax than either Bois or Beza since they treat προς το εὐσχημον as modifying λεγω and not as modifying εὐπαρεδρον.

At 1 Cor. IX.5 Bois refers to the Old Latin versions "a woman, a sister". He suggests on this basis that the TR ἀδελφην γυναικα is in inverted order "for in the prior place ought to be placed what is more general, in the latter what is more specific e.g. ἀνδρεσ ἀδελφοι". However, A.D. & H.[29] has suggested that ἀδελφην γυναικα means a Christian, or faithful woman so that ἀδελφη is being used as an epithet.

Bois' note suggests that the Final Committee here was concerned with the relationship between the two Greek words, rather than with the problem of translating γυναικα. If we accept the Bois/Vetus version, however, the sentence comes to mean "have we not the power to lead about a sister (who is a woman)?" Beza translates γυναικα as "uxor" in all his versions, maintaining (1598) that the Apostles could not honestly lead about women who were not their wives.

Of the English versions, Tyndale has "a sister to wife". Geneva and Tomson read "a wife being sister" which Tomson explains in the margin (after Beza and in agreement with A.D. & H.) as meaning "One that is a Christian and a true believer". Bishops' has "a sister, a woman"[30] in agreement with Bois. AV reads "a sister, a wife" and retains "woman" in the margin. This rendering is open to several interpretations: (a) a sister or a wife, (b) a good Christian woman who is a wife, (c) a good Christian woman,[31] and so leaves open the question of priests marrying. Explaining his translation in the 1598 N.T. Beza points out that the passage does not imply that the Apostles should desist from marriage. This, however, is denied by Clement, Paphnutius and Athanasius.

This point of interpretation was raised by Martin against Fulke.[32] Martin maintains that Beza uses the word γυναικα to signify a wife (1 Cor. IX.5) and not to signify a wife (1 Cor. VII.1) "both against virginity and chastity of priests". Fulke answers Martin's objection at 1 Cor. VII.1 saying that Beza's comment on γυναικος μη άπτεσθαι commends not only virginity in those who are not married but also continence in those who are married. According to Beza Paul does not condemn the coming together of man and woman through matrimony, but recommends it as remedy for those who cannot restrain from contact.³³ Thus "it is bad for a man to touch a woman unless she is his wife". This is in accord with Augustine's view but against Jerome who maintains that Paul forbids contact with women under any circumstances. Augustine asserts that if a man can touch food and drink, there is no reason why he should not be allowed to touch his wife.

At 1 Cor. IX.5 Fulke explains that άδελφην means Christian and that there is good testimony that the Apostles were allowed to marry. Thus γυναικα must mean "a wife" here. If the expression simply referred to a woman who ministered to the Apostles,³⁴ the word άδελφην would be sufficient.

At 1 Cor. IX.27 Bois refers to Chrysostom. Hom. 22 in Gen. p. 163. On this authority άδοκιμος is equivalent in meaning to άχρηστος. Beza has "reiectaneus" in his 1598 N.T. (earlier versions: "reprobus" in agreement with the Vulgate and Erasmus). Beza gives no reason for altering his translation but points out that this verse does not, as some have thought, question the decisiveness of election. Paul's concern here does not mean that his election is uncertain. Rather, his very uncertainty is an aspect of election for it was decided by God that election should be sustained through personal effort. Perhaps the word "reiectaneus" expresses the idea of exclusion from election less clearly than "reprobus" hence Beza's use of it in his later translation.

Bois' interpretation of άδοκιμος is different from Beza's.

Like Chrysostom, Bois emphasizes Paul's own uselessness in contrast to his preaching to others. Tyndale and Great adopt the same interpretation as late Beza and read "castaway". Geneva and Tomson read "reproved". Bishops' and AV both read "castaway" against Bois and Chrysostom.[35]

At 1 Cor. X.11 Bois suggests that the sentence should be understood ὡς τυποι ἡμων συνεβαινον ἐκεινοις thus taking τυποι to mean simply "examples". He objects to Downes' interpretation (after Augustine) which takes τυποι to mean "types and figures of the people of old", in other words, prototypes establishing a pattern for the future.

Beza in all his versions has "Haec autem omnia typice evenerunt eis", explaining (1598) that he takes τυποι in the sense of τυπικως "ut in duobus codicibus scriptum invenimus".[36] He goes on to say that these things were τυποι not with respect to the Israelites but to us. Related to this is the word ἀντιτυπα meaning prototypes of our sacraments. Thus manna to the Israelites was the sacrament of heavenly bread; our equivalent is the bread we break. We find that Beza is in agreement with Augustine and Downes, taking τυποι to signify things which establish a pattern, as opposed to mere examples. This is in accord with Beza's views on the relationship between the Old and the New Testament.

The Vulgate reads "Haec autem omnia in figura contingebant illis" and Erasmus has "Haec autem omnia figurae contingerunt illis".[37] All the English versions read "for examples",[38] thus omitting the prophetic nuance of τυποι. The AV, however, adds in the margin "or, types" which suggests some measure of support for the Bezan interpretation.[39]

At 1 Cor. X.17 Bois suggests that ὀντες should be supplied to complete the sense of οἱ πολλοι. He then adds "the exposition of Beza displeased us all for according to the sense of that exposition it ought to be written ὁτι εἰς ὁ ἀρτος".[40]

None of the English versions follows Beza here. The AV agrees with Geneva/Tomson/Bishops' reading "For we that are many are one bread and one body."

At 1 Cor. X.30 Bois comments that the interpretation "and if by thanksgiving", although rejected by Beza, has nonetheless been recommended by Downes. Beza (1598) reads "per gratiam" for χαριτι which he interprets to mean "If I am allowed by the grace to partake of some food, why should that which has been given by God's grace, be turned into something undesirable?" Beza objects to the interpretation "thanksgiving" (i.e. grace said before a meal) as in the Erasmus and Vulgate versions, because it is "forced". Of the English versions, Tyndale and Great agree with Vulgate/Erasmus reading "If I take my parte with thankes". Geneva, Tomson and Bishops' all agree with Beza, reading "If I through *God's* benefite be partaker" (Bishops' "by"). The AV also agrees with Beza but translates his reading literally "if I by grace be a partaker" thus removing the italics of the previous versions. The Vulgate/Erasmus alternative "or by thanksgiving" as suggested by Downes is inserted in the AV margin.

At 1 Cor. XII.29 Bois suggests that δυναμεις[41] is the use of the abstract for the concrete, cf. ἀντιληψεις in the preceding verse. Beza (1574) has "gubernationes" which Tomson translates as "powers". All the other English versions have "doers of miracles" (Rheims: "doctors"). AV has "makers of miracles" (cf. Matthew VII.22) but inserts "powers" in the margin. Beza keeps "gubernationes" in his 1598 N.T. which he explains as "Presbyterum ordinem declarat qui disciplinae et politiae Ecclesiasticae custodes erant...". We thus see that there is an agreement between Bois, Beza, Tomson and AV (margin) as regards the translation "powers" and its concrete signification. However, only Beza makes clear that he interprets δυναμεις as *Church* powers. The English versions leave this unspecified.

Galatians

At Gal. I.16 Bois suggests the translation "in me" but points out that others have "by me, to me". Beza agrees with the Vulgate here, reading "in me" in all his versions. In the 1598 N.T. he points out that ἐν ἐμοι means literally "mihi" but, when taken with the verb ἀποκαλυψαι it means the same as the Hebrew (hal mi), in other words, "significari Dei gratiam coelitus in animum ipsum".

Tyndale, Great and Bishops' all agree with Erasmus and read "by me" thus implying the meaning "revealing his son by means of me". Geneva, 1560, Tomson, Rheims and AV all agree with the Beza/Vulgate version and read "in me". This is ambiguous in English (and could be equally ambiguous in Latin although Beza denies it) meaning either "revealed in my mind" or "revealed by means of me". In connection with this it is interesting to see that Whittingham (1557) reads "to me" perhaps taking ἐν ἐμοι in its literal sense, as pointed out by Beza. It is difficult to tell whether Bois by "others" means other Revisers or other versions.

At II.2 Bois paraphrases τοις δοκουσιν as τοις κορυφαιοις. Beza translates τοις δοκουσιν as "iis qui sunt in pretio" in all his versions and paraphrases the Greek (1598) as τοις εὐδοκιμουσιν "quibus opponuntur οἱ ἀδοξουντες". He is opposed to the Vulgate version "Qui videbantur aliquid esse", i.e. τοις δοκουσιν εἰναι τι.[42] This, he suspects, is an interpolation from v. 6, unconfirmed by Jerome's commentary.[43] But even in his commentary Jerome did not recognize that τους δοκουντας means the same as τους εὐδοκιμουντας "quorum apud omnes praeclara est existimatio".[44] The Ambrose reading, "Qui sibi videbantur aliquid esse", Beza considers to be too difficult. His own translation agrees with that of Erasmus ("cum iis..."). Tyndale and Great read "with them which were counted chiefe". This is followed by Bishops' with substitution of "esteemed" for "counted". Geneva reads "with them that were chiefe" (retaining Erasmus' "cum") but Tomson has "to them that were the chiefe" which suggests that he follows Beza's reading here. AV departs from all previous English versions and has "to them which were of reputation" thus appearing to agree with Beza's interpretation of τους δοκουσιν as against Bois. However, when we consider that "chief" in English can mean "the best, the most prominent"[45] we can say that perhaps the AV reading strikes a compromise between Bois' and Beza's interpretation.

At Gal. II.4 Bois suggests the translation "And that because of" for δια δε. Others have "No, not because of" after the Greek Scholia which also link this verse with verse III.3 "which linking seems to agree not unsuccessfully with the intention of the Apostle". Downes thinks that there as in v. 6 the construction is ἀνανταπόδοτον. Camerarius (1572) thinks that it is an ellipsis and that "he was not compelled to be circumcized because of the false brethren" should be repeated. Beza in all his versions reads "nempe propter" (Erasmus: "propter"; Vulgate: "sed propter") suggesting (1598) that δε here is used in the sense of δη or δητα (i.e. "surely on account of"). He objects to Erasmus[46] removing δε ("Hieronymi opinione qui putavit redundare hoc loco quod non praecedat μην") as this is not a sufficient reason.

We see an agreement here between Tyndale, Great, Bishops', Bois and the AV. All these versions read "And that because of". Geneva version agrees with Erasmus reading "for all the" and Tomson translates Beza literally "to wit for the". Evidently the majority of versions agreed with the elliptical reading of the phrase.

At Gal. III.1 Bois suggests as alternative translation for προεγραφη "pictured, pourtraid, painted".[47] Beza in all his versions reads "depictus". He disagrees with the Vetus translation "proscriptus" unless it is taken in the sense of "written out on public documents". The interpretation "outlawed" adopted by Augustine, or "condemned" adopted by Ambrose Beza considers to be too difficult. Nor is he in favour of Erasmus' reading "praescriptus" (written before, about whom you have read before), which Erasmus took from Jerome. Beza points out that, other considerations apart, the usual Greek word for "praescribere" is παραγραφεσθαι not προγραφεσθαι and dismisses the Erasmus/Jerome interpretation as "etiam absurdior...quam superiores". He himself joins up προεγραφη with κατ' οφθαλμους.

All the English versions from Tyndale to Bishops' appear to agree with the Vetus (Vulgate) reading and have "was described". The AV reads "before whose eyes...evidently set forth" thus not only adopting Beza's translation of προεγραφη but also his syntax of linking that up with κατ' οφθαλμους. Bois' note here supports the Beza/AV version.

At Galatians IV.9 Bois takes παλιν ανωθεν in the sense of εκ παραλληλου. He then adds "In this he has combined the Gentiles with the superstitious Jews because they superstitiously observed days and times; at the same time therefore the Apostle mingles the superstition of both." Beza translates παλιν ανωθεν as "retrorsum" throughout. In the 1598 N.T. he explains that he takes the passage to mean that the Galatians were converted to the Gospel not from Judaism but from Paganism. However, as they "retreated" from the Gospel they were regressing into Judaism--hence the verb επιστρεφεσθαι - retorqueri. He objects to the Graeca Scholia interpretation that "elementa mundi" here means moon, sun and stars, and that Galatians, measuring hours and days by the planets, had reverted to their former idolatry. This interpretation Beza considers to be absurd.

It seems that Bois' note, linking the observation of days with Jewish superstitions provides an elucidation of Beza's exposition. Of the English versions Tyndale and Great read "affreshe" possibly agreeing with Erasmus' "denuo". All the other versions, including the AV, read "again".

At Gal. IV.15 Bois lists the following possible translations. "What is become then of the hapynesse that was ascribed unto you [or] your magnifying of yourselves, or thinking your selves hapy for my sake, your hapynesse that is talked or spoken of." He then explains ὁ μακαρισμος ὑμων as "by which others openly declared you happy, or you yourselves on account of the gospel having been received, or by which you openly declared me happy".

This note suggests that the Final Committee was considering only the translation of ὁ μακαρισμος ὑμων and that Bois wrote down the various possibilities. No mention is made in his manuscript of the variants που ουν / τις ουν ἠν[48] and the translation as written down by Bois implies that the Committee struck a compromise between the grammatical past and present. Beza in all his versions adopts the TR reading τις ουν ἠν[49] which he translates by the Latin imperfect "ubi erat...". This reading and translation suggest that the Galatians were only apparently happy during Paul's visit. This meaning is made clear in the marginal note to Beza's 1574 Latin version: "Quantus ubique rumor erat hominum vos beatos praedicantium." On the other hand Beza is in agreement with Bois in so far as he translates ὁ μακαρισμος ὑμων by "beatitatis vestrae *praedicatio*".

Of the English versions Tyndale reads "How happy were ye then?" agreeing with the TR. Geneva and Tomson also agree with the TR and take ὑμων as ordinary possessive adjective: "What was then your felicitie?" The Bishops' Bible agrees with the Vulgate text but also treats ὑμων possessively: "What is then your felicity?" The AV here adopts the Vulgate text more explicitly than Bois, reading "Where is then?"[50]

(i.e. your past happiness has turned to unhappiness) but inserting the TR reading in the margin. The Revisers are in full agreement with both Beza and Bois as regards ὁ μακαρισμος ὑμων which they translate as "the blessedness you spake of".[51]

At Gal. IV.17 Bois reads ἐκκλεισαι ὑμας and explains "which it is if it should be understood της ἐμης διδαχης or της ἐμης διδαχης ὑμων. Beza 1574, Vulgate and all the earlier English versions read ὑμας.[52] Beza in his 1589/98 N.T. reads "excludere nos". He explains that although "in omnibus Latinis codicibus scriptum est ὑμας (vos) poscit tamen sententia ut legamus ἡμας (nos)". He then compares the situation of Paul and Galatians to that of a love triangle with Galatians representing the young girl, Paul, the rival and Paul's enemies - the suitor. Beza suggests that it is more usual that the rival should be excluded from the girl by the suitor rather than the girl from the rival. In that case "nos" is more suitable grammatically than "vos".

Bois' note suggests that there was some uncertainty among the Revisers whether to accept the Bezan reading or that of the majority of versions. The Final Committee adjudicated in favour of ὑμας if it is taken to mean "they would exclude you from my teaching" or "they would exclude my teaching from you". If the passage is taken in this latter sense, Beza's metaphor of the rival being excluded from the girl is still relevant. Accordingly, the AV has "exclude you" in the text, but inserts the Bezan alternative "exclude us" in the margin.

At Gal. IV.18 Bois notes down the following alternative translations: "Now it is good to be had in admiration, or, to be imitated for, or, in that which is good all waies." Beza adopts the reading καλον δε το ζηλουσθαι in all his versions as opposed to the Vulgate/Erasmus καλον δε ζηλουσθε.[53] He explains his preference for the TR reading in the 1598 version saying it occurs in all the Greek MSS which he saw (presumably of the   type) "assentiente Syro interprete et Chrysostomo". The Vulgate reading, he claims, has the support of Ambrose, Jerome and the Latin version of Theodoret. Beza thinks here that the "old" Greek reading ought to be retained, even though the Apostle makes a sudden transition from the active to the passive. This transition is correct in the context since the Apostle is telling the Galatians that it *is* good *to be esteemed* by many, but two things are to be borne in mind, firstly that the course and the aim of the friendship be right, secondly that absent friends should be esteemed no less than present ones. In both these things the Galatians had sinned against Paul.

All the English versions agree with the TR reading here as against the Vulgate. However, there is a certain amount of discrepancy in the interpretations of ζηλουσθαι. Beza in his early versions has "praeclarum est vehementer amare" (which suggests the reading ζηλουσθε)[54] which by 1598 he alters to "Praeclarum est autem affectari". Tyndale and Great both read "to be fervent", (taking ζηλουσθαι in the sense of "to be impelled by zeal"). Bishops' agrees, reading "to be zealous". Geneva and Tomson agree with early Beza, "to love". However, we see that Bois' interpretation of ζηλουσθαι agrees with the *late* Beza, in that both take it in the strict passive sense. The AV, however, seems to prefer the middle interpretation of ζηλουσθαι reading "(it is good) to be zealously affected".

At Gal. IV.24 Bois paraphrases ἅτινα ἐστιν ἀλληγορουμενα as "Which things have this allegorical use". Beza here translates "Per quae aliud figuratur" in all his versions. The Vulgate has "Quae sunt per allegoriam dicta" and Erasmus "Quae per allegoriam dicuntur". Beza in his 1598 version explains "ego studui perspicuitati" and then mentions Erasmus' comment (after Chrysostom), that an allegory is totally fictitious, whereas here Paul is telling a *true* story "quae tamen aliud adumbravit magis reconditum mysterium".

Tyndale has "which things to be token mystery" thus showing an agreement with Chrysostom's definition of "allegory". Geneva and Tomson also agree with this, translating Beza literally "By the which things another thing is meant". Bishops' Bible agrees with the Great reading "Which things are spoken by an allegorye" and the AV has "which things are an allegorye"; the influence of Beza here does not extend beyond Tomson and Geneva.

We may perhaps suggest that Beza and the corresponding English versions were reluctant to use the word "allegory" in a Scriptural context and that Chrysostom here provided a useful corroboration. Evidently the Revisers did not feel that the word would cause any problems, and they seem to take "allegory" in the usual English sense of "a subject [not necessarily fictitious] representing another subject".

At Gal. V.7 Bois suggests an alternative translation "or, what beat you back". This would suggest that the marginal alternative ἀνεκοψε[55] (ἐνεκοψε in the text) is being proposed. The ἀνεκοψε reading occurs in the text of Stephanus and Erasmus and is followed by late Beza[56] who (1598) defines the word as "fecit ut inhibito cursu retro feramini" and translates it as "interrupit". He says that the word has a stronger meaning than ἐνεκοψε ("interpellavit") although he has seen ἐνεκοψε in the Vulgate and in a few Greek codices.

In view of the lack of support for ἀνεκοψε in the modern critical apparatus, Beza's statement appears rather surprising.

The English readings here suggest that all the versions adopted the ἐνεκοψε reading. Tyndale and Great have "who was a let unto you". Geneva and Tomson read "who did let you" (agreeing with early Beza). Bishops' agrees with Tyndale and Great and the AV has "who did hinder you". The Revisers, however, suggest "who did drive you backe" in the margin. This implies that they accepted Bois' suggestion which was based on the Stephanus/late Beza text.

Hebrews

Before considering the influence of Beza on the English versions of *Hebrews* we should point out that, at the time, the authorship of the epistle was attributed to Paul. We should also say that the Epistle did pose special difficulties concerning Old Testament quotations in Greek. Those are mainly taken from the Septuagint.

At Heb. I.3 Bois suggests "brightnesse or forthshining" as alternative translations for ἀπαυγασμα. Vulgate, Erasmus and early Beza all translate "splendour" but Beza in his 1598 version has "effulgentia" and explains this as "he in whom shines the glory and the majesty of the Father who is otherwise unknown and unseen" (cf. Coloss. I.15, 1 Cor. IV.4). All the English versions here, including the AV, read "brightness". Beza's suggestion "effulgentia" did not go beyond the Final Revision Committee.[57]

At Heb. I.12 Bois comments on the textual uncertainty, saying "In Hebrew" (i.e. the original O.T. Psalm 102, 26-28) "it is you will change" (i.e. ἀλλαξεις) "notwithstanding the Greeks have translated ἑλιξεις" (i.e. you will fold up) "looking back perchance to the place Isa. c. 34.4".[58] Beza in all his editions reads "circumvolves" but in the 1598 version he comments that the Hebrew phrase is [tachali phem] i.e. "mutabis". Beza thus agrees with Erasmus in thinking that the right reading is ἀλλαξεις as in the Latin versions. However, the Greek texts have the advantage of expressing what kind of change it was (as in Isa. XXXIV.4). Ἐλιξεις also occurs in the text of Chrysostom and Theophylactus.

It is interesting to see that Beza and Bois cover identical points in their respective notes, the Hebrew meaning, the Greek translation of it, and the reference to Isa. XXXIV.4. It would perhaps be presumptuous to say that Bois merely copies Beza's note in a shortened form, but there can be little doubt that he made a careful study of Beza here.

Tyndale, Great and Whittingham all read "change" probably under the influence of Erasmus' "mutabis". Geneva, Tomson, Bishops' and AV all adopt the reading "shalt fold them up" under the influence of Beza's decision to give priority to the *Greek* text.

At Heb. II.5 Bois gives Downes' definition of τὴν οἰκουμενην τὴν μελλουσαν. He takes this as concerning "the Messianic age [Jeme Hamaschiah] and compares this place with Is. IX.6". Beza has "mundum illum futurum" throughout and all the English versions have "the world to come". It is interesting to compare Downes' suggestion with Beza's remark at Heb. II.5 in the 1598 edition; he takes τὴν οἰκουμενην τὴν μελλουσαν to mean the happy world which was predicted by the Prophets, begun in the coming of Christ and has yet to be fulfilled (in other words, the Messianic age). There can be little doubt that Downes had read Beza but it is difficult to decide whether he was following Beza here, or whether both scholars were simply stating a current view.

At Heb. II.7.9 there are two problems; firstly the interpretation of ἐλαττωσις (v. 7, ἠλαττωσας; v. 9, ἠλαττωμενον) in relation to βραχυ. It can mean either "made a little less" or "made less for a short while". Secondly, there is the problem of interpreting δια το παθημα του θανατου δοξῃ και τιμῃ ἐστεφανωμενον. This can mean either that Christ was crowned with glory and honour because he had undergone the suffering of death[59] or, taking δια in the final sense, Christ was made lower than the Angels in order to undergo the suffering of death. Another possible interpretation is to take δια causally and read that Christ was made lower than the Angels because he suffered death.[60]

As regards βραχυ...ἠλαττωσας Bois takes ἐλαττωσις to mean the same as κενωσις at Philip.II.7. Taken in this way the word means "of no account". Bois does not comment on the relationship between that and βραχυ but quotes D.H.'s translation "a little lower". δια το παθημα is interpreted by the Final Committee as pointing to the reason for Christ's exaltation (cf. Phil. II.9). Bois is not altogether in favour of the other interpretation with δια being taken finally. For βραχυ...ἠλαττωσας the Vulgate reads "paulo minus". Beza, in his early versions has "paulisper inferiorem" which, by 1598, he changes to "parumper inferiorem". He does not comment on ἠλαττωσας but explains that βραχυ [Heb. mehat] can refer to the subject itself (aliquantulum) and to time. He prefers to use it in the latter sense because the Hebrew word has this meaning at Levi. XXV.32, Isa. X.25, Jere. LI.33 (also βραχυ τι at Acts V.34).

All the English versions except Bishops' take βραχυ in the sense of "aliquantulum" and translate the Greek phrase as "little lower than" or "little inferior to". The AV agrees with the majority of versions and the Final Committee, reading "little lower than" but it keeps in the margin the Bishops'/Beza alternative "for a little while inferior to".[61]

As regards δια το παθημα του θανατου... Beza in his 1574 N.T. has "propter mortis perpessionem" which is annotated by L'Oiseleur "ut mori posset". Beza retains this translation in all editions and in the 1598 N.T. he explains that δια here introduces a final clause thus giving the sense "Christ was made lower than the Angels for a short while so that he might die". He argues against the interpretation that the suffering of death brought about the lowering of Christ, saying that the lowering had consisted in incarnation and not in death. Otherwise a construction with διο would have been used here as at Philip. II.7.[62] However, Beza makes no mention of the interpretation which was later put forward by the Final Committee.

The Vulgate has "propter passionem mortis" and Erasmus "propter cruciatum mortis" on which he does not comment.

Tyndale and the Great Bible agree quite explicitly with Bois here and most probably account for the Final Committee's suggestion; both read "crowned with glory and honour for the sufferinge of death".[63] Other English versions from Whittingham to Bishops' read "through the suffering of death". This suggests the interpretation of lowering consisting in death but Tomson's version, which has "through"[64] in the text with the Bezan annotation "so that he might die" in the margin, suggests that "through" could be used with reference to result. The AV adopts the Tyndale/Bois interpretation and reads "for the suffering of death". The Revisers, however, insert "by the suffering" in the margin thus taking δια in the final sense after Beza. Bois' note confirms that there was a difference of opinion among the Revisers here "those" presumably referring to the other Revisers not to other versions in general.[65]

At Heb. II.16 Bois comments on the meaning of ἐπιλαμβανεται (it) "is to take hold of and to hold back to deliverance as those who grasp a falling man by seizing his cloak. See Graec. Schol." In view of this he proposes the translation "For he in no sorte took hold in [on] the Angels". Bishops' agrees with Tyndale and has "for he in no place taketh on him the Angels" and Geneva reads "For he in no sorte toke the Angels". Tomson includes Beza's explanatory note in his text, reading "For he in no sorte toke on him the Angels' nature". This is also the reading adopted by the AV ("he tooke not on him *the nature of* Angels"). It is doubtful whether the Revisers took this reading directly from Tomson, as they do not appear to have referred to his version in general. More probably, they adopted the same method as Tomson of combining Beza's text with his marginal annotation. The literal translation of the Greek "hee taketh not hold of Angels..." is given in AV margin.

At Heb. III.14 Bois annotates την ἀρχην της ὑποστασεως as "the beginning of our constant faith or constant hope". Downes suggests "the beginning of our constancy". Bois then points out that "there are those who accept here ἀρχην as head or chief; but then the contrast between ἀρχην and τελους will disappear". Bois makes no comment on the textual variants in this verse. Beza in all his versions reads την ἀρχην της ὑποστασεως which he translates as "principium illud quo sustinemur" thus taking ἀρχη in the non-temporal sense and assimilating it to ὑποστασις. He also points out the following textual variants; some Greek codices have την ἀπαρχην i.e. "primitias". The Vulgate adds ("initium substantiae eius") referring to Christ himself which does not occur in any Greek MSS. The Syriac version, however, suggests the presence of ταυτης in some MSS, for it reads ἐαν ἀπ' ἀρχης την ὑποστασιν ταυτην, in other words, "a principio ad finem usque constanter esse illud quo fulcimur sustinendum".[66]

Beza interprets ἀρχη here as meaning "the proper basis" "a quo nisi coeperis frustra quidpiam aggrediaris" [Heb. reschith) whereas he takes ὑποστασις to mean "foundation". According to this definition the phrase reads "that which is a foundation for other things (cf. II Cor. IX.4, XI.17). He finally cites Chrysostom who says that "fulcimentum" is the true doctrine of Christ apprehended by faith, or faith itself.[67]

Of the English versions Tyndale ("the first substance"),

Great and Bishops' ("the beginning of our substance") agree with Erasmus' "initium substantiae". Presumably, these English versions accordingly take the view that substance here is "our true nature" which is given to us through partaking in Christ. Geneva and Tomson translate Beza literally, "the beginning wherewith we are upholden". The AV takes a midpath between Bois and Beza reading "the beginning of our confidence".[68]

At Heb. IV.1 Bois comments that Downes "against Beza denies that καταλειπομενης επαγγελιας can be rightly translated 'forsaking the promise'--to which we have all agreed". Beza reads "derelicta promissione" in all his versions in agreement with Erasmus. (Vulgate: "relicta pollicitatione".) All the English versions from Tyndale to Bishops' 1602 agree with the Beza/Erasmus translation "forsaking the promise". The AV, however, adopts the Final Revision Committee's suggestion and reads "a promise being left us". Bois' note here as at Rom. V.12 shows that the Committee was continuously referring to Beza and that Bois thought it important to point out some places where they disagreed with the Genevan scholar.

At Heb. IV.2 Bois is in favour of the reading μη συγκεκραμμενους[69] "which reading bears a more commodious sense by far and it is assented to by Photius and the Graec. interp.". Bois then proposes the translation "for that they were not united by faith with them that heard it i.e. with those that believed it". He quotes a similar construction with συγκεραν-νυμι from Xenophon, liber 1 p. 13. Beza in all his editions agrees with the Vulgate and reads συγκεκραμενος. In the 1598 edition he shows knowledge of the -ους reading saying that it has the support of the Graecus Scholiastes, Photius, Theophylactus and five old codices. This reading is followed by the Complutensian Polyglot "the word did not help those who did not join themselves by faith with those that heard it". Beza

is against this translation saying that the Greek sets up an
opposition between τους ἀκουσαντας and τους πιστευσαντας i.e.
those that heard and those that believed. The people heard
the word but did not benefit from it because they lacked faith.
Bois' note suggests that there was a dispute among the Revisers here, some favouring the Complutension συγκεκραμ(μ)ενους
others inclining to συγκεκραμενος which had the merit of emphasizing faith as necessary condition for receiving the word
and of having the support of all the earlier English versions.
The Revisers finally gave priority to the TR συγκεκραμενος
reading translating it as "being mixed" (after Geneva). The
Graeca Scholia/Complutensian reading was relegated to the margin.

At Heb. V.2 Bois, in an attempt to define μετριοπαθης,
refers to Hesychius who considers it a synonym for ὁ συγγινωσκων ἐπιεικως (he who agrees reasonably). Beza in all
his versions has "Qui quantum satis est posset miserari". In
the 1598 N.T. he explains that μετριοπαθειν[70] indicates a disposition which can sympathize as much as necessary i.e. according to the greatness of the plight. Of the English versions
Tyndale and Great agree with the Vulgate ("qui condolere possit") and translate "which can have compassion". Geneva, Tomson and Bishops' all agree with Beza and read "sufficiently
have compassion". Bois is seen to agree with the Beza/Geneva
translation and cites the additional support of Hesychius.
The Revisers, however, finally prefer the Vulgate reading "who
can have compassion" which is inserted into the text. "Or,
who can reasonably bear with" figures in the AV margin.

At Heb. V.7 Bois' note suggests that the Revisers had
difficulty with translating ἀπο της εὐλαβειας. Bois pin-points
the problem saying that εὐλαβεια is difficult to translate in
this context, especially in conjunction with ἀπο. He then
lists the suggested translations of εὐλαβεια (fear, piety) and

the suggested translations of ἀπο (in behalf of, because of, for, from, after). Finally he suggests that the phrase should be read with the beginning of v. 8.[71]

Beza in his early versions reads "Exauditus esset ex metu" which by 1598 he changes to "exauditis precibus *liberatus ex metu*". The reading "metu" occurred in some Latin versions and in Gregory Nazianzenus. Both Vulgate and Erasmus read "pro sua reverentia" and this interpretation is followed by Tyndale ("because of hys godlynes") and the Great Bible ("because of his reverence"). Geneva, Tomson and Bishops' all agree with Beza and read "in that which he feared". This translation was attacked by Gregory Martin[72] who accused Beza of inconsistency in rendering εὐλαβεια sometimes by "fear" other times by "reverence". He was also against the translation of ἀπο by "from". Moreover, he asserted that the translation of the entire phrase was heretical "surely for defence of no less blasphemy than this, that our Savior Jesus Christ upon the cross was horribly afraid of damnation...and that this was his descending into hell, and that otherwise he descended not".[73] These objections were answered by Fulke; firstly that εὐλαβεια can mean both "fear" and "reverence" in Greek, secondly "from fear" can be paraphrased as "from that which is feared". Thirdly, the doctrine that Christ suffered the wrath of God in order to redeem our sins is perfectly sound. Hence his cry of despair on the cross "according to the sense of his humanity".

Possibly Beza emended his reading in 1598 to "*liberatus ex metu*" in order to avoid ambiguity which might lead to an accusation of heresy. The AV agrees with the early Beza/ Geneva reading (which has the additional support of the "moderate" Bishops' Bible), and reads "in that he feared" inserting "for his pietie" in the margin.

At Heb. VI.1 Bois glosses τον της ἀρχης του Χριστου λογον

as "the elementary doctrine". The difficulty which the Revisers were facing here evidently concerned the exact meaning of ἀρχη in conjunction with λογος.

Beza in all his versions reads "Qui in Christo rudes inchoat sermone" which he explains as "the first principles of Christianity which they call the Catechism". This shows that he takes ἀρχη in a non-temporal sense. The Vulgate has "inchoationis Christi sermonem". Of the English versions Tyndale and Great read "the doctrine pertayninge to the beginninge of a Christian man". Geneva, Tomson and Bishops' all have "the doctrine of the beginning of Christ" which is closer to the Vulgate reading than to Beza's. The AV, however, seems to base its translation on Beza's and Bois' explanatory notes and thus reads "principles of the doctrine of Christ",[74] thus making clear that ἀρχη is being used non-temporally and that it refers to λογος rather than to Χριστος. A literal translation of the Vulgate "the word of the beginning of Christ" is inserted in the margin.

At Heb. VII.19 the Final Committee was evidently trying to decide whether "Law" or "hope" was the subject of the second clause. Bois is in favour of the translation "but the further bringing in of a better hope [did make perfect]". He makes "hope" the subject of the second clause thus implying that the Gospel, or the priesthood of Christ provided a logical conclusion to the efforts of the Law. Bois finally points out that the noun ἐπεισαγωγη cannot be sensibly applied to "Law".

Erasmus has here (Lex) "verum erat introductio ad spem potiorem" but Beza in all his versions translates "superintroducta spes potior". In the 1598 version he claims that in 19b the author of the epistle is saying that Levitical priesthood was superceded by something better. Moreover, grammatically δε here should be taken in the sense of ἀλλα and the verb ἐτελειωσεν should be understood as repeated in both clauses ἀπο του κοινου. Similar constructions occur in the epistle at VII.28 where the verb καθιστησιν should be repeated and at X.27 with the verb ἀπολειπεται. Finally Beza states that the noun ἐπεισαγωγη as opposed to εἰσαγωγη is used with the express purpose of emphasizing something brought in from abroad.[75] Thus it cannot apply to the Law or to the Levitical priesthood which was already there and must be applied to the priesthood of Christ. Beza also mentions that the expression δε κρειττονος ἐλπιδος is obviously a translation of a "Hebraeorum idiotismus" for ἐπεισαχθεισα κρειττων ἐλπις i.e. "superintroducta spes melior". We can thus see that Bois had read Beza here and was in agreement with him as regards (a) hope as the subject of the second clause, (b) the theological significance of this, (c) ἐπεισαγωγη referring to hope but not the Law. Of the English versions Tyndale, Great and Bishops' agree with the Vulgate/Erasmus version reading "but was an introduction of a better hope" (Tyndale, Great) and "but was the bringing of a better hope" (Bishops'). Geneva and Tomson agree with Beza's interpretation, "but the bringing in of a better hope *made perfete*". The AV adopts Beza's phrasing as well as his interpretation ("but the bringing in of a better hope *did*") but it also inserts the more conservative version in the margin ("but it was the bringing in of a better hope").

At Heb. VIII.2 Bois' note suggests that the Committee was considering the exact translation of των ἁγιων. Bois translates it as "of the Sanctuary" finding this more acceptable on account of the things that follow.

Beza in all his versions has "Sanctuarii". In the 1598 N.T. he says that the Vulgate/Erasmus "sanctorum" is ambiguous as indeed is the Greek. However, he points out, Heb. IX. 11 suggests that the name "Sancta" applies to the heavens.[76] According to this interpretation Christ is the minister of the true Sanctuary (i.e. the heavens) just as he is a minister of the true tabernacle (i.e. his own body). Tyndale, Great and Bishops' agree with each other here and with the Vulgate/ Erasmus version, reading "of holy thinges". Although this translation is rather more ambiguous than Beza's it nonetheless remains open to the same interpretation.[77] The AV agrees with the more explicit translation, as put forward by Bois on the basis of Beza's N.T., and reads "of the Sanctuary" in the text, retaining "of holy things" in the margin.

At Heb. VIII.4 Bois suggests a possible translation "he should not so much as be a Priest, as long as the priests that offer gifts etc. remaine". He elucidates this saying "if the priesthood of Christ had been earthly, it could not have fallen out otherwise but that the two earthly priesthoods of the Levites, and of Christ, would have been crushed between themselves...". This note suggests that the Final Committee was specifically concerned with the meaning of the phrase. At the same time the translation as proposed by Bois, suggests that the Final Committee supported the *Bezan* text here,[78] as well as Beza's phrasing. Beza in all his versions has "Nam si esset in terra ne Sacerdos quidem esset, manentibus illis sacerdotibus qui secundum legem offerunt dona". He explains this in a way which agrees almost word for word with Bois' explanation. He points out that if Jesus were on earth he would not be a priest because earthly priesthood does not stem from the order of Juda (in which Jesus was born) but from the order of Levi. Thus, either Jesus himself could not be a priest or else the earthly priests would have to give their place to him.

None of the English versions follows Beza's translation verbatim here. The AV, however, follows Beza's Greek text inserting γαρ, των ιερεων and του νομου. Moreover, the *translation* which the Revisers do adopt (based on Geneva 1560) points clearly to the contrast between Christ's priesthood and earthly priesthood as outlined by Beza and Bois ("For if he were on earth he should not be a priest seeing that // there are priests that offer gifts according to the law." "// or, they are priests").

At Heb. IX.12 Bois glosses εὑρεσθαι as ἀνθ' ὧν ἔδωκε τις λαβεῖν. Downes here suggests the translation "having purchased". Beza in his early versions has "...redemptionem nactus" and this is glossed in the 1574 version as "Merito adeptus idque nobis". In the 1598 N.T. Beza reads "redemptionem adeptus". He adds a note stressing that "redemption" here means redemption for us. For εὑράμενος he proposes the same translation as at Rom. IV.1. There he points out that although εὑρίσκειν usually refers to that which was found by chance, here (and at Heb. IX.12) it is used in the sense of "obtaining something by an effort".[79] Beza thus emphasizes that εὑράμενος although middle has no personal reference such as "for himself" and that the redemption was not accidental. This latter point is also stressed by Bois' gloss and by Downes' suggestion, which could have been taken from Whittingham's N.T. Tyndale, Great and Bishops' translate the Greek word literally (in agreement with Vulgate and Erasmus) and read "founde". Geneva and Tomson agree with Beza's translation and interpretation, reading "obteyned eternall redemption *for us*". The AV also adopts this translation and interpretation, as it stands in the Geneva Bible.

At Heb. X.12 Bois expresses doubt with regard to punctuation: "It is not clear concerning το διηνεκες whether it ought not to be joined with προσενεγκας θυσιαν [or] with ἐκαθισεν. The prior construction fits better with the remaining argument, but the punctuation of every codex contends against it and indeed the major number of the translators."[80]

Both Vulgate and Erasmus associate το διηνεκες with ἐκαθυσεν. Beza, in all his versions, links εἰς το διηνεκες with προσενεγκας θυσιαν in agreement with Stephanus. He claims (1598) that he is somewhat uncertain which punctuation is the correct one, but he prefers the latter version because it is suggested by v. 14 (i.e. one sacrifice but for *all* time). The AV is the *only* English version to adopt the Beza/Stephanus punctuation. We thus see here full agreement between Beza, Bois and the AV translation.

At Heb. X.26 Bois comments that ἑκουσιως means "of set purpose". The Vulgate translates it as "voluntarie", Erasmus has "volentes". Both these translations convey the idea of "willingness" rather than "willfulness". Beza in his early versions has "ultro" but in the 1598 N.T. he says that ἑκουσιως is translated by the Hebrew [chinnam] and applies to those who do something without any cause, real or apparent. Thus here, says Beza, it applies not to those who simply sin knowingly (e.g. David and Peter) but to those who take delight in impiety such as Saul, Julian the Apostate, Arius "et alii quorum execranda est memoria". Thus there is not much difference between different versions so far as the interpretation of ἑκουσιως is concerned.

Of the English versions Tyndale, Geneva, Tomson and Bishops' all agree with the Erasmus/Vulgate translation and read "willingly". The AV and the Great Bible translate "wilfully". As we have seen both words can convey the idea of persistent and deliberate sinning.

At Heb. X.38 Bois defines ὑποστειληται as "if any man shrink back or withdraw him self for feare". See Sap. 6.7. Evidently the problem here was deciding the subject for ὑποστειληται. Erasmus and the Vulgate both took it to be ὁ δικαιος but Bois agreed with Beza in supplying "siquis" as subject.[81]

Beza in the 1598 N.T. supplies *siquis* in italics. He

also takes καὶ in the sense of ἀλλα on the basis of the corresponding place in Habbakuk where the faithful man is compared to the wicked. The Apostle here, claims Beza, keeps the Prophet's meaning although he changes the "collatio membrorum".[82] As for ὑποστειληται itself, Beza defines it as the equivalent of the Hebrew [huppelah] or "to retreat into a safer place".

Erasmus, although omitting μου from his text nonetheless takes ὁ δικαιος to be the subject of ὑποστειληται and translates καὶ by "et" not by "at". Tyndale, Great and Bishops' all agree with this reading "and if he withdrawe himself". All the English Geneva versions agree with Beza ("but if any withdrawe himself"). The AV agrees with Beza and with Bois, and reads "but if any drawe backe".

At Heb. XI.1 the problem lies in the exact meaning of the Greek. Bois proposes the following paraphrase "(faith) is a most sure warrant of things, is a being of things hoped for, a discovery, a demonstration of things that are not seen".

Beza in his early versions has "Est autem fides illud quod facit ut extent quae sperantur et quod demonstrat quae non videntur". By 1598 he has changed this to "Est autem fides illud quo subsistunt quae sperantur et quae demonstrat quae non cernuntur". He comments that the best interpretation of the phrase is by the Graecus scholiastes who says that Faith is the substance and the essence of things hoped for, which have no essence apart from Faith since it is Faith which brings them into being. Faith is also the proof and the demonstration of those things which cannot be seen, because it makes them visible to the mind.[83]

Beza then interprets Faith in the context of the passage; the author of the epistle is saying that Christ has always been the Saviour of those who believe. Thus ἐλπιζομενα refers to those things which the O.T. Fathers who had faith hoped *would* happen and which now we believe to have happened. Similarly τα μη βλεπομενα[84] can refer to things which they hoped would be seen and which we *have* seen. However, Beza adds, there is no difference between their Faith and ours since the objects of Faith change according to circumstances. We see here a fundamental agreement between Bois and Beza, not so much in matters of phrasing but in interpretation. Both take Faith as giving reality to things hoped for, and both dispense with Augustine's terminology: "substantia" for ὑποστασις and "argumentum" for ἐλεγχος. This terminology, however, is adopted by the Vulgate "sperandum substantia rerum argumentum non apparentium" and by Erasmus "earum rerum quae sperantur substantia, argumentum eorum quae non videntur".

None of the English versions follows the late Bezan paraphrase or interpretation. Tyndale and Great read "sure confidence...certayntie". Geneva, Tomson and Bishops' read "ground of things hoped for...the evidence...of things not seene". The AV reverts to the translation "substance" for ὑποστασις (adding in the margin "ground or confidence")[85] and translates ἐλεγχος as "evidence" in agreement with Geneva and Bishops'.

At Heb. XI.3 Bois adds a gloss "were made of things that were not extant".[86] Beza, in his early versions, reads "ut quae cernimus non sunt ex apparentibus facta". In his 1589/98 versions he alters "cernimus" to "videamus". He interprets this passage as meaning that the world which we see[87] was not made out of any already existent material but out of nothing. He therefore disagrees with the Vulgate "ex invisibilibus fierent visibilia" as he thinks it is not a question of things "invisible" but of things non-existent which only came into being with the creation of the world. He is more favourably inclined towards Erasmus' interpretation "Ut ex iis quae non apparebant, ea quae viderentur fierent" but questions its accuracy since Erasmus translates ὡς τε ἐκ μη φαινομενων rather than εἰς το μη ἐκ φαινομενων. We see full agreement between Bois and Beza here. The Vulgate translation here emphasizes that God, although invisible, nonetheless manifested himself in his works.[88] Tyndale and Great agree with the Vulgate, reading "things which are sene were made of things are not sene". Bishops' follows this, inserting only the past tense "were". Tomson and Geneva follow Beza verbatim with "the things we see are not made of things which did appear". The AV agrees with Bois' and Beza's interpretation of the creation altering the active to the passive "things which are seene...".

At Heb. XI.21 Bois inserts a gloss, "'Leaning upon the top' etc. See Mercer. Annot. In Santis. Thesaur. under the entry Mittah. Col. 1597." There were two problems connected with the Greek ἐπι το ἀκρον της ῥαβδου αὐτου; firstly there was the difficulty of translating ἐπι in this context. Secondly there was the problem of relating "staff" which occurred in the Septuagint and in Epistle to the Hebrews to "bed" which occurred in the Hebrew version of Genesis XLVII.31.[89] It is very likely that Beza as well as Bois consulted Mercer here since his *Thesaurus Linguae Sacrae* came out in 1577.[90] Certainly Beza's reading in all his versions ("adoravit super extremo baculo suo") is in substantial agreement with Mercer's exposition of ἐπι. Beza himself comments that ἐπι here "nihil aliud...declarat quam super", and objects to the Vulgate/Erasmus translation "Ad summum fastigium virgae eius". He further points out that Augustine was the only one of the ancients to see the true meaning of ἐπι. As for the transposition of "virga" and "lectum" Beza points out the difference between Septuagint/Hebrews and Genesis XLVII.31 but does not think it of much significance since in each case the same basic point is made, i.e. that Jacob worshipped (God).[91]

Of the English versions, Bishops' and Great agree, reading
"worshipped toward the top of his scepter". Tyndale, however,
has "bowed himselfe towarde the toppe of his cepter" which
although ambiguous seems rather closer to the Augustine/Beza
translation. Geneva and Tomson agree with Beza, reading
"*leanyng* on the end of his staffe he worshipped God" (*God* -
not in Beza). The AV has "worshipped *leaning* upon the top of
his staffe" thus reproducing Beza's reading exactly, with the
backing of Mercer and Bois.

This point of translation was raised by Martin against
William Fulke.[92] Martin claimed that only two ways of translating ἐπι το ἀκρον της ῥαβδου αὐτου were possible; either
"Jacob adored the top of Joseph's[93] sceptre" or "Jacob adored
toward the top of his (own) sceptre". According to Martin,
the Protestant translation goes against all the Fathers (except Augustine). It also adds two words which do not occur
in the Greek (*leaning* and *God*) thus departing from the Hebrew
construction "He worshipped towards the bed's head" at Gen.
XLVII.31. Fulke answers this point by point. Firstly, he
says, St. Augustine's rendition is the only sensible one since
"Jacob, as a weak old man worshipped upon the top of his
staffe". Secondly, although, in the Geneva Bible, the words
leaning and *God* are added, the sentence remains perfectly intelligible without them. Thirdly, αὐτου and αὐτου tend to be
interchangeable in the New Testament.

At Heb. XII.13 Bois maintains that the Apostle is continuing his argument from the previous verses exhorting "fortitude...in adverse circumstances". He is not speaking about
vacillating brethren who may threaten the course of Christian
life. In this case, Bois says, το χωλον and τοις ποσιν should
not be referred to different people but to one and the same
man; "lest that which is crippled i.e. lest the debility of
your mind be nourished and augmented by sloth". Beza in his

early versions has "ne quod claudum *est* abducatur a via", which by 1598 he changes to "ne quod claudum *est* deflectat de via". He takes the opposite view to Bois with regard to the interpretation of the passage. In the 1598 N.T. he makes clear that he does not refer to το χωλον and τοις ποσιν to one and the same person, saying that "the lame" (το χωλον) applies not only to those who were slow or negligent in doing their duty but also to those who were hesitant about accepting the full message of the Gospel.[94] The Vulgate has here "ut non claudicans quis erret" interpreting το χωλον as the weak brethren, and Erasmus "ne claudicatio aberret a via" which is open to both interpretations. Tyndale's translation is also ambiguous here ("lest any haltinge turn out of the waye") but the Great Bible has "lest any halting turn you out of the way" which suggests a reference to the weak. Geneva, Tomson and Bishops' all agree with *early* Beza here ("lest that which is halting be turned out of the way"). The AV also has this translation substituting "lame" for "halting". It is difficult to say whether the Revisers, in accepting early Bezan translation of the passage, also accept Beza's interpretation of it as against Bois'.

At Heb. XII.17 Bois explains μετανοιας γαρ τοπον οὐχ εὑρεν as "he could not bend the mind of his father, or persuade him so that having altered his determination he would recall and rescind the blessing with which he had blessed Jacob". Beza translates the Greek as "non enim reperit poenitentiae locum" which he explains as referring to the father's change of mind. According to Beza, those who refer the words to Esau's own repentance are wrong because "Esauum culpam suam minime agnosse".

Of the English versions Tyndale has "he founde no meanes to come therby agayne" thus making clear that it is not Esau's own repentance which is in question. Other versions, from

Great to AV read "he found no place of repentance". The AV, however, adds in the margin "// or, way to change his minde" (i.e. his father's mind). We thus see here a full agreement between Bois, Beza and the AV margin.

At Heb. XIII.3 Bois' note suggests that the Revisers were not sure how to interpret ὡς καὶ αὐτοὶ ὄντες ἐν σωματι. Bois himself interprets it "as being yourselves also subject to adversity" although adding that the Greek literally means "as being yourselves also in a body". Downes, on the other hand suggests the interpretation ὡς καὶ αὐτοὶ ἄνθρωποι ὄντες and others propose ὡς καὶ αὐτοὶ συγκακουχουμενοι. Beza in his 1574 N.T. has "acsi ipsi quoque corpore *afflicti* essetis". In his 1598 version, however, he translates the Greek literally "ut qui et ipsi sitis in corpore". He explains that the Apostle here wants his audience to sympathize with the captivity of their brothers by imagining that it is they *themselves* who are being held captive. For, Beza adds, we can only fully sympathize with the misfortunes of others when we feel them as our own. Therefore ἐν σωματι here means the same as "en personne" in French. The Vulgate has here "Tamquam et ipsi in corpore morantes" i.e. as if you yourselves are also subject to adversity. This reading is supported by the Syriac N.T. and accounts for Bois' interpretation. Erasmus has "veluti ipsi quoque versantes in corpore" and the "Doctissimus interpres"[95] takes ἐν σωματι as referring to the body of the Church (thus giving the meaning "you are all in the same body"). Beza approves of this latter interpretation "utpote quae universae huius doctrinae fontem aperiat" but inserts his own reading on grounds of simplicity. Tyndale ("which are yet in your bodies") and the Great Bible ("which are yet in the bodie") are rather ambiguous here but appear to agree with the Vulgate/Erasmus interpretation. Geneva and Tomson follow early Beza, reading "as if ye were also afflicted in the body". Bishops' makes quite plain its agreement with Vulgate/Erasmus, reading "as being yourselves also in the bodie subject to adversitie". Bois, although he mentions the literal rendition of the Greek is nonetheless in agreement with the Vulgate/Erasmus interpretation. The AV, however, agrees with late Beza as against Bois and the rest of the Committee, reading "as being yourselves also in the body".[96]

We can see from the instances discussed above that there was some difference between the Final Revision Committee's attitude to Beza and the use of Beza by the final version of the AV. This can be pinpointed by examining more closely the nature of the instances in which (a) a Bezan reading is adopted by the Committee and not by the AV text and (b) instances in which Beza is adopted by the AV as *against* the Committee. The main cases of (a) occur at Rom. I.28, XII.3, 1 Cor. VII.29, Heb. I.3, V.2, VIII.4, XII.17. In practically all these instances the Revisers choose a more conservative reading. At 1 Cor. VII.29 the AV rejects the evidence of Beza as backed up by the Committee and the Geneva and Bishops' Bible for the insertion of ὅτι. The reason for this is probably lack of MS support; not being able to explain Beza's "seventeen old codices" the Revisers reverted to the Erasmus/Vulgate reading. Their decision here is ratified by modern MS evidence.

At Heb. XII.17 the AV's only precedent for making clear that it is not Esau's own repentance which is in question, was Tyndale 1534. All the other versions (including Beza himself) translate the Greek literally "found no place of repentance". It would have been unusual therefore for the AV to sacrifice the Greek for the sake of a clear interpretation of the phrase as suggested by Bois. The interpretation, however, was inserted in the AV margin.

At Rom. I.28, Heb. I.3 the AV shows the same reluctance to accept the Committee's recommendation of a Bezan reading

if there is no support for it in any other English version.
Thus at Rom. I.28 no version follows Beza's rendering of εἰς
ἀδοκιμον νουν and the AV here is not more conservative than
Geneva in inserting "voyde of judgement" in the margin. At
Heb. I.3 Bois' suggestion of the Bezan "effulgentia" has no
supplementary support, and so the AV conforms with the earlier English versions, reading "brightness". The main cases
of (b) occur at Rom. III.25/26, Rom. V.12, Rom. XI.31, 1 Cor.
IV.9, Gal. IV.17, Heb. IV.2, V.7, X.12, XIII.3. Four of
those, Rom. XI.31, Heb. IV.2, V.7, X.12 are concerned with
either text or punctuation. At Rom. XI.31 the AV is the only
English version to adopt the Bezan punctuation (with the added support of Theophylactus). At Heb. IV.2 the AV prefers
the συγκεκραμενος reading after Stephanus and Beza, and it
relegates the Complutensian reading to the margin. At Rom.
V.12 the AV (with only the agreement of Tomson) inserts the
Bezan reading "in whom" in the margin. There could be two
reasons for this decision here; either some of the Revisers
insisted that "in whom" was a better translation for theological reasons, or they considered that it was a grammatically or
textually possible rendering of ἐφ' ᾧ. At Rom. III.25/26 the
AV adopts the more conservative theological interpretation
"remission of sins" (i.e. Christ declared God's righteousness
with a view to remitting past sins) inserting the Bezan theological interpretation (Christ demonstrated God's righteousness because in the past God had merely passed over men's
sins) in the margin. Although the latter interpretation is
taken to be the right one by modern scholarship, it is interesting to note that the Authorized Version had no precedents
for it at all.

We can see from this that there was a difference in the
AV's and the Committee's attitude to Beza. The Committee was
against a large number of Bezan readings on doctrinal and tex-

tual grounds. However, almost all the readings which were turned down by the Committee were accepted by the AV. There are also cases where a Bezan reading, having been accepted by the Committee, is turned down by the AV. However, as we have seen, such cases occur much less frequently than their converse. Thus it seems that Beza's authority, so far as the Revisers are concerned, is of crucial importance; so much so that the AV is, on occasions, less conservative than the Geneva Bible. The best instances of this are the AV marginal readings at Rom. V.12 and at Rom. III.25/26.

* * * * *

While the aim of this work has been to show Beza's influence on the English New Testament, we have been particularly concerned with his influence on the AV both in its final version and at various stages of Revision. The influence of Beza on the Geneva Bible of 1560 and on Lawrence Tomson's N.T. of 1576 was discussed briefly in the first chapter, sufficiently to show that both the versions relied on Beza almost totally for reasons of doctrine. This is hardly surprising since both were acknowledged as the official Puritan and Presbyterian New Testament. The AV of 1611 made no such claim; on the contrary, we learn from the instructions given to the translators that their aim was to avoid theological prejudice in any direction.

NOTES

1. For full details see Ward Allen, *op. cit.*, pp. 1-12. In this chapter I have followed Ward Allen's translation of the Greek and Latin except when it appeared to be inaccurate, e.g. at Rom. IX.6 his translation of οἱον τε ἀντι του δυνατον as "such a thing which may be compared with this" (see p. 118).

2. See p. 130. See also p. 15 for references to Beza's doctrine of the Eucharist.

3. Bois' references are to Henry Saville's Greek edition of Chrysostom.

4. Beza's 1565 N.T.

5. Neither Bois nor Beza mentions the variant προεχωμεθα which occurs in AL. Beza shows no knowledge of the D variant προκατεχομεν περισσον.

6. Beza makes this explicit in his comment on v. 26. Barrett's account of Rom. III.25.26 is in agreement with Beza's view of παρεσις (C. K. Barrett, *A Commentary on the Epistle to the Romans*, (New York, Harper, 1938).

7. N.E.B. also reads "justice" and takes παρεσις in the sense of "overlooking" not as a synonym for ἀφεσις.

8. He also says that there are no other instances of κατεναντι in the sense of ὁμοιως in the New Testament.

9. Both Erasmus and Beza draw attention to Ambrose's reading "credidisti". (Modern scholarship attributes the commentaries on Pauline Epistles not to Ambrose but to Ambrosiaster.) Neither Souter nor Nestle & Aland give this reading or any other variant with "credidisti". Erasmus mentions that Ambrose refers "credidisti" to the nation which Paul is addressing. In the 1535 N.T. he quotes Ambrose's comment "Ut unum deum omnium doceat alloquitur gentiles". The Bishops' Bible obviously based its reading on Ambrose's interpretation.

10. For theological differences between versions here see p. 24 above.

11. Beza leaves his criticism of "in quo" (i.e. peccato) anonymous, probably not wishing to openly criticize Augustine on this point.

12. Cf. N.E.B. "in splendour of the Father".

13. For Protestant translations of μετανοια see Fulke's *Defence*, ed. Hartshorne, pp. 429ff.

14. Erasmus (1535); "Sine poenitentia i.e. Quorum non possit poenitere eum qui dedit aut qui promisit, quasi dicas, impoenitibilia."

15. Souter and Nestle & Aland put the comma after ἠπει-θησαν and quote no variants. Cf. Tischendorf, II, p. 428.

16. Erasmus (1535) actually quotes Theophylactus' reading and comment. "Sic et illi non crediderunt ut vestra misericordia et ipsi misericordiam consequantur." *Commentum:* "Sed vestra misericordia et horum erit, aemulabuntur enim vos. Nec abhorret ab hoc Chrysostomi commentum docens utrumque populum vicissim fuisse incredulum, ac vicissim ad gratiam vocatum." Barrett, *Romans*, p. 222, is in substantial agreement with this interpretation.

17. N.E.B. has "at the moment of mercy".

18. See Barrett, *Romans*, p. 220.

19. Lit. "let each abound in his own sense" i.e. "let each use his reason to its fullest capacity". Contrary to what Beza says, this need not imply that men will rely solely on their own power of reason, without any recourse to God.

20. N.E.B. "everyone should have reached conviction in his own mind".

21. Souter and Nestle & Aland read ὑπερ ἁ γεγραπται and omit φρονειν. Nestle & Aland quote ℵ D G pm sy^P as reading υπερ ο and C ℵ 33 pm sy as inserting φρονειν. Cf. Tischendorf, II, pp. 475-6.

22. For modern discussion of this see J. Moffatt, *The First Epistle of Paul to the Corinthians*, (1951), p. 47.

23. For exact reference see Ward-Allen, *op. cit.*, pp. 45 and 115.

24. Moffatt has "doomed gladiators".

25. N.E.B.: "in a time of stress like the present". Moffatt, *1 Corinthians*, is in agreement with Beza's eschatological interpretation of the passage.

26. Souter quotes no variants with ὁτι. Nestle & Aland

quote Ψ D G pc sy Mcion but cf. Tischendorf II, praem οτι cum D E F G al mu ^{vid} Dam Thphyl, item it. vg ^{ms}. (ap. Lu. non am fu demid tol harl) syr utr. cop. basm. arm. Tert ^{marc} 5,7 et^8. Or int 2,172.

27. For the eschatological interpretation see Moffatt, *1 Corinthians*, p. 92.

28. Acc. Tischendorf II, ευπαρεδρον cum ℵ A B D E F G P al plus 30 Clem 573.631 Eus ^{dem} 31. Bas 3,640 et saepe al mu ...ς (= Gb Sz) : ευπροσεδρον cum K al plu. Chr ^{196}. (invito mosc^1) Dam ^{parall} 641. (non item ad h.l.) Oec. Similiter L προσεδρον, 5.6. ευπροσδεκτον.

29. For possible identity of the bearers of these initials see Ward Allen, *op. cit.*, pp. 10-11.

30. As this is the only place where Bodleian Bishops' and Fulman MS overlap, it is interesting to compare their annotations. In Bodleian Bishops' the Bishops' reading "a sister, a woman" is underlined and a reference is made to "p. 18". If the Bodleian annotator is disputing the Bishops'/Bois rendition here, this would support the hypothesis that the Bodleian Bishops' is later than the Fulman MS. (See p. 171 below.)

31. The word "wife" could mean both "spouse" and woman in 16th century English (S.O.E.D.). N.E.B. has "Have I no right to take a Christian wife about with me".

32. See Fulke's *Defence*, ed. Hartshorne, pp. 71, 115.

33. Cf. Beza's comment on ευσχημον above where he makes plain that marriage is the last resort.

34. This view was held by Ambrose who read "mulieres" here. Beza mentions this in his 1598 N.T. and finds it not acceptable.

35. Rheims; "my self should become reprobate".

36. Souter and Nestle & Aland have τυπικως in the text. Souter quotes no variants but Nestle & Aland mention ταυτα δε παντα τυποι συνεβαινον as occurring in most 𝕽 MSS. The D* reading here is παντα δε ταυτα τυποι συνεβαινον and Beza shows no knowledge of it. The Nestle & Aland text here was based on 𝔓 K 1611 pm latt sy hmg Irlat Or. Beza probably saw τυπικως in some Patristic MSS. (See also Tischendorf, II, p. 515.)

37. Erasmus explains "Et ad eum modum (i.e. ἡμων addendo) citat hunc locum Augustinus".

38. Rheims; "chaunced to them in figure".

39. Cf. "He offered wine not water in the type of his blood" (Jeremy Taylor, 1613, S.O.E.D.).

40. See also Ch. I, p. 15 above.

41. Cremer, *Lexicon*, gives two meanings for δυναμεις; "as designation of persons (1 Cor. XII.29)" and "as designation of supramundane angelic powers in N.T. and Hellenistic Greek usually conjoined with ἀρχη, ἐξουσια".

42. No Greek or Latin variant with ειναι τι is quoted by Souter, Nestle & Aland or Tischendorf.

43. Beza quotes Jerome after Erasmus (1535).

44. Cf. classical τα δοκουντα as opposed to τα μηδαν οντα (Euripides, *Troad*. 608). See also J. B. Lightfoot, *Saint Paul's Epistle to the Galatians* (1888), p. 103.

45. Cf. "The chieffe peers of the realme" (1536), S.O.E.D.

46. According to Nestle & Aland δε is omitted in Marcion.

47. Tischendorf, II, προεγραφη (47. εγραφη) sine add cum ℵ A B C 17*. 23*. 31. 38. 43. 52. 67**. 72. 73. 93. f am fu** tol syr sch. cop sah. Arm. Aeth. (Eus lat. ap Gall 4,489 quia ante oculos eorum descriptus est Jes. Chr. crucifixus) Euthal cod. Cyr esa 737. et glaph. 429. Thdrt 1,658. Archel 603. Aug; add. εν υμιν cum D E F G K L P al pler d e g vg cle. fu* demid harl go syr^P Ps - Ath 391. etc.

48. Souter and Nestle & Aland both have που οὖν in their text after p. 46ʄ L 1912 pm; τις ουν ην has the backing of ℵ D; που ουν ην occurs in G al it; που ουν εστιν in 103 f vg.

49. He confines himself to mentioning that he saw the που οὖν variant "in duobus vetustis codicibus". (See Ch. I, p. 7 above.)

50. On the relative merits of που οὖν / τις οὖν see Lightfoot, *Galatians*, p. 177.

51. Beza, in the annotations to his 1598 version, suggests that ὁ μακαρισμος ὑμων can mean either "how great and where was the rumour of men declaring you happy?" or "what was your dec-

laration that you were happy because of my coming?" He then says that the question points to Paul's amazement and that το μακαριζειν means to "profess happiness" in classical Greek, and the corresponding noun ought to be distinguished from μακαριστης meaning "happiness". This was first pointed out by Erasmus in his notes who, however, did not follow his own injunction in his translation.

52. Souter and Nestle & Aland both have ὑμας in the text and quote no variants (see Lightfoot, *Galatians*, p. 176).

53. Souter and Nestle & Aland read καλον δε ζηλουσθαι. Nestle & Aland quote the variants καλον δε ζηλουσθε in B ℵ pc vg Or and καλον δε το ζηλουσθαι in ℜ D G pm: cf. Tischendorf, II, p. 647.

54. See Lightfoot, *Galatians*, p. 177.

55. Neither Souter nor Nestle & Aland give any variants for ἐνεκοψε. Lightfoot, *Galatians*, p. 205 discusses the metaphor of ἐνεκοψε which he translates as "checked" and points out that the testimony in favour of ἐνεκοψε(ν) is overwhelming (TR; ἀνεκοψε[ν]) cum minusc vix mu (sed et Thdrt [ed]) acc. Tischendorf, II.

56. Early Beza; ἐνεκοψε.

57. But cf. N.E.B. "effulgence".

58. Both Souter and Nestle & Aland have ἑλιξεις in the text in agreement with p. 46 ABD[c], Syriac and Egyptian N.T., Origen and Chrysostom. Both quote as variants with ἀλλαξεις N* D* lat Irenaeus (lat.), Tertullian, Origen (lat.). J. Moffatt, *Epistle to the Hebrews*, (1968, reprint), comments that the variant also occurs in LXX MSS and attributes the change ἑλιξεις > ἀλλαξεις to ἀλλαγησονται (see *ibid.* p. 14).
   Sixteenth century scholarship, however, looked on ἑλιξεις as a variant, with ἀλλαξεις (from Ps. 102) being the "original reading". Erasmus (1535) strikes a compromise here, keeping ἑλιξεις in his Greek text but translating it as "mutabis".

59. See Moffatt, *Hebrews*, p. 24.

60. This view was held by several Greek Fathers. See Moffatt, *Hebrews*, p. 24.

61. Moffatt, *Hebrews*, also reads "for a little while". N.E.B. has "short while".

62. II.9.

63. Rheims version is even more explicit "because of the passion of death crowned with glory and honour".

64. Gregory Martin suggests that the Genevan translation here is intended to obscure the fact that Christ deserved his glory because of the suffering he had undergone and thus to deny the importance of works (see Fulke's *Defence*, ed. Hartshorne, p. 349).

65. Ward-Allen, *op. cit.*, p. 77.

66. Souter and Nestle & Aland both read την ἀρχην της ὑποστασεως in their text, quoting the variant αυτου as occurring in A 1912 pc f vg. On ὑποστασις being taken to mean Christ's substance, see Moffatt, *Hebrews*, p. 48.

67. This view took ἡ ἀρχη της ὑποστασεως to mean "the beginning of our true nature". Beza half-inclines to this by associating ὑποστασις specifically with faith ("in fide vero dicimur quidem stare", 1598), but takes ἡ ἀρχη in the non-temporal sense. (Acc. Tischendorf, II, 67** πιστεως.)

68. N.E.B. "our original confidence".

69. Acc. Tischendorf συνκεκερασμενος cum ℵ et...συγκεκραμενος (-μμενος 114) 31. 41. 114., item de vg $^{cle.}$ demid harl... hal syr $^{sch.}$ ar $^{e.}$ Cyr Lcif ^{215}...συγκεκερασμενους...cum A B C D* M 17 ^{vi} (dubium utrum -κεκερας-an-κεκρα-) 23. 37. 57. 71. 73. 116. 137. cat $^{txt.}$ Thdor $^{mop.}$ Euthal $^{cod.}$ Item Gb^1, συγκεκραμενους (48. 49. 106. 109. 120. 122. 139. 219. al ^{4} scr. 13 $^{lect.}$ - μμενους) cum D^c E K L P al plus^{70} etc. (See also Tischendorf, II, p. 791; Moffatt, *Hebrews*, p. 51 for comments on this.)

70. For full definition of μετριοπαθειν see Moffatt, *Hebrews*, p. 62. If we accept that "the thought of excess here is excessive severity rather than excessive leniency" then the Vulgate/AV translation is probably more correct than Beza's.

71. For exposition of the various interpretations of the phrase see Moffatt, *Hebrews*, p. 66. Some modern scholars agree with Bois in taking ἀπο της εὐλαβειας with what follows, but this is a difficult construction.

72. See Fulke's *Defence*, ed. Hartshorne, pp. 127, 151, 323. Rheims; "for his reverence".

73. Cf. translations of ἀρχη at Heb. III.14.

74. Cf. translations of ἀρχη at Heb. III.14.

75. In support of this he quotes Demosthenes' ἐπεισακτῳ σιτῳ i.e. "frumento aliis regionibus importato. Sic apud veteres dicebatur extrinsecus assumptum a croama ut Ribittus observavit (noster olim in academia Lausannensi collega) prolatis etiam ex Hermogene et Platone exemplis..." (for Jean Ribit see *Correspondance de Théodore de Bèze*, ed. H. Meylan and A. Dufour, [Geneva, 1963], I, p. 73, note 7).

76. See Moffatt, *Hebrews*, p. 104.

77. Erasmus (1535) interprets in the same way as Beza on the basis of Chrysostom and Theophylactus. The latter also admits the possibility of taking των ἁγιων as "sanctorum hominum".

78. Beza inserts γαρ which occurs in ℵ pl. He comments on the Vulgate "omission or neglect of των ἱερεων" (which is in fact omitted from ℵ pl. sy. τον νομον as in the text of Erasmus, Stephanus and Beza only occurs in ℵ D pm. Both Nestle & Aland and Souter read οὑν omitting γαρ των ἱερεων and τον (item Tischendorf).

79. For grammatical form and exact meaning of this cf. Moffatt, *Hebrews*, p. 121.

80. See Moffatt, *Hebrews*, p. 140.

81. Moffatt, *Hebrews*, p. 158 takes ὁ δικαιος to be the subject. And this is probably the only way to understand the Greek if we read μου ἐκ πιστεως in 38a. μου, however, is omitted from p. 18 ℵ pl; hence from Beza's text and the AV. It occurs in p. 46 ⅅ pc. vg$^{cl.}$ et al. (cf. Rheims; "my just").

82. For full definition of ὑποστειληται see Moffatt, *Hebrews*, p. 158.

83. Cf. Beza's definition of Faith in *Summe of the Christian Fayth*, translated out of French by Robert Fyll, (London, 1585).

84. Cf. Beza's definition of βλεπειν p. 54 and p. 100, n. 19 above.

85. Cf. translations of ὑποστασις at Heb. III.14.

86. Best MSS read ἐκ φαινομενων το βλεπομενον. This, however, was changed to τα βλεπομενα in D ℜ pl vg sy presumably to correspond with the other plurals. This is not mentioned by Beza or the Revisers.

87. See Moffatt, *Hebrews*, p. 162.

88. According to Augustin Marlorat, *Novi Testamenti catholica expositio Ecclesiastica*, (H. Stephanus, 1570). (Note on Heb. XI.3.) Calvin also interprets the passage in this way.

89. Ward Allen, *op. cit.*, p. 121 reproduces Mercer's note in full. The point made by Mercer, that the Septuagint read "virga" for "lectum" at Gen. 47 and that this was followed by the author of Hebrews, is confirmed by modern scholarship.

90. Beza certainly had a great respect for Mercer which he expresses in his preface to Mercer's *Commentarii in librum Job*, (Geneva, Vignon, 1573).

91. Cf. Moffatt, *Hebrews*, p. 178.

92. See Fulke's *Defence*, ed. Hartshorne, p. 539.

93. Neither Souter nor Nestle & Aland nor Moffatt quote αὑτου as variant for αὐτου. No mention of this variant is made by Beza, or Erasmus, or the English versions.

94. Modern scholarship is in substantial agreement with Beza. Moffatt assumes that the writer at v. 13 is making a specific reference to the Christian community which he is addressing. (See *Hebrews*, p. 206.) N.E.B. reads, [Then the disabled limb will] "not be put out of joint, but regain its former powers", taking ἐκτραπῃ in its medical sense. But the translation still does not make clear whether "the disabled limb" is a weak member of the community, or a weak spot within the individual.

95. See *Joannis Calvini Opera Quae Supersunt Omnia*, ed. W. Baum, E. Cunitz, E. Reuss, (Brunswick, 1896), vol. LV, 187. Beza, in his exegetical notes, never refers to Calvin by name, but always calls him the "Doctissimus interpres".

96. N.E.B. "for you like them are still in the world".

GENERAL CONCLUSIONS

In order to examine the exact nature of Beza's influence on the AV we investigated two documents which purport to represent two different stages in the making of the AV; the Bodleian Bishops' MS which deals with the Gospels and the Fulman MS which deals with the Epistles and which appears to represent the work of the Final Revision Committee. In the case of the Bodleian Bishops' we have had good reason to assume that it is connected with the AV because it contains typographical annotations for the insertion of italics which correspond almost exactly to the use of italics in the AV final version. Moreover, the two theological works of the Oxford Company translators which were examined showed agreement with the theology of the Bodleian Bishops' insofar as Church government and connection between the Gospel and the Law was concerned. As regards the connection of the Fulman MS with the AV we accept at the outset Prof. Ward Allen's conclusion that the Chrysostom pagination in the MS corresponds with the issue of the first volume of Sir Henry Saville's edition of Chrysostom's works and so with the date of the assembling of the Final Revision Committee.

In examining the MS annotations in Bodleian Bishops' our primary concern has been to establish the influence of Beza on these annotations and relate his influence on the Bodleian annotator to his influence on the finished AV. If the influence of Beza on the annotations and on the final version proved to be of a similar nature, this would support the evidence of·the typographical annotations and establish a close link between Bodleian Bishops' MS and the AV. Indeed, a detailed examination of the influence of Beza on the Synoptic Gospels reveals only very slight discrepancies between the two versions. Admittedly, we have seen that the Bodleian annotator is rather more reluctant than the AV to accept a few points of Beza's doctrine such as the status of the Law, or the nature of Mary's grace. However, on matters of text and style we see a remarkable measure of agreement and, as has been already pointed out, there are eight cases where the Bodleian Bishops' annotation provides the only parallel for a Bezan reading occurring in the AV. This argues very strongly that the Bodleian Bishops' cannot be a *later* collation of the Bodleian Bishops' and Authorized text, as some have thought hitherto. If, in addition to this evidence we remember the presence of the typographical annotations (and bear in mind the very fact that the agreement between the Bodleian annotations and AV is not total!) we must then conclude that the Bodleian Bishops' represents a late stage in the making of the AV.

In examining the Fulman MS where our object was the same as in the case of Bodleian Bishops', we were struck by the comparatively larger number of discrepancies between the Committee's attitude to Beza and the AV's attitude to him. Firstly we notice that in a *large* number of instances the AV goes against the Committee's advice by choosing a Bezan reading. Moreover, some of those readings are concerned with a fundamental point of Biblical exegesis (such as the question of παρεσις, or the meaning of ἐφ' ᾧ) while others (e.g. Rom. XI. 31) adopt a punctuation which has only Beza's support. Secondly, we notice that such Bezan readings as are recommended by the Committee are frequently turned down by the Revisers in favour of a more conservative version. This, however, seems to happen less often than the AV's rejection of the Committee in favour of Beza.

It must be borne in mind though, that there are cases where the AV concurs with the Committee's suggestion of a Bezan reading, and that there are also instances where the

AV strikes a mid-path between the Committee and Beza. This, however, does not obscure our basic point that so far as Bezan readings are concerned, the disagreement between the Fulman Committee and the AV is greater than the disagreement between Bodleian Bishops' and AV. We should perhaps mention here that the Synoptic Gospels would not, by their very nature, pose as many problems as the Epistles and hence they would give much less cause for disagreement. Yet, even taking that into account it does not seem reasonable that the Fulman MS, diverging from the AV as much as it does, should be considered the Authorized Version's immediate predecessor.

Thus, from the evidence examined, we conclude that, firstly, against first impressions, there is a very strong possibility (especially in view of the note at 1 Cor. IX.5) that Bodleian Bishops' annotations represent a later stage than the Fulman MS in the making of the AV. Secondly, that being the case, we see that the influence of Beza's doctrine, text and style becomes more prominent as the Revision reaches its final stages.

Generally, there seems to be no doubt that, so far as the Revisers were concerned, Beza's authority completely overshadowed that of any other New Testament scholar of the period. This does not imply that the AV is no more than an English version of Beza's 1598 New Testament. In matters of text, especially, the Revisers were unwilling to adopt a Bezan reading if it did not have authoritative support. In cases where Beza's text was accepted, the more usual reading was frequently inserted in the margin. Conversely, where a better known reading was adopted, the Bezan version was put in as a marginal alternative.

Although a similar procedure was followed in matters of doctrine, the theology of the AV is seen to be much more ambiguous than Beza's. The theological question of Mary's grace, for instance, is left completely open by the Revisers whereas

Beza makes it plain that no inherent grace should be attributed to Mary. As regards John's baptism the Revisers at first appear to accept Beza's view that the baptism of repentance is no less valid than the baptism whereby Spirit is given. However, this point is weakened by the Revisers' insertion of the more conservative interpretation in the margin. Concerning the hereditary nature of the original sin the Revisers put the more conservative reading in the text whilst putting Beza's interpretation in the margin. This is particularly interesting as the only English precedent for adopting the Bezan reading at this point is the New Testament of Laurence Tomson.

In matters of style, the Revisers, although taking over many of Beza's phrases (as has been seen above) nonetheless managed to attain to an individual style by frequent consultation of the other *English* versions and by their own inventiveness.

APPENDIX

Laurence Tomson 1539-1608[1]

In this study, we shall be chiefly concerned with Tomson as member of the English "Presbyterian" party, politician and theologian. We shall attempt to establish a link between his career and his theological works and also to throw some light on his function within the Elizabethan Puritan movement.

Certainly more records survive concerning Tomson's career as Politician than as Puritan leader. Whether this is due to the fact that political records are the ones most likely to survive, or the fact that Tomson's other activities were of a very clandestine nature--it is difficult to ascertain. The fact remains that Tomson as a second-line civil servant wielded a considerable amount of political power--not that this was in any way exceptional. As Patrick Collinson has pointed out,[2] "Virtually all the government servants employed at a high level in French and Dutch and one might add, Scottish diplomacy were puritans who looked to Leicester and Walsingham for support and preferment." So Tomson, in this respect ranks with Killigrew, Davison, Randolph and Beale--to mention only the most notable. He does differ from them, however, in that he appears to have been at the nexus of the presbyterian movement and to have had a long and active association with most of its leaders. In spite of this, his name is conspicuously absent from most of the Annals of the period. Tomson's name does not appear in Burnet's *History of the Reformation*, Strype's *Reformation Annals*, Brook's *Lives of the Puritans* or Neal's *History of the Puritans*.[3] Nowhere is he explicitly coupled with Cartwright, Travers or Gilby, and yet his standing must have been considerable with them as it was he who was instrumental in the downfall of Wilcox.[4] His role in the movement could thus be seen as that of a 'grey eminence', but his obscurity there is more than amply compensated for by his fame as a scholar, and especially as translator of Beza's Latin New Testament into English. This was published by Christopher Barker for the first time in 1576 and by 1587 it was accepted as the official New Testament in the English Geneva Bible. In view of this it is surprising that no attempt has been made so far at any biographical study of Tomson. Scott Pearson[5] confines himself to reproducing the biographical sketch in Wood's *Athenae Oxonienses* and Patrick Collinson only hints at the important role Tomson played in the presbyterian movement.

Laurence Tomson was born in Northamptonshire in 1539 and went up to Oxford in either 1553 (if we follow the Magdalen College Register)[6] or in 1556 (according to Wood) after being elected to a demiship and soon after became a "great proficient" in logic and philosophy. Magdalen, at the time under the presidency of Lawrence Humfrey, was the centre of Oxford Puritanism and it is worth noting that one of Tomson's contemporaries there was Francis Hastings, younger brother of Henry, the Earl of Huntingdon. Hastings was later to become one of the more effective Puritan laymen of the age and to cooperate with Tomson and Gilby in the Puritan movement.[7] Tomson took his BA on the 5th June 1559 and M.A. on 20th October 1564. He was admitted as Probationer Fellow in 1559 and attained to the status of Perpetual Fellow a year later. He was bursar from January until May 1565 when he and William Cole were given permission "unanimi consensu Domini Praesidis et officiariorum" to travel into foreign parts and to remain there for a year "studii liberioris ratione". They set out in July 1565 and were supposed to return within a year. But in December 1565 the governing body of Magdalen prolonged Tomson's leave until the first of July 1567. Unfortunately we do not know which "foreign parts" were the object of Tomson's journey. We do know that he accompanied Sir Thomas Hoby[8] on the latter's first and last embassy to France in 1566, which must have been the reason for the extension of his leave. The work with the Protestant diplomat was evidently Tomson's introduction to foreign affairs. In a letter dated 11th June 1566 Hoby tells Cecil that he "is sorry to hear their stir which is noised to be for the maintenance of Popish attire". Hoby was at the time engaged in discussions with the Duke of Anjou about the use of vestments in French Churches. Tomson probably became acquainted not only with the subject matter of those discussions, but also with the progress of affairs between France and Scotland generally. This knowledge he was to use later when helping Walsingham with the Mary Queen of Scots plot.

We do not know whether Tomson stayed abroad during the remaining months of his leave, after Hoby's death, or whether he returned to Oxford. If he did the former, it is likely that he spent some months as well as the first year of his leave, in Geneva, working on his translation of Beza's New Testament and giving public lectures in Hebrew which are alluded to in his epitaph.[9] Certainly such a pursuit would accord with the governing body's decree of "studii liberioris ratione". Unfortunately, owing to lack of evidence we can only make conjectures about this as well as about the question of Tomson ever coming into contact with Beza, while in Geneva. It seems unlikely that he would not have done, especially as Beza knew most of the leading English puritans personally, and a letter of his survives written to Walter Travers in 1580, asking for financial assistance for the city of Geneva, at war with Savoy. But there seems to be no extant correspondence between Beza and Tomson--not even a reference to Tomson is made in any of Beza's letters.

After returning to England in 1566 or 1567 Tomson spent about a year in Magdalen before setting off again--this time for Heidelberg where he is registered along with George Wither, Richard Seger and George Allen as a "nobilis Anglus". Tomson spent a year at Heidelberg and came back to England in 1569, when he resigned his fellowship in Oxford. Even so, his connections with the College were never totally severed and he was often consulted by the other Fellows in matters of difficulty. In a letter dated 24th July 1578 Richard Stanclyff writes to Tomson about the disorderly government and cheating in the University where he finds "injustice..malicious seeking of advantage and cruel subtilty". Many accuse Tomson of desiring the ruin of the colleges and especially of Magdalen. "They would talk as loud against Walsingham if they durst." Stanclyff goes on to say that he desires the appointment of impartial judges to decide the controversies respecting their statutes.[10]

More significant, however, is Tomson's connection with Laurence Humfrey, the President of Magdalen, who, along with Sampson, was "the original intellectual leader of Elizabethan Puritanism" and who, as tutor considered himself to be personally responsible for the care of "divers noblemen's sons". Although we do not know about Tomson's social origins there is no doubt that he came under Humfrey's care during his years at Magdalen. Interesting in this context is the letter which Tomson wrote to Humfrey in 1575, after the expulsion case.[11] It is a letter of very friendly advice which suggests close personal links between the two men. Tomson deplores the state of parties at Magdalen and censures Humfrey's proceding to such a severe measure as expulsion of Fellows in a case like this. This incident and Tomson's university career generally give us a good indication of the kind of course his life was to take. His two main interests, Puritanism and politics manifested themselves very early.

There are no details of his employment by Walsingham, but he must have attained to the office of Secretary around 1574. The importance of a man like Tomson holding this post cannot be under-estimated. Walsingham himself was a Marian exile, he was widely traveled and thoroughly acquainted with Continental Protestantism. In his biography of Walsingham, Conyers Read[12] says that the Queen's Secretary, although outwardly conformist did sympathize with the Reformers personally, and his household was a perfect hotbed of Puritanism. Apart from Tomson he employed Nicholas Faunt, a bitter critic of Whitgift's violent policy against the best and most zealous ministers, and Robert Beale who talked and wrote about the inquisitorial methods of the bishops and defied the archbishop of Canterbury. Beale was Walsingham's intimate friend, brother-in-law, and more than once, his substitute in office. In spite of that there is only one record of the Secretary registering any Puritan sympathies officially; his intercession to Whitgift on behalf of "one Wood, a Puritan". We can see, however, how acting as Walsingham's "right hand" would have given Tomson ample opportunities for manipulating the fate of English Puritanism--not just by means of recommendations etc. but also, indirectly, by political means. Particularly interesting in this context is Tomson's part in the Mary Queen of Scots affair, which we shall consider later.

A lot of work which he did for Walsingham, particularly in the realm of domestic and trade affairs was straightforward administration. In June 1572, when his name comes up for the first time in the Domestic Calendar of State Papers, Tomson campaigned for the establishment of a Mart Town in England and part of a historical description of a Mart Town in Flanders survives, written in his hand.[13] There he describes "the benefit to arise by the establishment of the same in England".

He was also involved in several trade matters and supported
(in December 1574) a charter of Incorporation of the Meer
Merchants who were conducting import-export traffic with
France (largely wine) to protect them against the encroach-
ments of retailers. In April 1576 he compounded a history
"of the matters in controversy between the Merchants of Hanze
Towns and the Merchant Adventurers". Tomson was M.P. for Weymouth and Melcombe Regis in 1575 and 1587 and for Downtown in
1588-9, but there is no record of whether he played any part
in the Puritan party activities prior to the opening of the
1589 Parliament.[14]

Far more involved, however, are Tomson's dealings in matters of foreign policy, and here it must be remembered that
Walsingham, "smooth organizer of an intelligence service equal
to that of Spain itself", set himself to wean Elizabeth from
her pro-Spanish Conservatism. He was convinced that England's
peril lay in a strong Spain, and her security in a free
Netherlands. On taking the office of Secretary he brought
with him a new group of Protestant enthusiasts who collective-
ly worked towards an Anglo-Netherlands alliance. Several
records of the period between 1577 and 1578 show that Tomson
was actively involved in this.[15]

William Davison, the former Secretary in Scotland to
Henry Killigrew was sent on a mission to the Netherlands in
1576 in order to finalize the alliance between Holland, Zee-
land and England. Some of the correspondence between him and
Walsingham (via Tomson) indicates that no efforts were spared
to aid and assist the Puritan cause during his stay in the Low
Countries. A letter written in June 1578 suggests that the
English agent was in touch with L'Oiseleur de Villers, a leading Dutch Presbyterian, protégé of Beza,[16] editor of annotations in Beza's New Testament and personal advisor to William
of Orange. Davison was sent two "advertisements" from Walsing-

ham and he was to "communicate that in French" to M. Villers. In October 1577 Merchant Adventurers wanted a chaplain and Walter Travers was nominated and sent over to receive Presbyterian ordination from L'Oiseleur de Villers and others. When, at a somewhat later date the governor of the Merchant Adventurers tried to put Travers to silence, Davison wrote to England on his behalf. This provoked a letter of encouragement from Tomson and eventually an open intervention from Walsingham in Travers' favour. Separately from that, Davison, acting on behalf of the English Congregation at Antwerp, wrote to Walsingham's Secretary, asking for a minister. Tomson handled the matter independently with no recourse to Walsingham; his reply to Davison points out that preaching is absolutely vital to salvation, and recommends that Davison should contact two people.[17] Apart from Davison, who was there in a diplomatic capacity, Rossell, a French Protestant and a secret agent in service to England was posted in the Netherlands whence he conveyed information to Tomson. Presumably Tomson would relay it to Walsingham at his discretion. In January 1578 Rossell reports that he was sent all the details of the negotiations between the Dutch and the Spanish, whereas Davison is handling the dispatch of the Ghent negotiations. Both Rossel and Davison repeatedly acknowledge their gratitude to Tomson and place their future fate and preferment in his hands. In 1590 Tomson was investigating reasons for discontentment in the Netherlands and he interviewed Evert Monkhoven[18] of Antwerp in connection with this.

Tomson made a detailed report of this interview which shows the extent to which he was involved. The general import of this report is as follows. Both the Nobles and the Commons are discontented in the Netherlands. The Nobles feel indignant about having been removed from government and the Commons resent the Spanish insolence and taxation. Tomson then asks

Monkhoven whether the burgesses of some towns including Antwerp, would be prepared to rise against the Spaniards. Monkhoven thinks that this could be effected, if the Marquess of Hensau, one of the more discontented Nobles, were prepared to lead them. Monkhoven, however, refuses to be the English agent for the purposes of suggesting the undertaking to the Marquess of Hensau and says that this would best be done by somebody of noble rank. He then proceeds to give Tomson a detailed breakdown of the Spanish garrisons stationed in various Dutch towns.

In interviewing Monkhoven, Tomson was obviously acting under orders to estimate the possibility of there being a revolt in the Netherlands in 1590.[19] From 1577-1590 Tomson was engaged in furthering the Anglo-Netherland alliance and so promoting the Puritan cause. He played a very similar part in the Mary Queen of Scots affair, where he actually did some intelligence work himself. In 1579 Walsingham, believing that the Pope was the root of all evil, dispatched Tomson to Boulogne for talks with the Papal Agent. He informed Tomson that the Pope intended to send an army against England under the leadership of Jacomo Bonacampanini[20] in order to deprive Elizabeth both of her throne and of her life. The enterprise was to be assisted by the Duke of Guise and other powerful princes and apparently had many supporters among the English themselves. This, however, was not the end of Tomson's investigations. His private report of meeting with the papal agent was incorporated into a much more comprehensive enquiry into "Practises to trouble her Majesty's state", based on letters to Mary Queen of Scots which Tomson intercepted. Emphasis is placed throughout the report, on the entente between Spain and the Pope seeking help from the "fifth column" of Catholics in England in order to put Mary Queen of Scots on the throne and depose Elizabeth. Implicit in the report is the suggestion that Elizabeth ought to abandon any political flirtations with Spain as her and England's safety lies only in the alliance with the Protestant Netherlands. Just how imminent this foreign invasion of England is Tomson illustrates by stating that the King of Spain has been in collusion with James Fitzmorris, the beginner of the rebellion in Ireland. Moreover ground is being prepared by large numbers of Catholic priests and Jesuits coming into England. Significantly Tomson asserts that the invasion will take place "as soon as (the King of Spain) should have brought the Low Countries to his obedience as appeareth in the direction and advise he gave Don Juan upon his commission in these words: 'Et par la dormera loy a tous ses voisins lequels a present luis tiennent le pied sur la gorge nourrissant cette guerre intestine pour opprimer la grandeur de sa Majeste.'"[21] Pope Pius V and the Duke of Guise are also implicated in this. Marriage, as another way of delivering Mary, was practiced by the late Duke of Norfolk "as by the confessions of sondrie persons and records appeareth". Tomson, in his report, claims that the "chief instruments herein were Roalph and Guerras, the one her agent for the Pope, the other for King Philip". His source of information for this was Julio Bussino, Florentine Secretary to Girauldi, the Portuguese Ambassador. The report on "Practises to trouble her Majesty's state" was evidently presented to Walsingham. Whether it went beyond that we do not know. Its overall Protestant tone and purpose, however, cannot be questioned and shows clearly the nature of Tomson's *political* involvement in the general cause of Puritanism.

There is also evidence for his involvement with the English Presbyterian movement. Although it is difficult to estimate the extent to which he was involved, we can, from the evidence available, point to two distinct periods when Tomson was active among the English Presbyterians; firstly, during the first spate of Puritan pamphlets from the secret press during the years 1572-4; secondly during the Puritan parliamentary campaign 1584-1589. During that period Tomson was M.P. first for Weymouth and Melcombe Regis, then for Downton. Tomson's name does not figure anywhere in connection with the vestments controversy but he probably had not yet engaged in Puritan activity at the time. From the Baker manuscript,[22] our best guide to Puritan affairs between 1572 and 1580, it transpires that the links between the groups of leading Puritans were very close. It also appears that the people who formed this group were Field, Wilcox, Sampson, Gilby, Cartwright and Tomson. The role played by Francis Hastings, although less explicit must have been, nonetheless, important. He is mentioned twice in the "Gilby correspondence", once by Tomson as "bringing the second Admonition to Gilby" and once by Humfrey who asks to be "commended to Mr. Hastings".

In 1572 Gilby is said to have met Wilcox, Sampson and others privately in London and agreed to help in the compilation of an "Admonition to Parliament". The conference resulted in two very bitter pamphlets declaring the Puritans' hostility towards episcopacy and demanding a constitution without Bishops. Field and Wilcox made an attempt to present it to Parliament and for this they were committed to Newgate in June 1572. Their correspondence with Gilby, dating from the period of their imprisonment, suggests a great deal of personal reliance on the rector of Ashby de la Zouche.[23] Wilcox writing in February 1573 mentions that the Commissioners caused "Beza his confession translated[24] into English to be burned in the Stationers' Hall...the pretence was, for that it was ill-translated but I suppose rather, because it overplainly dissolveth that Popish hierarchy which they yet maintain". He then entrusts his services to Father Gilby and asks for prayers.

Sampson, who became Master of Wigston Hospital in Leicester from 1567, after being deprived of the Christ Church deanery over the vestments controversy, writes to Gilby in 1584 thanking him "for his loving letter" and saying that he "has well advised upon [Gilbie's] counsel"--it is not stated over what matter. Humfrey, although not mentioned by Bancroft[25] as one of the "Admonition" conspirators also keeps up cordial relations with Gilbie and makes an arrangement with him as regards his son's coming to Oxford.

The tone of Tomson's letters to Gilby is different from all the others. All his letters date from the years 1572-1574 and we know that from 1572 until at least 1573 he was resident in Leicester. Unfortunately there are no details of his activities there; however, his letters suggest that he was in some way associated with the Puritan press. His letters to Gilby are impersonal in tone. They contain no acknowledgements of previous correspondence from Ashby de la Zouche, no personal reference to Gilby's family, and there is nothing in them which might throw a light on Tomson's own position or state of mind at the time--not even a general reference to the cause of "further Reformation". Every one of the four letters deals with a point of business and three of them in fact are concerned with Cartwright's *Reply to the Answer*.[26] The immediacy of the news in each letter would suggest that Tomson had links with sources of information (probably in London) via Hastings which were inaccessible to Gilby.

The letter dated Leicester, 1st March 1572, is obviously written in reply to Gilby and refers to Fulke's book *A Briefe and Plain Declaration containing the Desires of all those Ministers who seek Discipline and Reformation of the Church of England*. The letter implies that Christopher Goodman was in charge of the Puritan press at the time, but throws no light whatsoever upon Tomson's own connection with the press. All it makes clear is that Tomson had access to certain pamphlets before anybody else. This is corroborated by his letter to Gilby dated 21st March 1572 where Tomson communicates news of "another Admonition" to the hitherto ignorant Gilby and says that Francis Hastings will bring it to him. He then goes on to inform him about Whitgift's answer to the first Admonition "wherein he chargeth the Authors of it and all that favour it with Arianism, Puritanism and very often with Rebellion and Treason and joining hands with the Papists to subvert both the State ecclesiastical and Temporal....Greater bitterness of words I have not read in any, beside that he condemneth us as void of all learning (etc.)...." The next letter is dated 19th May 1573 where, with no acknowledgement of a reply from Gilby, Tomson says that the Queen has read Cartwright's *Reply to the Answer* and has forbidden "the enemy of truth", Whitgift, to answer it--"at least that is what is rumoured in London". The rumour is never officially confirmed in any way and does, in fact, seem rather dubious in view of the fact that on 11 June 1573 a royal proclamation enjoined the suppression of both the Admonition and its Defence. In December that year the Court of High Commission issued a warrant for the arrest of Cartwright who, consequently, fled the country and went at first to Heidelberg and then to Antwerp. Accordingly on 4th April 1574 Tomson wrote to Gilby. "We have heard of late from our Brother Thomas Cartwright, who, God be thanked, is well and thereupon we have taken such advice as God gives us. It was at the same time put unto you by our Brethren to draw forth a confession of our faith--that it may wel appeare to the world that we are in dede."

It is difficult to decide just how reliable a guide these letters are to the nature of Tomson's involvement in the Puritan Movement. It does appear from them, however, that Tomson was rather on the outside of the main movement, and was not on intimate terms with its leaders. His main contribution seems to have been the supplying of information, but because of the paucity of evidence, this could well be a tendentious conclusion.

It is interesting to note that, from the moment of his becoming Walsingham's Secretary, Tomson's direct contact with the Puritan divines appears to cease and, although he continues to demonstrate his Presbyterian connections, he does so by Parliamentary means. Not much information survives about his religious career during the late seventies and the early eighties. We know, however, that he was operative in bringing about the downfall of Wilcox when the latter went up before Aylmer, the Bishop of London, for contumacy. In the same year (1577) Tomson's name was put forward for the English Ministry Candidature at Antwerp, but Walter Travers was sent and ordained by Cartwright and L'Oiseleur de Villers. In 1576 he had published his translation of Beza's New Testament and also "A Treatise of the Excellencie of the Christian Man and how he may be knowen". This he translated from the "French of Peter de la Place" and dedicated to Mrs. Ursula Walsingham. Tomson got married sometime before 11th October 1579, a date on which N. Martin and N. Carey[27] in the name of the bailiff and jurists of Guernsey, wrote to Tomson concerning the complaints against their rule and sent him the petticoats made in the island, one for himself and one for his wife. In 1579 his translation of "the sermons of Calvin on Epistles of St. Paul to Timothie and Titus" was printed.[28] In 1582 Tomson was in attendance at court in Windsor, and then he moved to London.

He was elected M.P. for Weymouth and Melcombe Regis as nominee of the second Earl of Bedford--"a peer who for his charity and his Puritan sympathies may be likened to the Earl of Huntingdon, exercised a territorial authority not dissimilar to that of the Duke of Norfolk".[29] His influence was felt throughout the West Country and he nominated for Members of Parliament a whole series of Puritans with court connections; Francis Walsingham for Lyme Regis in 1563, George Carleton for Dorchester in 1571; so in January, 1576, on the death of a member, he nominated Tomson for Weymouth and Melcome Regis. In 1584 and 1586 Tomson secured his own re-election having access to court favours as Walsingham's secretary. In the Weymouth and Melcombe Regis documents[30] a draft of a letter survives informing Mr. Tomson that he has been chosen M.P. "as one in whom our onlye...confidence whollye relieth". There also survives a letter written in 1586 by the Mayor "to my Lord of Warwick". In it, the Mayor says that "he has given to him the motion of one of the Burgesses of Melcombe Regis side to be joyned with Laurence Tomson gent and with a nominee of the Earl of Pembroke and E. Phillipes gent". We know practically nothing about Tomson's work inside his constituency, but we do know that he played a fairly important part in the Parliamentary Puritan pressure groups. In 1584-5 classes conducted a survey of the ministries with the object of showing that the ministers who were being kept away were more competent than the ones appointed by Whitgift. Petitions for reform were drawn up and eventually Mildmay contravened his sovereign's orders and proposed a committee of thirteen moderate men to study the petitions. Later, "concerning the weight of this business required a greater number", the House doubled its size and a number of hard-core Puritans were added. Among those were Robert Beale, James Morice, William Stoughton and Laurence Tomson. Mildmay's committee met and the petition was presented to the Lords where it was answered by Whitgift in vitriolic and opprobrious terms. The Commons were not at all satisfied and Tomson is known to have commented on Whitgift's answer: "rather a discourse than any resolution of a divine". This particular parliamentary debate was followed by a spate of Martin Marprelate tracts and again, it is an open question to what extent, if at all, Tomson was involved in this. The only evidence that survives is a letter written by him "to Mistress Crane", from Laleham (near East Molesey) on 26th February 1585/6. The letter is signed "Your most obedient sonne Laurence Tomson"[31] and it has been written in haste to answer six questions of doctrine touching on the salvation of Papists, considering whether Papists dying as they lived (that is enemies of the doctrine of Christ) can be saved. Scott Pearson in his book *Cartwright and the Elizabethan Puritanism* suggests a connection between the early Puritan tracts of the seventies and the later Martin Marprelate pamphlets, common factors being the style and the person of John Field. Scott Pearson goes on to suggest that, most probably, material for the Marprelate tracts was being amassed as early as 1572. In view of this it is interesting to consider the extent of Tomson's information about the various 1572/73 tracts, and it seems perfectly possible that he had some connection with the central person or body responsible for amassing the material for the Marprelate tracts. Unfortunately, owing to lack of evidence we can only speculate about this.

Tomson's parliamentary activity continued and in 1585 he sat on the Committee responsible for reviving the bill for the establishment of the Geneva Prayer Book in place of the Elizabethan Prayer Book and setting up a presbyterian system of ministers and elders. Tomson retired on Walsingham's death in 1590, published *Tears of Mary* in 1596, died in Chertsey, Surrey, in 1608 and was buried there. His life and work suggest that Tomson, rather like L'Oiseleur de Villers, combined the functions of scholar, civil servant and Puritan. Although, as his reference to Cartwright[32] suggests, his sympathies were strongly presbyterian, all his actions in that sphere are characterized by care and caution. Thus, although Tomson trans-

lated Beza's Latin New Testament and associated himself with
Humfrey, his name is not associated with any of the truly
controversial Presbyterian tracts, and there is no suggestion
that he was ever "on the wrong side" of the Elizabethan government. Such work as he did for the English Presbyterians and
for the Puritan cause generally was either of an undercover or
of an official parliamentary nature.

So far we have outlined Tomson's political career and the
nature and scope of his involvement in the English Puritan
movement. We shall now examine his theological works in order
to discover his preoccupations in that sphere. We shall also
summarize the relationship between Tomson's New Testament of
1576 and the AV of 1611.

In 1576 Tomson published his translation of L'Oiseleur's
edition of Beza's New Testament. This version, as has been
said above,[33] showed a closer agreement with Beza than the
1560 Geneva Bible, particularly in matters of text. Although
Tomson also agreed with Beza on points of doctrine such as the
direct inheritance of the original sin it cannot be said that
either L'Oiseleur's edition or Tomson's translation of it contained anything controversial insofar as the question of Church
Government was concerned. In this context it is interesting to
examine L'Oiseleur's and Tomson's notes at 1 Cor. VI.1 and
1 Thess. V.12 and compare them with notes on the same places
in Beza's 1565 version.

    1 Cor. VI.1.

        L'Oiseleur: Tertia quaestio de forensibus iudiciis.
An liceat fideli fidelem ad infidelium tribunalia trahere. Respondet, non licere, propter offendiculum videlicet. Neque
enim per se malum est.

        Tomson: Third question of civile judgements.
Whither it be lawful for one faithfull to drawe an other faithful before the judgement seate of an infidell? He answereth

that it is not lawfull for offence sake, for it is not evill of itself.

Beza: having made the same point, he adds: "Istiusmodi audiendis disceptationibus minime adhibendos esse Pastores, Doctores, aliosve Ecclesiae Gubernatores aut Diaconos in suis sacris functionibus plus satis occupatos; sed alios potius quosvis ex iis quos postea *Laicos* vocarunt, commodius istis huius vitae negotiis illa igitur Apostolica doctrina... quod si attente, ut oportuit, a veteribus illis Episcopis... fuisset consideratum, neque seipsos tot laboribus fatigassent...neque suis posteris invadendae Magistratuum potestati aditum patefecissent."

Thus Beza here makes an explicit condemnation of the Canon Law, a condemnation which is not incorporated by either L'Oiseleur[34] or Tomson into their New Testament.

1 Thess. V.12.

L'Oiseleur: "Habenda magna ratio eorum qui verbi ministerio et Ecclesiae gubernationi praefecti sunt a Deo et officio suo funguntur."

Tomson: "We must have greater consideration of them which are appointed to the ministerie of the word and government of the Church by God and do their duetie."

Beza: makes the same point but adds "Apparet ex hoc loco et aliis a presbyterio fuisse in communi gubernatam ecclesiam, nondum Episcopatus ordine in superiorem gradu commutato."

Again, both L'Oiseleur and Tomson leave out Beza's overt reference to presbytery as the basic unit of Church government. It should be noted that both Tomson and L'Oiseleur, in the case of 1 Cor. VI.1 and 1 Thess. V.12, are simply reproducing Beza's annotationes minores (in accord with their general practice).[35] It is interesting to see, however, that neither of the two scholars chooses to add to the annotationes minores the more definite statements made by Beza in the annotationes majores.

In the same year (1576) Tomson's translation of *Treatise of the Excellencie of the Christian man* came out from the press of Christopher Barker. The French author of the book, Pierre de la Place, was "one of the King's Counsel and chiefe President of his Court of Aides in Paris". He was also one of the Huguenots murdered during the St. Bartholomew's Eve massacre in Paris. In Tomson's translation, the dedicatory epistle to Mistress Ursula Walsingham--on whose orders Tomson first perused the book--is followed by "a briefe description of the life and death of the said author to the end that everie one may knowe what he was". The 'briefe description' contains an account of La Place's conversion from Catholicism and his staunch upholding of the reformed faith.

The treatise itself concerns itself with the question: what constitutes a Christian man? La Place makes it plain that man is unable to become a Christian by his own powers, since he is unable to distinguish between good and evil. Man cannot distinguish between good and evil because he has been made corrupt through the fall of Adam, and therefore can rely only on the grace of God for enlightenment and salvation. However, La Place goes on to say, not all men can rely on grace. The 'Christian man' was chosen by God before the world was made "to...set him apart, to exempt him from the common state and condition of all other men". Before creating the world God foresaw that, as the first man was "pliable to good and evill having not that given to him to continue and stande steadily in that state wherein he was placed", he would inevitably fall. La Place then goes on to outline the attributes of Christian man in greater detail, and to specify the qualities of false or apparent Christians. This brief summary of the contents of the Treatise throws light on what seem to be the outstanding feature of La Place's theology: the supralapsarian doctrine of predestination and election. La Place's views here extend beyond Calvin's pronouncements on election, providence and the original sin (although they are in agreement with Beza's views on the doctrines). We do not intend to assert here that Calvin's doctrine of election and predestination taken by itself was different from that of La Place or Beza. However, it is important to remember that Calvin, in the 1559 edition of the *Institutio*,[36] links up predestination not with the doctrine of Providence but with the doctrine of Redemption. Both La Place and Beza in the *Tractationes Theologicae* link it up with the doctrine of God's eternal purpose.

Closely linked to the doctrine of predestination and election is the idea that God foreordained the fall of man. In Calvin's writings this idea is implicit, but he does affirm man's entire responsibility for the fall.[37] Both La Place and Beza,[38] on the other hand, stress the totally predetermined nature of the Fall.

We see from this that Tomson, in translating de la Place, was closer to the theology of Beza than to that of Calvin.

Three years later, however, in 1579, Tomson translated from the French, Calvin's sermons on Timothy and Titus. The work appeared under the English title[39] *Sermons of M. John Calvin on the Epistles of St. Paule to Timothie and Titus, translated out of French into English by L.T.* and was printed in London by G. Bishop and T. Woodcoke. In view of Tomson's earlier adherence to the more extreme doctrines of La Place and Beza his exact translation of Calvin's work seems rather surprising.[40] Moreover, it is difficult to find any event in Tomson's life or career that might have occasioned the translation of this particular work.

Before considering possible explanations, however, we shall give a brief description of both the translation and the original. For the purpose of this discussion we shall be concentrating on the epistles to Timothy.

Calvin's sermons contain a preface by Conrad Badius addressed exclusively to the Genevan people. The preface is followed by Calvin's summary of the doctrines contained in Timothy and Titus. The summary of 1 Timothy contains a condemnation of vain disputes such as those practiced by the Jews and by the Scholastic theologicans. In the summary of II Timothy Calvin makes the following points: (1) Paul says that all men should be prayed for publicly especially the princes and the magistrates (since God wants all men to be saved). (2) Having shown "combien c'est une charge excellente d'estre L'Eveque" Paul describes a proper Bishop and lists the qualities he should have. (3) Paul condemns false doctrines such as celibacy or fasting as useless fables.

Tomson does not translate any of Calvin's summaries, and appends his own preface saying that the reader may "take it as a great benefite to bee made partaker of that bread which is broken to thy fellowe brethren so farre distant from thee".

The actual text of Calvin's sermons is translated word for word by Tomson. Thus election is linked up with Christ and his work,[41] and Calvin's idea of Church government is expounded in full. This includes the definition of a Bishop and his duties. A Bishop, according to Calvin and Tomson, is not to be taken in the Papist sense of the word, but simply to mean a teacher and governor in the Church. There is no differentiation in the Scriptures between the functions of shepherd, minister, bishop and elder.[42] The office of Deacon is also described; although, primarily, deacons are appointed to take care of the poor, all church officers can be called deacons, i.e. ministers or servants.

A possible clue as to why Tomson translated Calvin's sermons on Timothy lies in the ambiguity of Calvin's views on

Church Government: although Calvin suggests that the office of a Bishop is no different from that of a minister, he does not, however, condemn the office in any explicit way. He also acknowledges tacitly a need for some kind of hierarchy in the Church.

Another clue may be found in Calvin's insistence on the necessity for civil order. Tomson, translating Calvin word for word, states explicitly, "Hereby we see that the state of Princes and the ministers of justice is not contrary to Christianitie as some phantastical heads have thought...."

Already in 1572, Tomson, writing to Gilby about Fulke's book *A Briefe and Plain Declaration containing the Desires of all those Ministers who seek Discipline and Reformation of the Church of England*,[43] pointed out, "I cannot tell what we should do with that book of M. Fulke's neither would I wish M. Goodman to let it go. For if it should chance to be put forth by them, it might hurt the cause. You know there are certain things in it not agreed upon and those of weight."[44] Tomson was evidently referring to Fulke's suggestion that higher assemblies were not necessary in church government and all important decisions should be referred to "the whole multitude".[45] Fulke's manuscript remained unpublished until 1584.

In 1566 *The Fortress of Fathers* had been published anonymously in England. The author of the book, calling himself J. B., was in favour of advocating some kind of resistance to the magistrate.[46] The same issue had been highlighted by the vestments controversy as a whole, and was, to some extent, resuscitated by the imprisonment of Field and Wilcox in 1572.

It is difficult to decide whether Tomson's restrained and ambiguous attitude to the issues of Church Government and civil law was an attempt to safeguard the Puritan cause as a whole or merely a strategem to protect himself. The problem becomes even more complex when we consider the existence of a copy of the 1574 edition of *Ecclesiasticae Disciplinae et Anglicanae Ecclesiae ab illa aberrationis plena e verbo Dei et dilucida explicatio*.[47] This book, printed by Adamus del Monte, is universally attributed to Walter Travers. One copy of it, however, sold in the Napier sale at Sotheby's, London, in March 1886, contains this MS note: "Laurentius Tompsonus. Oxoniensis theologus doctissimus est hujus libri author, 1574." No other external evidence points to Tomson's authorship of the *Ecclesiastical Discipline*. It is not inconceivable that Tomson might have collaborated with Travers on the book. It is even more likely that he was the instigator of the idea which Travers simply put into practice, seeing as Tomson was reticent and ambiguous about his views on Church Government, and that he was happy to translate both La Place's and Calvin's views on the doctrine of election.

We shall now discuss the *Ecclesiastical Discipline* and consider whether it is likely, in view of Tomson's career and his general involvement in the Puritan movement, that he was the grey eminence behind Travers' work.

The book is principally concerned with the government within particular congregations: the wider issues of Church Government are merely touched upon. Travers is in favour of the congregation being ruled by a consistory but he emphasizes that the consistory should comprise a few of the best and that only they should bear the rule. Travers is thus opposed to Fulke's idea that important decisions should be made by the multitude.

He then defines the offices within the congregation. He says that there are two kinds of Bishops (episcopi): doctors and pastors. The function of doctors is to expound the Scriptures and the function of pastors is to adapt the Scriptures to various occasions (ad varios usus accomodare). He defines deacons as those officers who fulfill all ecclesiastical duties "praeter eam quae in sermone versatur". The office of deacon is subdivided into *distributores* who are in charge of alms and *seniores* who look after the moral welfare of individuals.

We can see that Travers' views on Church discipline are less extreme than Fulke's and that they are not too far removed from those of Calvin. Travers does not openly condemn the office of Bishop and, like Calvin in Timothy, says that the name covers a variety of church offices. He defines the office of deacon rather more closely than Calvin but agrees with the Genevan leader in saying that the particular duties of a deacon are concerned with the poor.

In view of this large measure of agreement between Calvin and Travers, we find it not unlikely that Tomson might have instigated the composition of *Ecclesiastical Discipline*.

It now remains to summarize the influence of Tomson's 1576 New Testament on the Revisers, which has already been discussed in the earlier chapters. We should remember that, by 1611, Tomson's New Testament had been incorporated into the Geneva Bible, albeit not in its entirety. For the purposes of this discussion, however, we shall be referring to both the Geneva 1560 New Testament and to Tomson's New Testament. We have already examined the influence of Beza on the AV books of Matthew (pp. 44-65) and Romans (pp. 113-123). We now propose to review the AV readings in Matthew and Romans discussed above, and estimate (a) the number of readings which come directly from Beza, (b) the number of readings which come from Beza and have the support of the Geneva Bible, (c) the number of readings which come from Beza and have the support of Tomson. AV readings where the influence of Beza is not clear will not be considered here.

In Matthew we notice an agreement between Geneva and Tomson in the case of 15 readings (II.11, IV.10, V.47, VI.2(2), VI.34, VII.3, VIII.18, X.9, XI.28, XIII.11, XV.5/6, XVIII.19,

XIX.28, XX.23, XXI.37). Only three of those, however (II.11, IV.10, VIII.18), show an agreement between Geneva and Tomson and Beza. Thus Tomson and Geneva go against Beza in twelve cases. We see, on the other hand, that Beza seems to influence directly 16 readings in the AV Matthew (V.18, V.21, V.47, VI.2, VI.2(2), VI.34, VII.3, IX.16, X.9, XI.28, XIV.2, XV.5/6, XVIII.19, XIX.28, XX.23, XXI.37). Eleven of those readings are the ones where both Tomson and Geneva go against Beza (V.47, VI.2(2), VI.34, VII.3, X.9, XV.5/6, XVIII.19, XIX.28, XX.23, XXI.37). There are eight readings in the AV where the Bezan influence may be traced to Geneva and Tomson (II.16, V.29, VI.2, VI.7, VII.23, IX.16, XII.18, XIV.2 [margin]). There are three readings where the Bezan influence may be traced to the Geneva version (II.6 [margin], III.9, VIII.32) and three readings where the Bezan influence is also shown by Tomson's N.T. (IV.12, XVIII.26, XXVI.26).

In Romans there are four cases (I.1, I.20, III.9, XI.31) where Geneva and Tomson show mutual agreement but differ from corresponding AV readings. In the case of three of those readings (I.9, I.20, III.9) Geneva and Tomson agree with Beza whilst the AV adopts another reading. In one case (XI.31) Geneva and Tomson go against Beza whereas the AV adopts a Bezan reading.

There are four readings in AV Romans (I.9 [margin], I.28, IV.17, XII.26) where the Bezan influence is also shown in the texts of Tomson and Geneva. There is also one case (V.12 [margin]) where the AV Bezan reading may be traced to Tomson.

From this, it is difficult to estimate how much independent influence Tomson had on the Revisers. We can see, however, that, especially in Matthew, the Revisers seem to be more influenced by Beza than either Geneva or Tomson. This does not necessarily mean that they are more Puritan when we consider that the readings in question are concerned with stylistic and textual rather than with doctrinal points, and that the Revisers do not append any doctrinal notes in the margin. We can also see a large measure of agreement between Tomson and Geneva, which suggests that Tomson must, at least, have referred to the 1560 Geneva when translating L'Oiseleur's edition of Beza's Latin New Testament.

We have now examined Tomson's life and career, his works and the relationship of the 1576 New Testament to the English Geneva Bible and the AV. We have seen that Tomson's involvement with the Puritan leaders of his day was characterized by caution. We have also discovered that while his views on the doctrines of election, predestination, original sin and the Eucharist were more extreme than Calvin's, yet his views on Church government were no less conservative than those held by Calvin. He was against Fulke's notions of Church discipline and he translated Calvin's sermons on Timothy, compromising his earlier view of election in order to put across a more restrained view of Church government. A large measure of agreement between Calvin's and Travers' view on this suggests that Tomson might well have instigated the composition of *Ecclesiastical Discipline*.

So far as his New Testament is concerned, Tomson avoids statements on Church Government and shows a large measure of agreement with the Geneva version although he is more "Bezan" than the Geneva translators in his pronouncements on the Eucharist and the original sin. His views on the latter are incorporated into the AV margin, although, generally speaking, his influence on the AV is not significantly different from that of the Geneva version.

NOTES

1. First published in a shortened form, under the title of "Laurence Tomson (1539-1608) and Elizabethan Puritanism", *Journal of Ecclesiastical History*, 28 (1977), pp. 17-27.

2. Patrick Collinson, *The Elizabethan Puritan Movement*, (1971), p. 166.

3. G. Burnet, *The History of the Reformation of the Church of England*, 3 vols. (Dublin, 1730). B. Brook, *The Lives of the Puritans*, 3 vols. (London, 1813). D. Neal, *The history of the puritans or protestant non-conformists from the Reformation under Henry VIII to the act of Toleration under William and Mary with an account of their principles*, 2 vols. (London, 1754). J. Strype, *Annals of the Reformation and establishment of religion and other various occurrences in the Church of England with an appendix or repository of original papers*, 3 vols. (London, 1709).

4. See Collinson, *op. cit.*, p. 238.

5. A. F. Scott Pearson, *Thomas Cartwright and Elizabethan Puritanism 1535-1603*, (Cambridge, 1925).

6. J. R. Bloxam, *The Magdalen College Register*, (1873), IV, p. 138.

7. For full account of Hastings' role in the Puritan movement see M. C. Cross, "An Example of Lay Intervention in the Elizabethan Church", *Studies in Church History*, II, pp. 273-82.

8. Sir Thomas Hoby (1530-1566). Studied at St. John's College, Cambridge, died in France in 1566. He translated Martin Bucer's *Gratulation unto the Church of England for the restitution of Christ's religion* (see *Calendar of State Papers*, Foreign, 1566-8).

9. The epitaph is reproduced in A. Wood's *Athenae Oxonienses*, II, (ed. Bliss, 1815), p. 44.

10. Bloxam, *op. cit.*, IV, p. 141.

11. Bloxam, *op. cit.*, IV, p. 142.

12. Conyers Read, *Mr. Secretary Walsingham and the Policy of Queen Elizabeth*, 3 vols. (Cambridge, 1925), II, p. 261.

13. Bloxam, *op. cit.*, IV, p. 142.

14. J. Neale, *The Elizabethan House of Commons*, (1949), *passim*.

15. *Calendar of State Papers*, Foreign, 1577-78. The documents suggest that the English Puritans supported the cause of Anjou only as long as it was also Elizabeth's cause.

16. For relations between Beza and L'Oiseleur see M. J. de Vries, *Pepinière du calvinisme hollandais*, (1918), II, p. 204.

17. *Calendar of State Papers*, Foreign, 1577-1578, p. 384.

18. MS Cotton, Galba D. VII. fol. 163.

19. For full account of the 1590 revolt in the Netherlands, see Pieter Geyl, *The Revolt of the Netherlands*, (1958), pp. 219ff.

20. MS Cotton, Caligula C. V. fol. 113.

21. MS Perrot 9772, fol. 27.

22. MS Baker XXXII.

23. See for instance Field's letter to Gilby written in August, 1572 (MS Baker XXXII), where Field says "So our present Calamitie and the trouble threatened against the Churche of God, compell me to wryte unto you, as to one in whome all the godlie have conceived such opinion, as of a Father...."

24. Theodore Beza, *A briefe and pithie summe of the Christian faith made in forme of a confession*, translated by R.F., (London, R. Hall, 1563, 1565, 1566, 1572, 1585, 1589).

25. Richard Bancroft, *Daungerous positions and proceedings, published and practised within this island of Brytaine, under pretence of reformation and for the presbiteriall discipline*, (London, J. Wolfe, 1593).

26. Thomas Cartwright, *A replye to an answere made of m. doctor Whitgift Agaynste the Admonition to the Parliament*, (Wandsworth, J.S. c. 1574).

27. *C.S.P.*, Domestic, *Addenda* 1566-79, p. 563-8.

28. Bloxam, *op. cit.*, IV, p. 140.

29. Neale, *op. cit.*, p. 196.

30. H. J. Moule, ed., *Descriptive catalogue of the charters, minute books and other documents of the borough of Weymouth and Melcombe Regis A.D. 1252 to 1800*, (Weymouth, 1883), II, 58, 72.

31. A. Peel, ed., *The Seconde Parte of a Register...* (Cambridge, 1915), II, 48.

32. MS Baker XXXII. Letter from Tomson to Gilby, April 1574: "We have heard of late from our Brother Tom. Cart. who God be thanked, is wel." Cartwright during his exile was evidently in secret communication with Tomson.

33. Ch. I, pp. 18-28.

34. Although L'Oiseleur was a Huguenot, he was also a refugee and hence had to proceed carefully if he was to attain status in England.

35. For full account of this see Ch. I, pp. 18-28.

36. *Inst.* 1, 15.8.

37. *Inst.* 1, 15.8.

38. Note on Luke XXII.22 in the *Annotationes*.

39. *Sermons de Jean Calvin sur les deux epistres de Sainct Paul à Timothée et sur L'Epistre a Tite*, (Geneva, Jean Bonnefroy, 1563).

40. It is difficult to know how much emphasis should be placed on this. Tomson, after all, was not a "systematic" theologian but a public servant susceptible to pressure from patrons.

41. Tomson, *op. cit.*, 3rd sermon on 1 Timothy ch. 2, p. 154.

42. Tomson, *op. cit.*, 20th sermon on 1 Timothy ch. III, p. 237.

43. At that time Fulke, after narrowly missing the mastership of St. John's, Cambridge, was appointed chaplain to the Earl of Leicester and was given the livings of Warley in Essex and Dennington in Suffolk. The links fostered between Fulke and Gilby by Leicester's common patronage would make Gilby personally concerned with Fulke's book, apart from its general importance to the Puritan cause.

44. MS Baker XXXII.

45. See also Collinson, *op. cit.*, p. 108.

46. See Leonard J. Trinterud, ed., *Elizabethan Puritanism*, (1971), pp. 67-126.

47. In the Bodleian Library (8° Rawl 1072). The book was printed at La Rochelle.

BIBLIOGRAPHY

Primary Sources

(a) MANUSCRIPTS

   MS Baker XXXII (now in Cambridge University Library)

   MS Cotton, Caligula C.V. fol. 113 (British Library)

   MS Cotton, Galba D. VII. fol. 163 (British Library)

   MS Perrott 9772 fol. 27 (Bodleian Library)

(b) PRINTED BOOKS

Abbot, G. *An exposition upon the prophet Jonah contained in certaine Sermons preached at S. Maries Church in Oxford,* (Richard Fell, London, 1600).

Bancroft, R. *Dangerous positions and proceedings published and practised within this island of Brytaine, under pretence of reformation and the presbiteriall discipline,* (London, F. Wolfe, 1593).

Beza, Theodorus Vezelius. *Confessio Christianae fidei et eiusdem collatio cum papisticis haeresibus,* (Geneva, E. Vignon, 1587).

Beza, Theodorus Vezelius. *A briefe and piththie summe of the Christian faith made in forme of a confession,* (London, R. Hall, 1565).

Jesu Christi Domini nostri Novum Testamentum Graece et Latine Theodoro Beza interprete, (Geneva, H. Stephanus, 1565).

Novum Testamentum Theodoro Beza interprete; additae sunt summae breves doctrinae in Evangelistas et Acta Apostolorum, item methodus apostolicarum epistolarum ab eodem authore; paucis etiam additis ex Joachimi Camerarii notationibus in Evangelistas et Acta, (London, Th. Vautrollier, 1574).

Jesu Christi Domini nostri Testamentum sive Novum foedus, Cuius graeco textui respondent interpretationes duae; una, vetus; altera, nova, Theodori Bezae. Eiusdem Theodori Bezae annotationes, (Geneva, E. Vignon, 1598).

Master Bezaes Sermons upon the three first Chapters of the Canticle of Canticles, (Joseph Barnes, Oxford, 1587).

The Holy Bible (Bishops' black letter, with the original MS corrections prepared for the new edition appointed by King James I), (London, R. Barker, 1602).

Bullinger, H. *Commentarii in...Pauli Epistolas atque etiam in Epistolam ad Hebraeos*, (1582).

Camerarius, J. *Notatio figurarum sermonis et mutatae simplicis elecutionis in apostolicis scriptis ad perspiciendam sententiam auctorum accuratam*, (Leipzig, 1572).

Sermons of M. John Calvin on the Epistles of S. Paule to Timothie and Titus translated out of French into English by L. T., (G. Bishop & T. Woodcock, London, 1579).

Sermons de Jean Calvin sur les deux Epistres de Sainct Paul a Timothee et sur l'Epistre a Tite, (Jean Bonnefroy, Geneva, 1563).

Camerarius, J., *Commentarius in Novum Foedus*, (1642).

Cartwright, T. *A Commentary upon the Epistle of Saint Paule written to the Colossians*, (London, Nicholas Okes, 1612).

The Bible and holy Scriptures conteyned in the Olde and New Testament translated according to the Ebrue and Greek, (Geneva, Roland Hall, 1560).

Novum Testamentum ab Erasmo Roterdamo recognitum et emendatum, (Basle, Froben, 1535).

La Bible qui est toute la sainte escriture du Vieil et du Nouveau Testament, (Geneva, 1588).

Junius, F. *Apostolorum Acta ex Arabica translatione Latine reddita cum notis*, (Leyden, 1578).

Junius, F. *Pauli apostoli ad Corinthios epistolae duae ex Arabica translatione Latinae facta cum notis*, (Leyden, 1578).

Articuli Lambethani, Ex Typographeo Thomae Henrici Gymnasii Typographi, Impensis Johannis Junioni Amsterdamensis Librarii, (Amsterdam, 1613).

Place, Pierre de la. *Treatise of the Excellencie of the Christian Man*, Englished by Laurence Tomson, (Christopher Barker, London, 1576).

Stephanus, R. της καινης διαθηκης απαντα...*Novum Jesu Christi Domini nostri Testamentum*, (Lutetia, 1550).

Tomson, L. *The New Testament translated out of Greeke by Theodoroe Beza whereunto are adioyned brief summaries of doctrine and also short expositions on the phrases and hard places*. Englished by L. Tomson, (London, C. Barker, 1576).

Travers, W. *Ecclesiasticae Disciplinae et Anglicanae Ecclesiae ab illa aberationis plena e verbo Dei et dilucida Explicatio*, (Adamus de Monte, 1574).

Tremellius, E. *Testamentum Vetus Biblia Sacra, Scholiis illustrata ab E. Tremellio et Fr. Junio; accesserunt libri Apocryphi Latine redditi a Fr. Junio, quibus adiunximus Novi Testamenti libros ex Sermone Syriaco ab eodem Tremellio in Latinum Conversos; ed. septima; quibus adjunximus Novi Testamenti libros ex sermone Syro ab eodem Tremellio et ex Graeco a Theodoro Beza in Latinum versos*, (Havoniae, 1624).

Tyndale, W. *New Testament published in 1526; being the first translation from the Greek into English by W. Tyndale; reprinted verbatim; with a memoir of his life and writings by George Offor*, (London, 1836).

Whittingham, W. *The New Testament conferred diligently with the Greke and best approved translations*, (Geneva, Badius, 1557).

Secondary Sources

Allen, P. S., ed. *Opus epistolarum Desiderii Erasmi Roterodami*, 11 vols., (Oxford, 1906). Vol. XII, *Indices*, edited by B. Flower & E. Rosenbaum, (Oxford, 1958).

Allen, W., ed. *Translating for King James*, (Nashville, Vanderbilt University Press, 1969).

Anderson, Christopher. *Annals of the English Bible*, 2 vols., (London, William Pickering, 1845). Edited and rev. by Hugh Anderson, (London, Jackson, Walford & Hodder, 1862).

Armstrong, E. *Robert Estienne Royal Printer*, (C.U.P., 1954).

Barrett, C. K. *The Gospel according to St. John*, (London, SPCK, 1955).

Barrett, C. K. *A Commentary on the Epistle to the Romans*, (London, 1971, reprint).

Baur, Dom Chr. *Saint Jean Chrysostome et ses oeuvres dans l'histoire litteraire*, (1907).

Berger, S. *La Bible au seizième siecle*, (Paris, 1879).

Blass, F., ed. *Acta Apostolorum sive Lucae ad Theopilum liber alter*, (Göttingen, 1895).

Bloxam, J. R. *The Magdalen College Register*, (Oxford, 1873).

Brook, B. *The Lives of the Puritans*, 3 vols., (London, 1813).

Burnet, G. *The History of the Reformation of the Church of England*, 3 vols., (Dublin, 1730).

Butterworth, C. C. *The Literary Lineage of the King James Bible, 1340-1611.*

Cadier, J. *Calvin*, (Paris, 1967).

Collinson, P. *The Elizabethan Puritan Movement*, (London, 1971).

Creed, J. M. *The Gospel According to St. Luke*, (London, Mcmillan, 1930).

Cremeans, C. D. *The Reception of Calvinistic Thought in England*, (1949).

Cremer, H. *Biblico-Theological Lexicon of New Testament Greek*, translated by W. Urwick, (Edinburgh, 1962, reprint).

Cross, M. C. "An Example of Lay Intervention in the Elizabethan Church", *Studies in Church History*, II.

Dresselhuis, J. Ab Utrecht "Pieter Lozeleur des Prinzen
   Raad en Hofprediker", *De Gids*, II, (1846).

Fulke, W. *A defence of the sincere and true translations of
   the Holy Scriptures*...[1583], ed. C. H. Hartshorne,
   (Cambridge University Press, 1843), (Parker Society).

Ganoczy, A. *Bibliothèque de l'Académie de Calvin*, (Geneva,
   1969).

Gardy, F., ed. *Bibliographie des oeuvres de Théodore de
   Bèze*, (Geneva, 1960).

Geisendorf, P. F. *Théodore de Bèze*, (Geneva, 1949).

Gerdesius, D. *Miscellanea Groningana*, 4 vols., (1736-45).

Gould, E. P. *A Critical and Exegetical Commentary on the
   Gospel according to St. Mark*, (T. & T. Clark, 1961),
   I.C.C.

Greenslade, S. L., ed. *The West from the Reformation to the
   Present Day*, vol. III in *The Cambridge History of the
   Bible*, (Cambridge, 1963).

Hall, B. "Calvin against the Calvinists", *John Calvin*,
   (Sutton Courtenay Press, 1966).

Harnack, A. von. *History of Dogma*, 7 vols., (London &
   Edinburgh, 1894), (Theological Translation Library).

Hooker, R. *The Works*, 3 vols., (Oxford, 1807).

Kickel, W. *Vernunft und Offenbarung bei Theodor Beza*, (1967).

Legg, S. C. E., ed. *Novum Testamentum Graece, Evangelium
   Secundum Matthaeum*, (Oxford, 1940).

Legg, S. C. E., ed. *Novum Testamentum Graece; Evangelium
   Secundum Marcum*, (Oxford, 1935).

Lightfoot, J. B. *St. Paul's Epistle to the Galatians*,
   (London, Macmillan, 1887).

Lock, W. *A Critical and Exegetical Commentary on the
   Pastoral Epistles*, (Edinburgh, 1966, reprint), (I.C.C.).

McNeile, A. H. *The Gospel according to St. Matthew*, (London,
   1938).

Metzger, B. M. *The Text of the New Testament*, (Oxford, 1968).

Metzger, B. M. "The Influence of Codex Bezae on the Geneva Version of the English Bible", *Historical and Literary Studies*, (Leiden, 1968).

Moffatt, J. *A Critical and Exegetical Commentary on the Epistle to the Hebrews*, (Edinburgh, 1968, reprint), (I.C.C.).

Moffatt, J. *First Epistle of Paul to the Corinthians*, (New York, Harper, 1938).

Moule, H. J., ed. *Descriptive catalogue of the charters, minute books and other documents of the borough of Weymouth and Melcombe Regis, A.D. 1252-1800*, (Weymouth, 1883).

Moulton, J. H. *A Grammar of New Testament Greek*, 2 vols., (Edinburgh, T. & T. Clark, 1967).

Moulton, J. H. & Milligan, G. *Vocabulary of Greek-Testament illustrated from the papyri and other non-literary sources*, (1914-29).

Neal, D. *The history of the puritans or protestant nonconformists from the Reformation under Henry VIII to the act of Toleration under William and Mary with an account of their principles*, 2 vols., (London, 1754).

Neale, J. *The Elizabethan House of Commons*, (1949).

Nestle, E. & Aland, K., ed. *Novum Testamentum Graece*, (United Bible Societies, London, 1971, 25th edition).

The New English Bible, (Oxford, Cambridge, London, 1974).

Pearson, A. F. Scott. *Thomas Cartwright and Elizabethan Puritanism, 1535-1603*, (Cambridge, 1925).

Pollard, A. W., ed. *Records of the English Bible*, (New York, H. Frowde, 1911).

Pollard, A. W. & Redgrave, G. R. *A Short-Title Catalogue of Books Printed in England, Scotland and Ireland and of English Books printed abroad, 1475-1640*, (London, 1926).

Porter, H. C. *Reformation and Reaction in Tudor Cambridge*, (Cambridge, 1958).

Raitt, J. *The Eucharistic Theology of Theodore Beza*, (Grand Rapids, 1971).

Read, C. *Mr. Secretary Walsingham and the Policy of Queen Elizabeth*, 3 vols., (Cambridge, 1925).

Sabatier, P., ed. *Bibliorum Sacrorum Latinae Versiones Antiquae seu Vetus Italica*, 3 vols., (1743).

Scrivener, F. H. A. *Authorized Version of the Bible, 1611*, (Cambridge, The University Press, 1884).

Scrivener, F. H. A., ed. *Bezae Codex Cantabrigiensis, being an exact copy in ordinary type of the celebrated uncial Greek-Latin Manuscript of Four Gospels and Acts of the Apostles written early in the sixth century and presented to the University of Cambridge by Theodore Beza, A.D. 1581. Edited with critical introduction, annotations and facsimiles*, (1864; rpt. Pittsburgh, The Pickwick Press, 1978).

Souter, A., ed. *Novum Testamentum Graece*, (Oxford, 1947, second edition).

Strype, J. *Annals of the Reformation and establishment of religion and other various occurrences in the Church of England with an appendix or repository of original papers*, 3 vols., (London, 1709).

Tischendorf, C., ed. *Novum Testamentum Graece*, 2 vols., (Leipzig, 1869). Vol. III, *Prolegomena*, compiled by C. H. Gregory, (Leipzig, 1894).

Trinterud, L. J., ed. *Elizabethan Puritanism*, (O.U.P., 1971), (A Library of Protestant Thought).

Turner, N. *A Grammar of New Testament Greek*, III, (Edinburgh, T. & T. Clark, 1963).

Turton, H. *The Text of the English Bible*, (1833).

Vermiglius, Peter Martyr. *In Epistolam S. Pauli ad Romanos Commentarii*, (Basle, 1558).

Vries, d, H. J. *Pepinière du Calvinisme hollandais*, 2 vols., (The Hague, 1924).

Weigle, L. A., ed. *The New Testament Octapla*, (1962).

Wendel, F. *Calvin*, (1963), (Fontana Library Theology and Philosophy).

Westcott, B. F. *A General View of the History of the English Bible*, (3rd edition, revised by W. A. Wright, 1905).

Williams, C. S. C. *A Commentary on the Acts of the Apostles*, (London, 1971, reprint).

Willoughby, E. E. *The Making of the King James Bible*, (Los Angeles, Printed for Dawson's Bookshop at the Plantin Press, 1956).

Wood, A. *Athenae Oxonienses*, (ed. Bliss, 1815).

Wordsworth, J. and White, H. J., ed. *Novum Testamentum Domini Nostri Jesu Christi Latine*, 4 vols., (Oxford, 1913-41).

INDEX

Index of New Testament Passages Discussed

MATTHEW

I.	11	11, 44, 90
II.	6	45
II.	11	4, 45, 89
II.	16	46
III.	8	46, 90
III.	9	47
III.	11	4
IV.	10	4, 5, 48
IV.	12	48, 91
V.	18	4, 5, 49, 90
V.	21	50
V.	29	51
V.	33	4
V.	36	4
V.	44	4
V.	47	4, 51f., 90
VI.	2	20, 52f.
VI.	6	20
VI.	7	14, 23, 53
VI.	14	23
VI.	16	20
VI.	34	53f.
VII.	1	4
VII.	3	54
VII.	6	4
VII.	13	4
VII.	14	4, 54f., 90
VII.	19	4
VII.	23	55
VIII.	8	4
VIII.	18	56
VIII.	32	56
IX.	11	4
IX.	16	56f.
IX.	38	21f.
X.	1	12
X.	9	57f.
X.	18	58

MATTHEW (continued)

XI.	28	58
XII.	18	58f.
XIII.	11	59
XIV.	2	59f.
XV.	5-6	60f., 92
XVIII.	19	61
XVIII.	26	61f.
XIX.	28	62, 89
XX.	23	63, 89
XXI.	37	63
XXIII.	2	63f.
XXIV.	31	64
XXVI.	26	64f.

MARK

I.	34	65f.
II.	23	66
IV.	40	67
V.	23	67
VI.	10	67f.
VI.	19	68
VI.	52	69
VI.	56	69
VII.	2	69f.
VII.	3	70f.
VII.	15	71
VIII.	24	71f.
IX.	16	72
X.	42	72f.
XIV.	3	73f.
XIV.	31	74, 90
XIV.	49	75
XIV.	72	75
XV.	3	75f., 89

MARK (continued)

XV. 28......76
XVI. 15......21

LUKE

I.   4......76f.
I.   17......77f., 90f.
I.   28......78f., 91
I.   36......23
I.   39......23
I.   45......79
I.   50......23
I.   77......79f., 90
I.   78......80
II.   9......80
III. 15......80f.
IV. 29......81
VI.   7......81f.
VI. 40......82
VII. 30......82f.
VIII.14......83f.
VIII.18......84
VIII.29......84
IX. 22......85
IX. 46......85
X.   22......85f.
XI.   3......86
XVII.20......86f., 91
XVII.21......87, 91
XVII.36......88
XVIII.7......88f.

JOHN

I.   15......26
VII. 16......20
XII. 32......12
XIV. 1......23

ACTS

II. 46......16
XVII.11......16
XX.   7......16f.
XXII.14......17

ROMANS

I.   9......15, 113
I.   20......113f.
I.   28......15, 114, 158
II. 27......10
III. 9......115
III. 25-26....115f., 159
IV.   2......10
IV.   9......12
IV. 17......12, 116f.
V.   12......24f., 117, 159
V.   14......11
VI.   4......118
VI. 12......11
VII. 6......24
VII. 7......22
VII. 22......118
IX.   6......118f.
XI. 29......119f.
XI. 31......120f., 159
XII. 3......121f.
XII. 6......122
XIV. 5......123

1 CORINTHIANS

IV.   6......123f.
IV.   9......125
VI.   1......188f.
VII. 1......10, 129

1 CORINTHIANS (continued)

VII.	26	125f.
VII.	29	126f.
VII.	35	127
IX.	5	128f.
IX.	27	129f.
X.	11	130
X.	17	15, 130f.
X.	30	131
XII.	29	131

GALATIANS

I.	16	132
II.	2	132f.
II.	4	133
III.	1	133f.
IV.	9	134f.
IV.	15	135f.
IV.	17	136
IV.	18	136f.
IV.	24	137
V.	7	138f.

PHILIPPIANS

I.	1	95
I.	10	26f.

1 THESSALONIANS

V.	12	189

HEBREWS

I.	3	139, 158f.
I.	12	139f.
II.	5	140
II.	7-9	140f.
II.	16	142f.
III.	1	15
III.	14	143f.
IV.	1	144
IV.	2	144f.
V.	2	145
V.	7	145f.
VI.	1	146f.
VII.	19	147f.
VIII.	2	148f.
VIII.	4	149f.
IX.	12	150
X.	12	150f.
X.	26	16, 151
X.	38	151f.
XI.	1	152f.
XI.	3	153f.
XI.	21	154f.
XII.	13	15f., 155f.
XII.	17	156f., 158
XIII.	3	157f.

1 PETER

III.	18	25f.

INDEX OF PERSONS AND SUBJECTS

Abbot, George, 94, 96ff.
Admonition to Parliament, 182ff.
Allegory, 137-138.
Ambrose
- criticized by Beza, 10f.
- doctrine of the eucharist, 11.
ἀποθανοντος, 24.
Augustine
- in Beza's theology, 11.
Authorized version, *passim*.
- and the Bodleian copy of the Bishops' Bible, 89ff.
- Final Revision Committee, 109ff., 158ff.
- principles for italics, 28ff.
- the translators, 28
- treatment of theological questions, 171f.

Baptism of John, 78, 80, 91.
Beale, Robert, 177.
Bishops' Bible, 93f. & *passim*.
Bishops' Bible: Bodleian copy, 1, 28ff., 169ff.
- MS annotations, 28f.
- typographical annotations, 29f., 43
- mentioned, 34, 44, 89ff.
Bois, John, 34, 105 n. 73, 109ff. & *passim*.

Calvin, John
- *Lectures on Jonah*, 96ff.
- *Sermons on Timothy and Titus*, 191ff.
Camerarius, Johannes, 19-22.
- his annotations preferred by L'Oiseleur de Villers, 20.
- mentioned, 119, 133.

Cartwright, Thomas, 102 n. 44, 184, 200 n. 32.
Christ
- as servant, 59.
- priesthood of, 149-150.
- sacrifice of, 150
Church government, 95f., 188, 189, 194f.
Codex Bezae, 3, 7, 14, 46, 48, 67, 70, 73, 75, 88, 106 n. 91.
Cole, William, 174.
Complutensian Polyglot, 75-76 & *passim*.
Confessio Christianae Fidei, 49.
Crane, Mistress, 187.
Creation, 153-154, 190-191.

Davison, William, 178-179.
Deacons, 192, 194f.
Disciples, 82.
δωρον, 60f.
Douai - Rheims version, *see* Rheims.
Downes, Andrew, 119, 120-121, 130, 140.

Ecclesiastical Discipline Napier copy, 194.
ἐφ' ᾧ, 24f.
Election, 129, 190-191, 192.
Erasmus
- his annotations a model for Beza, 8.
- attitude to the Fathers, 8
- attitude to Origen, 39 n. 32
- N.T., *passim*.
Estienne, *see* Stephanus.
Eucharist
- Calvin's and Beza's doctrine, 15, 40 n. 50.
- mentioned, 64-65.

Faith, 51, 122, 143, 144-145, 152-153.
Fathers
- Greek and Latin editions available to Beza, 8-9.
- Beza's attitude to, 9ff.
- Beza's references to their works in *Romans*, 38 n. 31.
- as witnesses to the Greek text, 11f.
Faunt, Nicholas, 177.
Field, John, 182, 187, 193
Fortress of the Fathers, 193.
Fulke, William, 104 n. 71, 105 n. 72, 112, 146, 155, 183, 193, 194.
Fulman MS, 34, 109ff., 169ff.

Geneva Bible, *passim*.
- English version 1560, 13, 160.
- marginal notes in, 14ff.
- reliance on Beza's N.T., 27ff.
- French version 1558, 14ff.
Geneva Prayer Book, 187.
Gilby, Anthony, 182ff.
Glory, earthly and divine, 52-53.
Goodman, Christopher, 183.
Grace of Mary, 78-79, 91.
Greek MS sources, 2ff.
- and the annotations in Bodleian Bishops', 31f.

Harmar, John
- translation of Beza's *Sermons*, 94f.
Hastings, Francis, 174, 182
Hebrews, 139.
Hoby, Sir Thomas, 175.

Humfrey, Lawrence, 174, 176, 183.

Incarnation, 141f.

Jerome (Vetus interpres) *passim*.
- Beza's and Erasmus' attitude to, 10, 39 n. 33.
- mentioned, 48, 129, 132.
Judgement (last), 55, 62.

King James' Bible, *see* Authorized version.
Kingdom of God, 86f., 91.
Knowledge, 114.

Lambeth Articles, 107 n. 102.
Law (O.T.), 24, 49ff., 90, 96f., 147f.
L'Oiseleur, *see* Villers.

Magistrates, 64, 193.
Marprelate tracts, 187.
Marriage of priests, 129.
Martin, Gregory, 104 n. 71, 146, 155, 166 n. 64.
Mary, Queen of Scots, 180f.
Matthew
- 'Ang' and 'Rom' annotations, 32.
Mercer, Johannes, 154.
Messianic age, 140.
Miracles, 59f.
Monkhoven, Evert, 179f.
μυστηρια, 59.

Origen
- Beza's attack on, 10.
- doctrine of the original sin, 25.
Original sin, 24f., 117, 190-191.
Oxford Company, 44, 93ff.

Place, Pierre de la, 190.
Prayers, 53, 100 n. 17.
Predestination, 63, 83.

Pre-existence (of Christ), 26.
Puritan pressure groups, 186.

Rabbinic learning, 20.
Redemption, 150.
Repentance, 46f., 90, 119f.
Resurrection, 25f., 97.
Rheims version, 106 n. 84 & 87, 163 n. 35, 164 n. 38, 166 n. 63 & 72.
Ribit, Jean, 167 n. 75.
Rossell, 179.

Sampson, Thomas, 182, 183.
Saville, Henry, 110.
Scaliger, Joseph, 125.
Scribes
 - as successors to Moses, 64.
Sin, 51, 102 n. 44, 151.
Stanclyff, Richard, 176.
Stephanus, Henri, 2, 35 n. 8.
Stephanus, Robert, 1-2.
 - MS sources used by, 3ff.
 - mentioned, 24, 44 & *passim*.

Substance, 143f., 153.
Supralapsarianism, 191.

Textus Receptus, 6, 13, 37 n. 21.
Tomson, Laurence
 - translation of Beza's Latin N.T. 1576, 18ff., 160, 174, 188ff.
 - annotations, 22f.
 - text, 23f.
 - agreement with Beza, 27.
 - influence on the AV, 195ff.
Travers, Walter, 175, 179, 185, 194f.
Tyndale, William (N.T.), *passim*.

Vestments, 95, 175, 193.
Villers, Pierre L'Oiseleur de and his version of Beza's N.T., 18ff., 178, 185, 188f.

Walsingham, Ursula, 185, 190.
Wilcox, John, 174, 182.

www.ingramcontent.com/pod-product-compliance
Lightning Source LLC
Chambersburg PA
CBHW070249230426
43664CB00014B/2462